CR

With This Ring

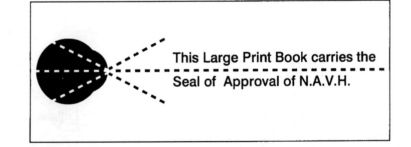
This Large Print Book carries the
Seal of Approval of N.A.V.H.

With This Ring

A QUARTET OF CHARMING STORIES
ABOUT FOUR VERY SPECIAL WEDDINGS

Lori Copeland
Dianna Crawford
Ginny Aiken
Catherine Palmer

Thorndike Press • Thorndike, Maine

Published in 1999 by arrangement with Tyndale House
Publishers, Inc.

Thorndike Large Print ® Romance Series.

The tree indicium is a trademark of Thorndike Press.

The text of this Large Print edition is unabridged.
Other aspects of the book may vary from the original edition.

Set in 16 pt. Plantin by Minnie B. Raven.

Printed in the United States on permanent paper.

Library of Congress Cataloging in Publication Data

With this ring : a quartet of charming stories about four
very special weddings / Lori Copeland . . . [et al.].
    p.   cm.
  ISBN 0-7862-1921-1 (lg. print : hc : alk. paper)
  1. Love stories, American.   2. Christian fiction,
American.   3. American fiction — Women authors.
4. Weddings — Fiction.   5. Large type books.
I. Copeland, Lori. Something old.
  PS648.L6 W58   1999
  813'.085083823—dc21   99-14362

Contents

Something Old

Lori Copeland

Therefore shall a man leave his father and his mother, and shall cleave unto his wife: and they shall be one flesh.
GENESIS 2:24

Chapter One

Brooklyn, New York, November 1887

"A simple wedding, Anna. Nothing complicated."

Anna nodded, her heart overflowing with love. She'd waited months for Adam to propose. They were of the same conviction that God would be the cornerstone of their relationship. She had had no idea when they'd slipped away from church for a late afternoon dinner that he was going to propose! A simple ceremony would be fine with her!

"I know the stone is small, Anna, but someday I'll buy you the biggest diamond in the state of New York."

"Johan Adam Wilhelm, stop this nonsense! It's beautiful!" She proudly studied the engagement ring he had slipped on her finger. So like Adam to be worried over the size. Size meant nothing to her; it was sentiment that counted. Giddy with love, she looked into her future husband's bright blue eyes filled with promise. "It couldn't be more perfect."

"Then your answer is yes?"

She had prayed for this moment. The man she loved with all her heart sitting across from her, romantic music played by a violinist moving slowly between the tables. Could anything be more perfect?

"Yes, yes, a thousand times yes." She leaned across the table and gently touched his cheek, her gaze traveling over his rich, sand-colored waves of hair. "I've loved you from the first moment we met."

He kissed the palm of her hand, chuckling. "I'm grateful you find a poor, working man attractive."

She smiled and pulled her hand away, glancing around the cozy restaurant at onlookers looking their way. Did they have any idea how ecstatic she felt? Snow fell outside the plate-glass window, giving the cold November day a winter wonderland ambiance. "I always felt the Lord had a hand in our meeting. If we both hadn't decided to teach children's Sunday school . . ."

"And if you weren't such a tender heart for the disadvantaged, accepting a teaching position here in Brooklyn instead of a nice New York neighborhood . . ."

"Oh, Adam." She thought her heart might burst. "You were always there waiting for me, looking so handsome." She felt her cheeks warm. "Every week you brought me the biggest, reddest apple you had — and remember how I told you, 'You'll never get rich giving apples away to every girl who comes along'?"

He squeezed her hand, love shining through his blue eyes. "There are other women in the world?"

Twirling the ring on her finger, she sighed, watching it sparkle in the candle-light. Meeting unchaperoned with Adam was daring, and she felt guilty. But considering the occasion, she was willing to risk a few whispers. "It's going to be a lovely wedding."

"How soon can we be married?" he whispered.

"When do you want to?"

"Tomorrow."

She shared his impatience, but she knew it wasn't practical. Planning a wedding was no simple task! "Tomorrow wouldn't give Mother and me much time — I was thinking perhaps early spring."

He shrugged. "If I must wait that long, I must. But I don't have to like it, do I?"

"I'd like nothing better than to marry you tomorrow." She leaned closer, lowering her voice. "But first you must ask Father for my hand."

Adam frowned. "Your father?"

She sat up straighter. "Yes — it's only proper."

"But I've met the man only twice in my life. I talk to your butler more often. Can't I ask Giles for your hand in marriage?"

She grinned. "Silly goose. Do my parents scare you?"

His features sobered. "They're so affluent, Anna. They're Upper West Side New York, and my family is Brooklyn Borough. I don't want them to be ashamed of your choice in a husband."

She understood his concern, but Father wasn't an ogre. He was a good man, merely preoccupied with his political campaign. She wanted the kind of marriage Adam's parents shared. They worked together, loved together. Her parents were fine people, but they had little time for home life and domesticity, or for each other, it seemed. As an only child, she longed for a house full of babies and all that family life offered — real family life, not just big, empty houses, servants, and a garage full of fancy carriages.

"My parents will learn to love you as much as I do. Father's bark is much worse than his bite."

"He bites, too?"

12

Her hand felt tiny beneath his as he rubbed his thumb across her knuckles. "Don't worry. I'll be right beside you when you ask for my hand — just as I will for the rest of our lives."

"What if your father won't approve of me?"

"Who could not approve of you? You're one of the hardest-working men I know. Father respects hard work."

Adam ran his hand over the back of his neck. "You have so much, Anna-Marie — I have so little to offer —"

"Oh, Adam. It's your love I need, not material things." Couldn't he see that? Didn't he know she wanted nothing more than to spend the rest of her life with him, regardless of his financial status?

"You have my soul, Anna-Marie, but I want to give you so much more. Someday I will have many grocery stores — all over the state. I'll be prosperous. We'll live in a grand house — even bigger than the one you live in now. We'll own a motor carriage —"

"Shhhh." She silenced him with a light touch of her fingertip to his lips. She knew he had strong Christian values, but at times she wondered if he'd grown so comfortable in his faith he only went through the motions of turning tomorrow over to the Lord.

Material things seemed far more important to Adam than they did to her. "Such talk. I don't need a big house or lots of grocery stores — I need you." She was warmed by the tenderness her words brought to his smile. "Now, let's talk of other things. When Father consents to our marriage —"

Adam's expression turned serious. "I'm afraid he would have a fight on his hands if he didn't."

"He will, darling — but there are a million things to be done. The church, flowers, attendants . . ." She leaned back and sighed. "If it were up to me, I'd be content with a simple wedding, but Mother will probably insist on more. She must think her only child is destined to be an old maid."

"Twenty-one is not old."

"To Mother it is." Her parents had married when her mother was only sixteen. Many times Anna had been told of how beautiful Luellen Stewart had been swept off her feet by Broderick Martin, a prominent attorney some believed destined to become president.

Anna sighed again. "And I'm afraid she'll want a big enough wedding that all of Father's Republican Party cohorts can attend."

Her parents were generously charitable to

worthy causes, but they led such a busy life that family matters came second — unless they might enhance her father's political career. A big, expensive bash to celebrate Broderick Martin's only child's wedding certainly would do that.

"Sounds complicated." Adam toyed with a menu. "I mean it, Anna. Let's keep the ceremony small and simple."

She patted his hand. "Don't worry. I don't want a lot of fuss either. To honor Mother, we may have to compromise occasionally, but we'll be firm —"

"It won't be just *your* parents," he warned.

"Oh?"

"My family has deep-seated customs from the Old Country. Grandmama Wilhelm will come from Munich; since I'm Grandpapa's namesake, she'll expect certain proprieties to be carried out. . . ."

Grandmama. Anna liked the sound of that. She'd never known her grandparents because they had died before she was born. And Adam's family fascinated her. While he was modern in thought, his behavior was still steeped in Old Country ways.

"Don't worry, Adam." She touched his hand warmly. "I want to honor your parents too."

"Of course. And I shall honor yours. I see

no reason why we can't do both, do you?"

"Not at all." She felt her spirits lift. Of course they could do both! They were all adults.

The waiter refilled their water glasses and asked if they were ready to order. Anna-Marie felt too giddy to eat, but she decided on a small salad. Adam chose a seafood chowder.

When the waiter left, he edged forward in his chair. "Now about these family customs. Are you sure you don't mind? Grandmama is strong on tradition. It could conceivably cause problems."

She waved his concerns aside. "Nothing could *ever* cause problems between us, Adam. We love each other too much." She just prayed that Grandmama's German customs meshed well with the Martins' upper-class, Anglo-Saxon ways.

"Don't be so sure." He laughed. "You don't know Grandmama."

She smiled. *And you don't know Mother.*

"Then there's the fact that our parents have never met," he mused.

Well, there was that. Over the months, they'd continued to see each other without informing the parents of their deepening relationship. With all the teachers' meetings, picnics, and social events, they were chaperoned but out of their parents' eyes.

"I'm sure that can be worked out. Mother will probably insist on hosting a get-acquainted dinner, and then you can ask Father for my hand."

He frowned. "I was thinking Mama would want to do that."

When Anna frowned back, he calmly folded his napkin and set it aside. "On second thought, your parents might be uncomfortable eating in the back of the store."

Her family intimidated him. He had never actually said as much, but she had detected it in his tone of late. If only he knew how much she admired *his* family and the closeness they shared. In lieu of gatherings around the family table, the Martin celebrations were observed in Luellen's favorite restaurants. The atmosphere was often commercial and sterile, not at all like the warm, boisterous family times Adam enjoyed telling about.

"Adam, if you're uncomfortable with the idea of your parents eating at my home, then we'll come to yours. Mother will understand."

She wasn't at all sure her mother would understand; she was only hoping. But, though a bit of a snob, Mother was reasonable and only wanted her daughter's happiness.

Adam lightly touched his lips to the back of her hand. All she ever needed to know was bared in his eyes as he gazed back at her. "If you don't mind," he said, "I'd prefer neutral territory when we break the news. I'll make reservations for six at Delmonico's. Will Saturday night be too soon?"

"*Delmonico's?* In the city?" The upscale New York restaurant was outrageously expensive — a place her father would take his political friends, not somewhere a struggling young grocery clerk should be squandering his hard-earned money.

Adam smiled. "Nothing but the best for the woman I love."

"But the cost, Adam." He didn't need to impress her parents in order to please her! "Delmonico's isn't necessary. We can eat at Monroe's; it has —"

His stern look silenced her. "Just make certain your parents are in attendance Saturday night."

Well, Delmonico's certainly wasn't a problem. It was Mother's favorite haunt.

Concern shadowed Adam's handsome features. "Your parents will approve of me, won't they?"

"Of course they will. I'm sure they'll grow to love you as much as I do." They might have a few reservations about her sudden

18

engagement, but they'd come around. Eventually.

"My parents may take a bit of getting used to," Adam said. "Papa is a great jokester, and Mama is so conservative — and Grand-mama, well, Grandmama is different." He picked up his water glass and studied the contents, his voice guarded now. "She can be headstrong at times, especially where tradition is concerned."

Anna-Marie smiled, tapping a spoon. "Have I mentioned my godfather is a dress designer?"

He raised an eye.

"Quite a successful one," she went on. "Have you heard of *Jacob's Couturiers?*"

He shook his head.

"Uncle Murray — well, he's not really my uncle, he's my godfather, but I've always considered him to be my uncle — he's been designing my bridal gown for years." Seeing the change in Adam's expression, she hurried along. "Uncle Murray has no idea when I'll marry, but wedding gowns are dear to him. He's made gowns for royalty, you know. He and Mother have had their heads together for years, trying to come up with the perfect dress for me. . . ." Her voice trailed off when she saw his growing discomfort. "Is something wrong?"

"No . . . it's just —" He took a deep breath. "I have a feeling Grandmama will want you to wear the dress she married Grandpapa in."

"Oh?" She felt sick. Mother would have her heart set on a traditional gown, and Uncle Murray would be hurt to the bone if he didn't design it. "Does it matter awfully?"

"There is only one thing that matters to me," he said as he gathered both of her hands into his large, protective ones.

"What?" she whispered.

"That I marry you." He kissed her fingertips. "And that you have my children." He kissed her index finger. "And that we raise them together." He kissed her ring finger. "And that you love me until we're very old and very crotchety —"

"And very set in our ways," she finished, sealing the vow with a brief kiss to his thumb. Her heart was fairly bursting with joy. Everything would be fine. He'd see!

Chapter Two

"What's this 'personal matter' you have to discuss with your mother and me?" Anna-Marie's father patted his trim stomach, then checked his pocket watch, frowning. A large, authoritative figure, he ruled the Martin household with a firm but loving hand. "I've a political event to attend shortly."

Anna-Marie took her father's arm and led him to his favorite chair. "They'll not start without you, Father. This is important — probably the most important event in my whole life." She turned to her mother. "You'll probably want to sit for this too."

Mother, looking her usual elegant self in an electric blue Murray Jacobs tailored suit, gingerly perched on the edge of a straight-back Queen Anne chair. Fashionably trim with wonderfully coifed silver-gray hair, her six-foot stature towered over her daughter's petite frame. "Good heavens, Anna-Marie, whatever you do, don't upset your father. This is a significant night for him. Senator Gardner is hosting a party at his townhouse; the governor is going to be in attendance."

Father held up a hand to silence his wife. "Let the girl speak, Lu."

Anna-Marie cleared her throat. "There are some people I want you to meet."

Her mother sat up straighter. "Here — now? Really, Anna-Marie, you should not bring guests in without notice."

"No, Mother, they're not *here*. Saturday night. I want you to meet them Saturday night . . . over dinner." Anna-Marie glanced around the ornate sitting room with a sinking heart. What would Adam's parents think when they saw the Martins' affluent lifestyle? The Chinese Chippendale furniture, the massive mahogany staircase gleaming beneath finely cut crystal chandeliers. Rugs from the Orient, faint blue-tinted Waterford vases that were personal gifts from the Waterford family. Would the Wilhelms flee in panic?

"I'm afraid we have plans for Saturday night, dear," her mother said. "Senator Hoskins is hosting another dinner for your father's campaign."

Anna-Marie released a noisy breath. "Well, you'll just have to change your plans, because this is extremely important to me. I ask very little of you —"

"It's okay, Lu." Her father smiled. "She does have to put up with a lot of political business." He turned to his daughter. "These people? Are they Republicans? voters?"

Anna-Marie put her hand on her father's shoulder. Adam's parents were Democrats, but she'd worry about that later. "I'm sure they vote — but that's not important. They're Klaus and Elfie Wilhelm, Adam's parents."

Mother ran a well-manicured fingernail up the sides of her coifed hair. "Adam? Is that the young man you teach Sunday school with — the one in Brooklyn? Really, Anna-Marie, if you insist on forming a friendship with this young man, we must arrange for you to be more properly chaperoned —"

"I see him more than occasionally, Mother. We're in love."

Father's jaw dropped. "In love — you can't be in love! He's a *grocer's* son, isn't he?"

Anna-Marie felt her spine stiffen. "The grocery business is a respectable profession —"

"That's not what your father meant, dear." Mother fussed with the collar on her blue silk blouse. "I'm sure Adam is . . . well, whatever he is. It's just that we have higher aspirations for your future. We don't want you to marry a man —"

"Adam asked me to marry him, and I accepted."

The statement ricocheted off the walls like a rubber bullet.

Father jumped to his feet and paced back and forth on the Persian carpet. "Anna-Marie, you *can't* be serious. Why . . ." He was blustering now. "Well. Your mother and I have discussed sending you to Elmira Woodmire's Finishing School — perhaps it is time to pursue the matter!"

Anna-Marie's chin lifted stubbornly. "You're not listening to me. I'm in *love* with Adam. He's going to ask you for my hand in marriage Saturday night, and I want — no, I *insist* that you say yes." She lifted her hand to display the tiny diamond. "I've already accepted his ring."

"Engaged to a *grocer's* son!" her father snapped. "Nonsense. You'll break the engagement immediately."

Tears sprang to Anna's eyes. She had known it would take time for them to accept Adam. But accept him they would, or she would . . . she would —

"You could send me to the ends of the earth, and I'd still be in love with Adam. And I'd find a way to marry him — with or without your approval." Her jawline tightened. "I would prefer the former, of course."

Mother rose and took Anna-Marie's hand to see the ring. She strained to glimpse it, then she lifted her spectacles, which hung on a jeweled chain around her neck. She squinted closer.

Anna-Marie saw disappointment spread across her mother's features. "It's beautiful, isn't it, Mother?"

"Unique," her mother said, looking as if she were about to faint.

"I love the simplicity of it."

Her father's shoulders slumped. "Anna-Marie, have you taken leave of your senses?"

"I've never been so certain of anything in my life, Father." She searched her parents' eyes, imploring their approval. "Please be happy for me. Adam is all I ever want; he's good, kind, gentle. You'll love him as much as I do once you know him."

Mother grabbed the arm of a nearby chair and eased herself down. "Dear heavens. Our daughter married to a grocer's son? What will our friends think?" She looked from her daughter to her husband, calamity mirrored in her eyes.

"Well." Father sighed deeply. "It appears she's got her mind made up, Luellen. She's twenty-one. Hardly a child anymore." He gazed at Anna. "Are you certain this isn't merely a whim?"

Anna-Marie ran to his side and flung her arms around his neck. She felt his hesitation, but eventually one hand came up to pat her on the back, then the other wrapped around her waist. Affectionate displays were foreign to the Martins; her father's hug brought tears to Anna's eyes. She even saw a smile flicker at the corner of her mother's mouth at the sight of father and daughter embracing.

Father pulled a snowy white handkerchief from his trouser pocket and blew his nose. The ragged honk shattered the strained silence.

"Where's this dinner supposed to take place?" he asked gruffly.

"Delmonico's."

Mother sat up straighter. *"Delmonico's?"* She got up, smoothing her hand across her silk skirt. "Well — Delmonico's. I'll need a new dress —"

"No, Mother, please. Wear something simple."

Her father let out a loud guffaw. "Simple? Your mother doesn't own anything simple."

"Really, Broderick," her mother scolded, wiping her eyes.

Anna-Marie felt her cheeks warm. She hadn't meant to be so blunt, but she didn't want her mother's flamboyance to make

26

Adam's parents uncomfortable. "There's no reason to buy a new dress. You always look lovely, Mother."

Mother smiled. "Thank you, dear." She cast a disapproving glance at her husband. "I'm glad someone in the family appreciates my eye for style."

Father checked his watch, frowned at the lateness, and hurried out into the night. As soon as Luellen closed the door behind him, Anna-Marie latched onto her mother's hand. "Now we'll go upstairs, and I'll help you pick out something to wear Saturday night." A nice *plain* black dress, she thought.

"Oh, dear . . . you're certain this is what you want?" Her mother's hand covered her heart. "To marry a man who has nothing? What about that nice Ted Mercer — Congressman Mercer's youngest son?"

"Mother, I don't love Ted Mercer. I love Adam, and he loves me deeply. What more could I ask? I'm rich in the only way that matters. I'm rich in love. Besides, Father wasn't wealthy when you married him."

Mother slowly climbed the stairs with Anna-Marie supporting her arm. "I'm thinking white. White sets off my hair. I've been told white becomes me."

"It does. White it is. And, Mother? Adam and I want a simple wedding. Okay?"

27

"Certainly. Five bridesmaids and —"

"One maid of honor, Mother. And one groomsman."

"Oh, dear."

Adam's parents took the news of his engagement stoically. But when Saturday night arrived, Adam was nervous about the dinner. As he dressed, he was painfully aware of his living quarters. His gaze traveled the cluttered area in back of the store, imagining how it must appear through Anna-Marie's eyes. He'd been born and raised here; Mama had tended his hurts, nursed his sicknesses, and she and Papa had helped him grow into a man here. He'd learned reading, writing, and arithmetic, as well as the Golden Rule, right here in these tiny rooms. Never once had he noticed the couch was worn and the tables had more nicks and scratches than smooth places. Until tonight.

The old tabby cat lay on the back of the threadbare sofa, his tail gently flicking the tattered green-and-bronze afghan Grandmama Wilhelm had knitted twenty years ago. A fireplace across the north wall struggled to provide warmth to the drafty room. Wind whistled through the cracks and around the eaves of the run-down frame building.

Papa's overstuffed chair with a tear in the armrest was scooted close to the cheery fire. A pair of glasses, a spring seed catalog, and his Bible lay next to the lamp on the table. A pair of well-worn slippers were shoved beneath, awaiting tired feet.

Adam's gaze moved to his mother as she emerged from the bedroom. His heart sank when he saw she was wearing her old coat. "Mama, is that your best coat?"

His mother straightened the collar on the threadbare garment. "And vat is the matter vit vat I'm vearing?"

Adam took a step backwards, perusing the tired apparel. "I wish you would let me buy you a new one."

Mama tucked a lock of salt-and-pepper hair into her chignon, then she smoothed the serviceable black wool over her ample hips. Pale green eyes stared back at him. "I need no new coat. This coat is special — your father bought it for me vit the first profit from the store." She crossed the room, straightening magazines and fluffing pillows as she went.

He grinned, thinking of how Mama was noted for organized chaos. She'd kept everything she'd ever owned. Magazines, mail, pieces of wrapping paper, ribbons, catalogs, books, and plain old junk littered the living area. To her credit, she could locate a requested item at any given time, although Adam didn't know how.

"Mama, you're going to be too warm. Why don't you take off your coat? Papa hasn't even finished shaving."

"Don't vant to be late for important dinner vit fancy people."

"They aren't fancy, Mama. They're just different than we are."

"How do you mean, different? This Anna — she is very rich?"

Adam stepped to the mirror hanging over the bureau. "Her parents are well off, but money's not important to Anna-Marie. She wants to bring the light of Christ's love to Brooklyn and to children less fortunate than her." That's what he loved about her. She was open, and honest, and generous to a fault. Wealth was in her heart, with love and caring for others. She volunteered long hours at the hospital and gave tirelessly to the church.

"Hummpt. And her mother and she picked *you?*" Mama raised her brows. "They know you are a poor man?"

"We're in America, Mama. Unlike the Old Country, women in the upper class marry for love, not just for social prominence."

30

his talk must cease if ve are to catch
n," Papa announced. His eyes twin-
ischievously as he gazed at his wife.
e, Mama, I vill hold your hand as ve

ching for his jacket, Adam said a silent
r. So much was riding on this night.
a, Mama —"

pa held up a beefy hand, silencing him.
smile faded from his round face. "It is
good for son to be ashamed of his mama
papa."

dam sobered. "I'm not ashamed of you,
pa."

"*Gut.*" His father's sunny disposition re-
rned. "I am not ashamed of you, either."

As Adam walked out the door, Papa
weaked his behind.

Adam rolled his eyes. *Please, God. Of all
nights, let him behave.*

"But your fiancée — she vill judge your mama by the coat I vear?"

"Of course not. She's not materialistic."

"Then vy do you vorry so much over a coat?"

"I'm *not* worrying over a coat. I just think it's time you had a new one."

Elfie threw up her hands. "Vill never understand America."

Adam mentally groaned. What would Broderick and Luellen Martin think when they met Klaus and Elfie Wilhelm for the first time?

Papa's booming voice filled the room as he joined the conversation from the water closet where he shaved. Arms the size of small hams deftly worked the straight razor as he maneuvered it around snow-white muttonchops. Cobalt blue eyes twinkled with mischief as he fitted his two-hundred-twenty-pound frame around the sink. "So! My son, he is ashamed of his mama's coat? It is not good enough for Miss Anna-Marie Martin?"

Studying his father in the mirror, Adam formed a loop with his tie. "Mama's coat is worn out, Papa. She should have a new one."

"Perhaps my son, the millionaire, vill buy her one, *ja?*"

Adam winced, dreading the coming dinner. "Please, Papa. None of your corny jokes tonight. I want you and Mama to make a good impression on Anna-Marie's parents."

"Ah." Papa lifted his chin to shave carefully under his neck. "Not to vorry, my son. The vomen, they all love Klaus, eh, Mama?"

Elfie scoffed, moving to the kitchen sink to rinse a dish. "This fancy restaurant — it is costing you a fortune, *nein?*"

"Not so much, Mama."

She tsked. "And I have *Kartoffelpuffer* going to vaste."

Kartoffelpuffer. Potato pancakes hardly seemed a meal appropriate for such a special occasion. Adam doubted the Martins had ever heard of *Kartoffelpuffer,* much less ate it. "You deserve a night out, Mama."

"For my son's engagement, I could have made nice *Streusel*," she fretted.

"Mama." Adam jerked the knot in his necktie loose and started over. "Anna-Marie and her parents can order anything they want at the restaurant."

"They cannot order *Kartoffelpuffer.*"

"No, but they'll have other choices."

"Is not the same. A family should not eat the stuff they put out in restaurants. Ve vill all be sick by morning."

Adam changed the subject, hoping to

temper her mood befor restaurant. He didn't through her food as if the in a conspiracy to make t George?"

"Your brother is at the li He ate *Kartoffelpuffer* for sup

Adam gave her a gentle wai

She sniffed. "After he ate, She folded a dishcloth, then h on a towel holder beside the aroma of potato pancakes hung air. "He has important test tomo walked to Adam, straightened hi patted his cheek. "You must get to tonight. Vit all this vedding talk, forgotten you vill be helping fill giving baskets at church in the morni

"I didn't forget, Mama. Anna and will be working on the project."

"Hummpt."

Papa emerged from the water clc shrugging into a robin's-egg-blue s jacket. The tight fabric strained beneath broad shoulders. Adam groaned. Why *tha* coat? It made him look like a bouncer at a tawdry bar.

"Vedding vill be big one?"

Adam straightened the tie, frowning. "I hope not."

Chapter Three

Elfie Wilhelm carefully examined the silverware on the well-appointed table setting at Delmonico's, frowning. She promptly shook out the white linen napkin and proceeded to polish a fork and spoon.

Adam blocked her hand. "Mama, what are you doing? They'll be here any moment!" He refolded her napkin and placed it next to her plate. "And put your purse under your chair."

"I vill keep it right here, thank you." She patted her arm where the wide black strap of her pocketbook rested. "One can never be too careful."

Adam checked his watch, then glanced toward the entrance. Anna and her parents were late.

Papa patted Mama on the shoulder. "You look especially lovely tonight, my Elfie Delfie."

"Papa, do you have to call Mama Elfie Delfie?"

His father's brows shot up. "I've called your mother Elfie Delfie all our married life

— now suddenly my son, the professor, vants me to stop?"

"Papa, I just want this evening to go well for Anna."

"First your mother's coat isn't fancy enough, now my pet name —"

"Mama's coat is fine." Adam watched her shrug it up over her shoulders. "I wish you'd let me hang it in the cloakroom for you, Mama."

"So drafty in here," she said, tightening the collar around her neck. "They should spend a little less on silvervare and more on heat."

"Shhh . . . there they come now." Adam rose and pulled a chair out for Luellen Martin, then Anna. He squeezed Anna's shoulders and leaned close to her ear as he seated her. "Remember, whatever happens, I love you."

She smiled up at him, her lips silently forming "I love you."

To Adam's horror, Papa gave Broderick Martin a hearty slap on the back, knocking the man's spectacles askew. "Klaus Vilhelm," he announced in a boisterous voice. "This is my vife, Elfie."

Adam was mortified. Mr. Martin's eyeglasses hung loosely on one ear as his father pumped the man's hand as if *he* were running for office.

36

Mr. Martin cleared his throat and hooked the earpiece back into place. "Klaus, Elfie," he acknowledged, then he held his hand up to summon the waiter.

"I'll have the trout," Luellen announced after consulting her menu. She sipped from a long-stemmed, crystal water glass. "I find it quite warm in here — are you ill?" she asked Adam's mother, obviously eyeing her coat.

"I understand the trout is excellent," Adam interrupted. "I believe I'll have the same. What about you, Mama?"

Mama painstakingly read the menu through, then laid it aside. "I have perfectly good *Kartoffelpuffer* going to vaste."

"Mama, the chicken is good here. You must have some." He turned to the waiter and nodded. "The lady will have the chicken and braised vegetables. Papa?"

Papa turned to Mr. Martin and slapped him on the back again. "Vat're you having, Brod?"

Broderick unabashedly ordered the biggest steak on the menu.

Silence fell over the table as they awaited their dinners. Adam decided it was a nice respite, but after a while the silence became embarrassing. He sensed Mr. Martin was looking for the nearest exit, and Mrs.

37

Martin looked as if she detected a faint, unpleasant smell.

Eventually, dinner was brought, and they began to eat.

Adam felt compelled to break the stalemate as he buttered a roll. "So, Anna-Marie tells me you're running for public office, Mr. Martin."

"Yes." Her father warmed to the subject. "We need to unseat a few of the blasted Democrats who are sucking us dry —" He stopped short when Adam's mother choked on a piece of chicken.

Papa bolted from his seat to give her a swift whack on the back. The offending morsel popped out on her plate, and Papa reseated himself.

"You're a Republican?" Mama managed to strangle out.

Adam started to get up, but Anna-Marie restrained him. "It's all right," she said calmly, then she turned to her father. "Let's not talk politics tonight, Father. Adam has something he wants to ask you."

Her father gave her a dismissive glance, addressing his remarks to the Wilhelms. "Am I to presume you're *not* Republicans?"

"Certainly not," Mama declared. "Ve're Democrats — hardvorking Democrats."

Adam tapped the side of his water glass

38

with his fork. "Please, it doesn't make any difference what our political affiliation is —"

Mr. Martin tossed his napkin on the table. "It certainly *does* make a difference!"

"But not tonight, Father," Anna reminded him under her breath.

Adam saw the look she centered on her father, pleading for consideration. Luellen Martin had the same pained look.

Red faced, Mr. Martin resumed eating.

Adam reached for his water glass, indicating a toast. "Mr. Martin, I have brought you here tonight to ask for Anna-Marie's hand in marriage. I love your daughter with all my heart, and I will do my best to provide well for her. I have plans to expand the grocery. . . ." His voice strengthened as Anna took hold of his hand to show her support. "I assure you, sir, I will move heaven and earth to make her happy."

It seemed an endless span before Broderick Martin finally lifted his eyes to his wife. She bit back tears, nodding. Reaching over, she patted his hand, her eyes mutely indicating they would adjust. Somehow.

Broderick cleared his throat. "Never had a Democrat in the family before." He sucked his breath in noisily, then released it.

"Her mother says yes."

"And you, Father?" Anna asked.

Adam waited as Broderick drained the last of the water from his glass. "You are quite sure this is what you want, Anna-Marie?"

She gazed at him with all the love Adam ever hoped to see in her eyes and whispered, "Very sure, Father."

"Then you have my blessing."

Papa slapped Broderick on the back, making his head bob. "*Sehr gut,* don't you think, Brod? Elfie Delfie and I have vaited long time for grandbabies!"

Adam glanced at his mother and saw she was frowning. "You vish to be married soon? Mother Vilhelm vill vant to be here."

"There's plenty of time for her to make the voyage. Anna would like a spring wedding."

Luellen's eyes moved to Anna. "Mother Wilhelm?"

"Grandmama," Adam explained. "She will be coming from her home in Munich. There are many customs she will share with us . . . if that's all right with you."

"Customs?" Luellen lifted her hands to her temples.

"Adam's bride vill vear Mother Vilhelm's vedding dress," Mama said.

Luellen's sickly look turned hostile. "Murray Jacobs will design Anna-Marie's gown. Why, as her godfather, he would be devastated if she wore another dress."

Mama shook her head, sucked her breath in, and stared straight ahead. "Adam ist Grandfather Vilhelm's namesake — *ist* first-born. Bride vill vear Grandmama's dress."

"Certainly not! My daughter will wear a Jacobs Couturier gown!"

Papa tossed down the last of his water. "Now, now, ladies. *Mutter's* gown vill arrive in plenty of time. No need to make new one —"

"It isn't a matter of *need*," Luellen sputtered.

Anna rose, and all attention focused on her. "Adam and I will decide what dress I will wear," she announced in a firm voice. "No one is to worry; everything can be worked out."

Adam wished he felt as confident as she sounded. "Anna, Grandmama will insist on —"

She put a fingertip to his lips. Turning back to her parents, she stated, "We are all going to be one, big happy family. I'll have it no other way."

"Good grief," Broderick muttered.

Dessert was refused. By now everyone

41

had lost their appetite.

"Come, dear," Broderick extended his arm to his wife as the dinner party broke up. He nodded good-night to the Wilhelms.

As the Martins turned to leave, Papa arose from his chair. "Vill see you soon, huh, Brod?"

Adam mentally groaned. He held Anna's hand tightly, ignoring the throbbing headache at his temples as both sets of parents filed out ahead of them.

"Well," Anna said, giving his hand an affectionate squeeze, "the worst is over."

Thanksgiving approached, and with it a deep snow. New York was blanketed with six inches of white powder, with still more predicted to fall.

Anna jumped Friday evening when Adam caught her around the waist and stole a kiss in the church vestibule. Tonight they were decorating for the upcoming holiday.

"Adam!" she scolded.

He helped himself to another hug. "I don't get to spend nearly as much time with my favorite girl as I'd like," he teased.

She sighed, agreeing with him. They'd hardly seen each other at all this week. The children were working on a holiday cantata, and two unexpected missionary projects had popped up. She'd barely had time to catch her breath.

She handed him a large paper pilgrim. "Make yourself useful."

Taking the pilgrim, he tacked him to the wall. "Can we find a few minutes for ourselves after service tonight? There's something I'd like to show you."

"Oh, Adam . . ." She hated to refuse him, but she felt deceitful when she spent more time with Adam than she did in mission work.

"There's a beautiful coat in Patton's Department Store window I want you to have. If you like it, I'll purchase it for you."

"The coat I have is perfectly good, Adam."

He stepped back to admire his handiwork, frowning when he saw the pilgrim's hat was lopsided. "Yes, but it isn't from me. I want to give you nice things, Anna."

Leaning close, she kissed him lightly on the ear, then put a colorful fat paper pumpkin in his hand. "How many times do I have to tell you? I love *you*, Adam. Not what you can buy me. The Lord has given us something money can never buy." She gave him another quick peck on the cheek, then picked up the box of decorations to move on. "Remember, he says that life doesn't consist in the abundance of our possessions." She winked. "Besides, having your love makes me the richest woman on earth."

Thanksgiving Day, Anna pulled a navy blue wool dress out of the closet and studied her image in the mirror. A knot that felt as large as a goose egg lay in her stomach as she worried about the dinner today. Adam told her not to worry, but how could she not? His parents were a big part of her future.

She frowned. She loved Adam more than life itself. But lately she was starting to wonder if love alone was going to be enough to see them through this wedding. Just this morning, Mother had insisted she have three bridesmaids and the groomsmen to escort them. Sighing, she closed the closet door, hoping that today differences would be set aside and blissful unity would rule the Thanksgiving celebration.

The doorbell rang as she came down the stairway a few minutes later. Giles, dressed in a white coat and black trousers, shuffled across the foyer to answer it. The stooped, gray-haired servant had served the family for more than forty years.

Touching her hand to her hair, Anna took

a deep breath as the butler admitted the Wilhelms. Adam caught sight of her and winked, making her heart trip wildly.

Clad in a black coat, Elfie Wilhelm, sturdy black purse over her arm, marched into the foyer. She paused beneath the crystal cut chandelier, her dark eyes roaming her elegant surroundings. Her gaze landed on the pretentious round marble tub holding a dried wheat-and-baby's-breath bouquet the size of a bathtub.

Klaus's booming voice accompanied the noisy entrance. *"Guten Tag!"* He stomped the snow off his boots onto the black-and-gold Oriental rug and reached to shake Giles's hand. "Klaus Vilhelm."

Giles gingerly accepted his greeting. "Mr. and Mrs. Martin are receiving in the parlor."

Klaus nodded, knocking his hat on the side of his overcoat. Snow fell in clumps on the polished floor. "Nice place you got here."

"Sir. May I take your coat?"

"Nein, I'll just throw it over the couch." Klaus glanced around the polished foyer. "Don't vant to cause any bother."

"Mr. and Mrs. Wilhelm." Smiling warmly, Anna descended the stairway. "Welcome to our home. How nice of you to spend Thanksgiving with us."

Elfie nodded, and Anna could see the woman felt out of place and uncomfortable with the surroundings.

Joining Adam at the bottom of the stairs, Anna took her fiancé's arm, then looped her other one through Elfie's and followed Giles into the parlor.

Anna's parents rose as their visitors entered the room. Anna noticed her father quickly reach up and secure his spectacles. She prayed Klaus wouldn't be quite as buoyant with his salutations today.

Adam held tightly to Anna's arm, his warmth penetrating her cold fingers as he greeted her parents. "Good evening, Mr. and Mrs. Martin. Thank you for inviting us to share your holiday."

Father and Klaus shook hands as Mother nodded pleasantly to a stone-faced Elfie.

Introductions over, the Martins asked their guests to be seated. Klaus tossed his coat onto a nearby chair and helped Elfie out of hers. Then Klaus and Elfie sat down on the straight-back sofa, crossing their legs in unison.

The clock over the mantel ticked away the seconds. The families sat in the elegant parlor, hands folded, staring straight ahead.

Finally, Adam cleared his throat. "Papa,

Mr. Martin is fond of chess."

Klaus nodded. "This is *gut?*"

"Very good." Adam smiled at Anna.

Klaus perked up. "I play checkers."

"Checkers?" Anna's father shook his head. "Never took to the game."

Klaus sank back down.

Mother smoothed her hair, then said, "Anna, have you told Mrs. Wilhelm that Murray is working around the clock on your dress?"

Anna sat up straighter. The gown was the *last* thing she wanted to discuss. Adam's mother would get upset, then her mother would take offense, and . . . she had to steer the conversation in a safer direction. "Mother, have you decided on the color of your dress?"

Ignoring her, Mother smiled at the Wilhelms. "You remember? Murray Jacobs — the designer, Anna's godfather?"

"Don't know him," Klaus admitted, glancing at Elfie. "I bought my Elfie's coat at Gutmeister's."

Anna interrupted. "Perhaps I could wear both gowns? Uncle Murray's during the ceremony, and Grandmother Wilhelm's during the reception?"

Elfie frowned. "Vat? Vear *two* gowns? This is silly. Mother Vilhelm vill bring dress she married Father Vilhelm in." She glanced at her son. "It is tradition. Adam's bride vill vear Grandmama's dress."

Mother's eyes darted to her daughter. "Anna, you can't wear an *old* dress — what will your father's associates say?"

"Old?" Elfie frowned. "Vat *old?* Is good dress."

Patting her mother's hand, Anna tried to smooth the moment. "Mother, please. Adam and I will handle this."

"Mama." Adam took a firmer stance. "We're not prepared to say which gown Anna will wear. We will consider both possibilities."

Elfie's eyes narrowed. "Not vear your grandmama's gown? You make joke, *nein?*"

"*Nein,* Mama." Adam stared straight ahead, a muscle working tightly in his jaw.

When Giles appeared in the doorway to announce dinner was served, Anna nearly wilted with relief. It was going to be a long day.

As Christmas drew near, church activities took up all of Anna's spare time. Her mother reserved the sanctuary at St. Luke's Church and proceeded with wedding arrangements in a whirl of preparations. The wedding party had grown to six brides-maids, six groomsmen, maid of honor, best man, two flower girls, and a ring bearer. Nuptials between Adam and Anna-Marie would be exchanged at four o'clock in the afternoon on Saturday, March 17.

At times Anna found herself resentful, and she had to stop and pray for patience. It seemed it was more Mother's wedding than her own. Elfie Wilhelm had entered into the fray, insisting her dear friend Helga Frack bake the cake.

The matter of Anna's gown remained unresolved. Murray was hard at work on a creation proclaimed by Mother to be the "most heavenly gown on earth." Sleeves full to the elbow of rich white satin, fastened with pearls and silver bangles looped together in a mass. The petticoat of lustrous white satin with pleating of thick white gauze at the hem made a striking contrast against the soft silk gauze overskirt, drawn up in places to form a drapery of festoons thickly set with pear-shaped pearls. The tulle veil fastened with orange blossoms looked to be the most exquisite ever fashioned.

Elfie had sent for Grandmama Wilhelm with the explicit instruction to arrive early in February with the dress in which she'd married Adam's grandfather.

By now, Anna's and Adam's nerves were frayed. They argued over small things and made up less easily. They rarely slipped away alone now. Anna insisted Agnus Bennet, head of the children's ministry, accompany them wherever they went.

Over the holiday, the Wilhelms returned the Martins' hospitality. Anna and her parents were invited for a late supper after the traditional Christmas Eve communion service. The Wilhelms' Brooklyn church was smaller than St. Luke's, and Anna realized her mother noticed. Her snobbish side was showing. Anna resented her mother's attitude. After all, Anna spent all her time at the Brooklyn church, and she felt it was an important part of her life.

Klaus welcomed Anna's parents with a huge bear hug that rattled Father's teeth and dislodged Mother's fancy hairdo. Gathering coats, Klaus tossed Mother's fur and Father's cashmere topcoat over the back of the worn sofa. Shoving a stack of magazines aside, he motioned for the Martins to have a seat. Mother eyed the family cat and promptly burst into a fit of sneezing.

Elfie served eggnog she'd prepared from her mother's recipe in huge German beer steins.

Anna discreetly checked her watch, her

gaze drawn to Adam. She could sense his discomfort, and she longed to put him at ease. She longed even more to feel the warmth that was once between them before all this wedding madness had started.

Mother lifted her mug to her mouth and was trying to drink around the hinged metal lid when the cat suddenly leapt into her lap. She lapsed into a fit of sneezing, the stein flew out of her hand, and Anna watched, horror struck, as the sticky eggnog splattered her mother's coat draped over the back of the sofa.

"My fur!" Mother sprang to her feet, causing Father to choke on the *Apfelkuchen* he'd just bitten into.

Adam sprang from his chair, mopping at the sticky sweetness as Anna tried to calm her mother. The cat screeched, bounded off the sofa, and darted between Elfie's legs as she was returning from the kitchen with a tray of *Linzertorte*.

Mother whirled on Anna's father. "I want to go home — now. I have a splitting headache."

"But you haven't had dinner," Elfie protested. She hurriedly picked up the cat and carried it to the door.

"I'm sorry," Anna's father apologized. "My wife is highly allergic to cats."

51

Anna glanced at Adam and, with a heavy heart, realized there was little anyone could say or do to salvage the evening.

"We'll do this another time," she apologized softly.

Slipping into her coat, she helped her mother put on the soiled fur. As they stepped into the cold winter's night, the last thing she heard was Klaus calling "*Gute Nacht* — and Merry Christmas!"

Merry Christmas indeed. Hot tears stung Anna-Marie's eyelids as she prayed through gritted teeth. *Father, forgive me, but right now the last thing I feel is merry!*

Chapter Four

January 1888

"Are the rolls fresh, Adam?"

"Just out of the oven, Mrs. Alder."

The stout redheaded matron ordered a dozen as Anna waited for Adam to sack the customer's purchase. He looked tired, and her heart went out to him. Three weeks into the new year, and she'd seen him twice since Christmas. The second job he'd taken at Sader's Deli left practically no time for courting. Now, if she wanted to see him, she had to come to the deli for lunch. She hated slipping away, unchaperoned, but she couldn't keep imposing on Mrs. Bennet to oversee their luncheons. The big day was only weeks away, and nothing had been settled about the gown. Mother had commandeered the flowers and guest list, so there was little left for Anna to do.

"Is that a new watch you're wearing?" she asked when the rush was over.

Adam lifted his arm, showing off his latest purchase. "I bought it for a song. It's a lot like your father's, don't you think? Except for the diamond in his — but someday —"

"Adam —" she closed her eyes, praying for patience — "listen to yourself. Your having a fancy watch means nothing to me if I can't spend time with you. You work too hard for your money to spend it on foolish baubles." She immediately wanted to bite her tongue when she saw his smile fade.

"I thought you would be happy I'm doing so well." He studied the watch, and she could see he was admiring the way its gold etchings caught the shafts of light streaming through the open doorway.

"I *am* happy. It's just that I miss our times together." She couldn't believe it when Adam had taken the part-time job at the deli. Work took up all his spare time — including his weekends. He had even gotten a substitute teacher for his Sunday morning class. He insisted the money was needed for their future, but so far he'd purchased items totally unlike him. Gifts for her, and now the watch. What was he thinking?

"We'll have time together, darling. Mr. Sader has agreed to let me stay on after we're married. Combined with my wages from Mama and Papa, it won't be long before we can open the second Wilhelm's Market — and then a third. We'll travel, we'll eat at the nicest restaurants, we'll . . ."

She sighed, letting his voice fade away. All he talked about lately was business, travel, and his obsession with a ridiculous motorized carriage a friend from Germany had told him about. What nonsense. She pictured horses bolting for cover when such a contraption sped down the streets.

". . . you will want for nothing, Anna."

Her eyes were drawn back to Adam's. The love she saw there did little to still her fears. "I want for nothing now — nothing but you."

"You *have* me," he said softly. "Are you sure you want to wake up with a grocery clerk every morning?"

"I want nothing more." She studied him a moment. "A handsome grocery clerk who's not had enough sleep lately."

"Sleep is for old men who have everything they need." He kissed her hand, then he ran his thumb over the engagement ring. "Someday you will wear diamonds and gold to rival a queen."

She jerked her hand back. "Stop it, Adam. I love this ring, and I don't ever want another."

"But your mother looks so elegant in all her finery."

"I'm not my mother." She checked her sharp tongue and forced a smile. He only wanted to please her. Without hurting his feelings, what could she say to make him realize she was content to be a storekeeper's wife? "Impressing my parents isn't necessary. I don't want an extravagant lifestyle. I want a simpler life — like your parents, Adam."

"But don't you see, Anna? I want to give you the kind of life *your* parents have — the kind of life you deserve." His voice became excited again. "And I will, with a big house and lots of room for babies."

"Lots of babies?" This was a subject dear to her heart. "We don't need a big house to have lots of babies — we only need each other. My friend Betsy mentioned an apartment that's for rent in her building. It would be close to the grocery store for you, and I love the area. It's small, but it's perfect for us."

Maybe it was only because he looked so tired, but she detected an air of impatience, as if all his plans were being discounted.

"You'll see, Anna. We will need more than each other. Children need clothes, schooling. I don't want your father to think I can't provide well for my family —" His attention was drawn to a customer entering the deli. "Be right with you," he called out, then turned back to her. "I'll ask Mr. Sader if I can get off early. We can go for a walk in the park."

"And listen to your expansion plans and how you are going to buy out all the jewelry stores for me? No, thank you," she said. "If you leave early, I suggest you go home and sleep." She jerked her cloak tighter around her neck and walked out the door.

Adam stood with his mouth agape. Anna-Marie had never said a harsh word to him. What had he done? He only wanted to give her things she was accustomed to. Even though she said material possessions meant nothing, he knew she would grow weary of a poor man's life. He wanted to make her happy — and make her father proud to have him as a son-in-law. Broderick Martin respected a man of means, he could see that. One day he would be a man of means — a man Anna could be proud of.

"Yes, sir, what can I get for you?" he said to an older man blowing on his fingers.

"Coffee. The hotter, the better."

Adam poured the black liquid into a cup, his mind more on Anna than his duties. "Cream?"

"Just a little sugar."

Staring out the deli window, Adam absently spooned sugar into the coffee and thought of Anna out in the cold, waiting for the train home. She had risked her parents' censure by coming here alone to spend a few minutes with him, and once again they had argued. God forgive him, he didn't want it this way. He wanted Anna happy, smiling, the way she used to be. He would make it up to her. He would take a whole day off very soon and do anything Anna wanted. Maybe he would borrow the prototype motor carriage his former schoolmate was trying to interest him in. Of course, he couldn't afford to buy it right now, but it was exciting to think about owning such a novelty someday. It was patterned after the three-wheeler Karl Benz built in Germany a couple of years before, but his friend had added a seat on the back to carry extra baggage.

Adam's daydream brought a smile to his face. He pictured Anna and himself cruising along the boulevard and waving at awe-struck passersby. His friend said the one-cylinder, internal-combustion engine powered the chassis along at almost eight miles an hour. *Eight miles an hour. Think of that!*

"Ahem!"

Adam jerked his head around to see the old man staring at him.

"I said a *little* sugar, son. You've shoveled

in six spoons full already. Sader'll have your hide for being so wasteful."

"Sorry, sir. I'll fix you another."

⚭

Sleep would not come that night, no matter how tightly Anna squeezed her eyes shut. She finally got up, donned her robe, and slipped down to the kitchen for warm milk. *Adam.* She loved him so much, and it broke her heart that they had argued again. *So silly.* How could she be upset with someone who only wanted the best for her? But she *was* angry. Adam was changing right before her eyes. He wasn't the same man she'd fallen in love with. He was suddenly driven by materialistic values — values she found offensive. She thought God had sent her Adam, that they had the same goals. How could she have been so wrong? Did God make mistakes? Or were all the problems she and Adam were having God's way of telling her Adam was not the man for her? And Mother. Why was it suddenly *Mother's* wedding and not hers?

She carried her glass of milk into the library, pulled the Bible from the shelf, and curled up in a large, high-backed leather chair. As she sipped the warm beverage, she flipped through the pages, searching for consolation. Her gaze focused on the familiar verse in Genesis. *Therefore shall a man leave his father and his mother, and shall cleave unto his wife: and they shall be one flesh.*

What did that mean? What was the Lord saying to her? Was Adam to disregard his parents' feelings in order to satisfy hers? That hardly seemed fair. Was she to disregard her parents' feelings in order to be a dutiful wife? How could she honor her parents and yet make them so unhappy at the same time?

Troubled, she put the Bible back on the shelf and returned to bed.

⌘

In the living quarters behind the grocery store, Adam lay in his bed, staring into the dark as he listened to George's soft snores. He envied his brother's peaceful slumber. Anna's face was all he could think about. Where was the happy couple they once had been? He longed to see the excitement in her eyes when they met, hear her soft giggle when he kissed her neck just below her ear. Desire flooded him when he thought of his fiancée. He loved her, of that he was sure. But was love enough? Perhaps they were too opposite, had too many obstacles to overcome. There was a time he thought she had been sent from heaven just for him to love and cherish. What had gone wrong? He only wanted the best for her — to buy her pretty things, to give her anything her heart desired.

Tossing the covers aside, he rose and tiptoed into the kitchen for a glass of water. As he passed Papa's chair, he noticed the open Bible where Papa always left it. Adam felt a twinge of guilt. With all the hours he was putting in at work these past weeks, he'd been remiss in studying his Sunday school lessons. Touching a match to the coal oil lamp, he sat it on the kitchen counter. Leafing aimlessly through the pages of Scripture, he stumbled across a verse in Hebrews he had read a dozen times before. *Let your conversation be without covetousness; and be content with such things as ye have: for he hath said, I will never leave thee, nor forsake thee.*

Sitting down at the table, he buried his head in his hands. Was that what he was doing? Putting material possessions before the people he loved?

February

Anna huddled beside Adam on the dock and watched the ship carrying his grandmother glide into port. Overhead, a dark

61

blustery sky heightened her gloomy mood. Excited onlookers awaiting the arrival of the large vessel strained for a closer look, jumped up and down, waved and shouted to loved ones who lined the railing on the ship's upper deck. A cold wind whipped coats and sent fur hats skipping along wooden planks.

Huddling deep inside her cloak, Anna forced back tears, feeling miserable. Adam had barely spoken two words to her on the ride over. How could he, when he was fighting like a man possessed to control the wheel of that ridiculous motor carriage? Anna was sure her hair looked as if it had been whipped with an eggbeater, and the wind had stung her nose a bright red.

A deafening whistle sounded from the upper stacks of the ship as the gangplank lowered. Passengers streamed off, eyes eagerly searching the crowd. Hugs and happy tears escalated into a holidaylike atmosphere.

"Grossmutter!" Adam shouted, waving to a stout-looking woman making her way down the gangplank, a black purse securely strapped over one arm, a large suit box tucked beneath the other.

The old woman spotted them, her face splitting in a big grin. *"Enkel!"* She rushed off the gangplank and engulfed her grand-son in a bear hug. Anna smiled, watching the exchange and thinking how much Grandmother Wilhelm favored her son, Klaus: short, stocky, and with a smile that spread from ear to ear.

"Grandmama." Adam drew Anna to his side. "This is my fiancée, Anna-Marie Martin."

Mrs. Wilhelm smiled, shaking her head up and down. "*Ja, ja. Ist* lovely." She handed Anna the box. "*Ist* your dress. My English not so *gut*."

"Thank you, Grandmother Wilhelm, and your English is just fine." Anna kissed her on the cheek, shooting Adam a desperate look. He shook his head, and she took his warning to mean he didn't want her to go near the subject of dresses right now.

As Adam rounded up his grandmother's trunk, Anna took the suit box, then she turned Grandmother Wilhelm in the direction of the motorcar. As they walked toward the silly-looking contraption, the older woman's eyes widened.

A crowd had gathered, oohhing and ahhing over the machine. Small children ran their hands over the shiny black fenders. The three-wheeled, open-aired monstrosity caused quite a commotion. Anna wished she could share their enthusiasm. They'd obviously never ridden in one.

"What is that?" a man in the crowd shouted.

"A motor carriage," Anna called back, hurrying Grandmother Wilhelm along. The little woman's short legs could barely keep up.

"There's nothing to be frightened about," Anna explained when Grandmother Wilhelm appeared hesitant to go near it. "Adam's thinking of purchasing it." Taking her arm, Anna helped the elderly woman into the backseat, then she climbed onto the front bench and sat down. Turning around, she checked on the old woman's comfort. Adam's grandmama sat stiff as a poker, black-stockinged feet straight out in front of her, hands gripping the side of the bench tightly. Anna could see that the poor woman was scared to death. She could just choke Adam!

"Are you all right, Grandmama?"

"*Ja,* very *gut!*" she said in a squeaky voice.

Adam squeezed the trunk in beside her, grinning. "We'll be home soon, Grandmama."

He climbed in, and Anna latched onto her hat as off they wheeled in a cloud of snow, scattering people, scaring horses, and causing a horrible ruckus with seventy-two-year-old Grandmother Wilhelm in the backseat, hanging on for dear life.

That night, Anna-Marie closed the door to her bedroom and hurried to her wardrobe. Dragging the suit box off the top shelf, she carried it to the bed. The box was old and worn, evidence of a treasured keepsake. She'd delayed looking at Grandmother Wilhelm's wedding dress all afternoon. What if it were truly ugly — worse yet, what if it were sizes too big for her? Mina Wilhelm was a stout lady and three inches shorter than her. Anna-Marie sank down on the side of the bed, her eyes focused on the box. Which dress should she wear? Visions of the gown hanging in Uncle Murray's workroom taunted her. The design was breathtaking, every girl's dream, with its yards of satin and lace and an elegant train.

She buried her face in her hands. The wedding was only weeks away, and she still had no idea in which gown she would vow to love and obey Adam.

Biting her lower lip, Anna closed her eyes and carefully lifted the lid. When she allowed herself to look, her gaze fell on a wedding veil, a lovely wreath of dried red and white roses, with myrtle entwined.

Tears burned her eyelids as she peeled aside yellowed tissue to reveal a simple gown of white toile nestled among the wrapping.

Setting the wreath aside, she removed the garment and examined it, her breath catching at its simplistic beauty. Large puffy sleeves, billowing skirt, nipped tightly to a small waist. Grandmother Wilhelm had once been very tiny. Anna's gaze focused on an object lying in the bottom of the box, and she reached for the strange-looking ring. The pattern was ornate and charming: figures of Adam and Eve, and the Tree. The symbolism escaped her, but it must mean something special for Grandmother Wilhelm to have kept it all these years.

Slipping the ring on her finger, she discovered it was a perfect fit. Was it Grandmother's wedding ring?

A knock sounded at the door, and she removed the ring and placed it back in the box. "Who is it?"

"Mother, dear. Dinner is served in five minutes."

"Coming, Mother." Anna folded the dress and laid it carefully back in the box. Placing the veil of dried roses and myrtle on top, she replaced the lid.

March

A round of bridal showers and elaborate teas kept Anna busy throughout the month of February. As she hurried along the sidewalk on her way to meet Adam, she fretted. At times, she wondered if every bride felt as she did — torn, heartbroken that she couldn't please everybody. It seemed at the moment she was pleasing no one — not herself, not Adam, and most certainly not God. The strain between her and Adam was palpable, and she'd ignored her friends something awful. There didn't seem to be enough hours in the day to do what was expected of her.

A brisk wind snatched her hat and sent it sailing. She chased it down the street for most of a block before she caught up with it. Jamming it on her head, she hurried to the restaurant. As she entered, her gaze eagerly searched for Adam. She needed his strength today, his calm assurance. She stiffened when she saw him sitting at a small table, a pretty German-speaking waitress bent over his shoulder, pointing out the day's special. The girl's honey blond curls touched his light brown waves. Jealousy consumed her as she approached the table. What would happen if she were to lose him to another?

She couldn't bear the thought. The past months had been so strained — was he wishing he'd never asked for her hand in marriage? Would he rather have a pretty German girl for his bride?

Adam glanced up, and she saw his blue eyes soften when he spotted her. "Hello, darling."

"Hello, Adam." Love oozed through her like rich, warm honey. Today was going to be different; today there wasn't going to be an ounce of disharmony between them — if she had to tape her mouth shut, she would refuse to talk about *anything*, however trivial, that would lead to another disagreement.

Today harmony would reign.

She slid into the chair opposite him and removed her gloves. She glanced at the waitress, hoping her jealousy didn't show.

"*Guten Tag.*" The young woman smiled.

Anna knew enough German to return the greeting. "Good afternoon."

"*Ist* nice day?"

Anna touched her hair and laughed. "Not so nice. It's very windy."

The waitress nodded, took their order for tea, and disappeared.

Adam reached for her hand across the table. His eyes glistened with love as he looked at her. "Your cheeks are red from the cold, and you're very beautiful."

"And you're very handsome — and the new waitress noticed, I'm sure." She casually perused the menu. "And she's very German."

Drats. The words were out before she realized she'd spoken.

Adam glanced over his shoulder. "Is she? I hadn't noticed." His brow lifted. "Are you jealous?"

"Should I be?" She snapped the menu closed and decided she'd better change the subject. "Your grandmother's dress is lovely."

"You finally looked at it? Grandmama's been asking for days — do you like it?"

"It's very pretty," she confessed, ignoring his expectant look. It *was* pretty, but certainly it was not Mother's taste. When Mother saw the dress, she remarked she'd been to a festival once where the yodelers wore similar clothing. That was Mother's way of dismissing the dress, but Anna didn't feel that way, nor had she felt like *yodeling* when she'd tried it on.

Disappointment softened Adam's face. "Why did you take so long to tell me?"

"I didn't want to say anything for fear I'd have to make a decision —"

"Anna." His voice turned patronizing. "I would never force you to wear a gown you didn't want to wear. I only want you to consider the possibility —"

"It's unfair of your parents to insist that I wear it!" she blurted.

"My parents have as much right to insist we follow tradition as your parents do —"

"It's *my* wedding!"

"It's *mine,* too, but you'd never know it! Your mother has taken over —"

"*My* mother! What about yours? She insists that friend of hers, Helga Frack, bake the cake!"

His eyes snapped with impatience. "You have been in a foul mood for weeks, *Miss Martin.*"

"Me? What about you — and don't tell me you didn't notice that waitress was pretty. You're not blind."

He busied himself with the tableware. "You're jealous — and you need to comb your hair."

"Comb my hair!" Her hand flew to her hat, aware she should have tidied herself before she came to the table. She sucked in her breath through clenched teeth. "How *dare* you talk to me this way, Adam Wilhelm."

He'd never uttered an unkind word to her, and now he was *insulting* her hair. She stood up, hurling her napkin down on the table like a gauntlet. Diners turned in their seats to stare.

Adam stood up. "When have I *ever* insisted you wear one gown or the other?" Their eyes locked in a heated duel.

"It's in your *voice*. I know you want me to wear your grandmother's gown, and Mother insists I wear Uncle Murray's —" She blinked back tears. "Sometimes I wish I didn't have to wear either one!"

There. She'd said it: the dark thought that had consumed her lately. Either gown she wore was certain to doom her to eternal misery!

Adam got very quiet, looking at her as if he couldn't believe she would behave so badly. She squirmed beneath his perusal, aware she'd gone too far.

"Adam — I didn't mean —"

He signaled for the check. "Perhaps this meeting was a mistake. You aren't yourself today."

"Adam —"

"Another time, Anna."

As they left the restaurant, Adam hailed a cab, paying the driver after giving her parents' address. For once Anna was thankful Agnus Bennet wasn't with them to witness this spectacle.

"Adam . . ." Anna caught the sleeve of his jacket, desperately ashamed of the way she'd acted. She didn't know what had gotten into her!

He calmly shrugged her hand aside. "I'll use Mr. Sader's telephone and call you later." He put her in the cab and shut the door.

As the carriage pulled away, Anna huddled miserably beneath the blanket. *Nothing* was going as planned. She buried her face in her hands and wept.

And so much for a harmonious day.

Chapter Five

When Giles announced a visitor for Anna that evening, she cringed. Her eyes were red and swollen from crying, and she was dressed in her robe and gown, ready for bed.

"Is it Betsy?" she asked, blowing her nose on a linen handkerchief.

"No, Miss. It's the young Mr. Wilhelm. He apologized for calling so late but says it's urgent he talk to you."

Anna forgot about her appearance and fairly flew down the stairs to the foyer.

"Adam! I thought you were going to call from Sader's."

He studied her face, then he reached for her hands and pulled her to him. "You've been crying. I don't want you crying —"

She sagged against his chest, comforted by his presence. Life would be meaningless without him. "Oh, Adam, what is happening to us?"

Holding her close, he smoothed her back. "I didn't call, just because I wanted to see you. I . . . I didn't want to go to sleep with this anger between us."

"It's so late, Adam, and you have to get up early in the morning —"

"No, I don't. I've asked Papa for the day off." He tightened his arms around her waist and pulled her closer. "Tomorrow we will go on a picnic."

She buried her face in his shirtfront, amused. "Adam, have you forgotten this is March? It's hardly picnic weather."

He laughed. "Where's your spirit of adventure, young lady?"

It felt so good to hear him laugh again, Anna thought as she hugged him tight. "Come into the parlor, and we'll talk."

"No, it is very late. I only wanted to say good-night." He tipped her face up and kissed her. "I have rented a sleigh. Tomorrow we will spend the day together and talk of nothing but our future." His eyes softened. "Just you and me, Anna."

She walked him to the door, her arm looped through his. This was the old Adam — the Adam she fell in love with.

"I'll be up at the crack of dawn," she whispered.

He looked down at her, smiled, and touched his lips, then hers, with his fingertip. "Make that half past dawn. I could use the extra sleep."

★ ★ ★

Anna woke to bright sunlight streaming through the bedroom window. It was a glorious morning. She hadn't slept so well in weeks. Too excited about spending an entire day with Adam, she discounted the eggs and hotcakes Cook had prepared. Instead, she drank a small glass of juice and ate two bites of bread and jam.

"Is Mother up yet?" she asked as she passed Giles, who was polishing the mahogany banister to a blinding sheen. For once she was going to explain that she and Adam were going to spend the day alone to discuss wedding plans.

"She and Mr. Martin left the house early this morning, Miss Anna. Something about checking on arrangements for the reception."

"Oh, yes, the reception." She felt a prick of disappointment. She wanted to settle the matter of the dress before she met with Adam. "If they return before I do, please tell them I'm spending the day with Adam."

Giles smiled. "Seems like a nice chap, that Adam. He's quite smitten with you."

She loved Giles' clarity. He had the ability to sum up things in a minimum of words. Adam was certainly a nice "chap" — at least he was when she'd met him — and she had no doubt he loved her as much as she loved him. But if they couldn't resolve their problems before they married, what would it be like afterwards?

❧❧

"First time I see you smile since I step off ship." Grandmama Wilhelm buttered a piece of Elfie's sweet roll. "You alvays my pretty-faced boy — no vant you frown."

Adam laughed. "Grandmama, men don't have pretty faces — they have handsome faces."

"Don't be fresh vit Grandmama. You alvays my pretty boy." She bit into the hot bread.

Adam dropped a kiss on the top of his grandmother's head. "Sorry I can't eat breakfast with you this morning, but I have an appointment."

"Vit pretty girl, Anna, I bet. You vear pullover I knit you?" she called. "*Ist* cold!"

"Yes, Grandmama."

As Adam gathered articles for the picnic lunch and put them in a basket, he felt a wash of guilt over leaving Mama and Papa to run the store by themselves, especially with Grandmama visiting. But it was necessary to quell tension between him and Anna. March seventeenth was closing in, and still there were so many problems.

Elfie came in yawning, and Adam kissed her good morning. His father was a couple of steps behind. "I'll work the early shift tomorrow, Mama. George can help me. He doesn't have classes. You and Papa can spend time with Grandmama Wilhelm."

"That is not my vorry, my son," his mother said.

Adam glanced at his father, who was staring at him with the same censuring expression on his face as Elfie's.

"What?"

"Ve are vorried about you."

"Me? I'm fine. Why?" Adam asked.

His father turned around and looked him up and down. "Your clothes."

Adam glanced down at his apparel. "What's wrong with my clothes? I'm wearing the sweater Grandmama knitted."

His father pointed at him. "Your new pants, your new jacket, your new coat —"

"Your new vatch, your new hat," his mother finished.

"I just want to look nice for Anna," Adam said.

"So — you didn't look nice two months ago?" his father asked indignantly. "The clothes your Mama and I vear are not *gut* enough anymore? Suddenly, you look down on your parents?"

"Oh, Papa — Mama, I would never be ashamed of you. I love you."

"Ve never see you anymore," Elfie said, sniffing back a tear. "You vork, vork, vork. You have to have money for this, money for that. You buy us foolish presents. Vere do ve go to vear new coats, new shoes? Ve don't know you anymore."

Adam would rather cut off his right arm than to have his parents disappointed with his behavior. How could he explain that he only wanted to be prosperous, to provide a good home for his new wife, to make Mr. and Mrs. Martin proud of him — to make *them* proud of him?

"I am your son. I will always be your son."

His father swiped a dust rag across the counter. "Our son used to be happy vit vat he had. Our son didn't put vorldly possessions before all else. Our son used to tell us that loving each other vas the greatest gift of all."

The verse in Hebrews flashed through Adam's mind. *Was* he dwelling on money too much? He only wanted the best for those he loved.

"Please, Mama, Papa, don't be upset. The wedding will be over soon, and we'll be back to normal."

Elfie crossed the room and put her arms around him, giving him a brief, forgiving hug before handing him a sack. "Some *Linzertorte* for Anna. Give her our regards. Ve have missed seeing her around — and, Son?"

"Yes, Mama?"

"Leave everything to God. He vill guide you. He never fails."

The sun was shining, the air brisk. Anna snuggled under the blanket and leaned closer to Adam. "Where are you taking me? Is it far?"

"A park. It should be deserted this time of year."

She giggled. "Wouldn't surprise me."

"There." He pointed. "We're almost there."

She sat up to see a snowcapped pavilion standing in the middle of a white field. "We'll freeze, Adam."

He pulled the sleigh to a stop. "I brought a quilt to wrap around our shoulders." He hugged her tightly. "I'll keep you warm."

She snuggled close to him. "I wish it could be like this all the time."

"This cold?"

She laughed. "I mean you and me. Just you and me."

He put his arms around her, cradling her

to his chest. She felt warm and safe in his embrace.

"Soon, my love," Adam said. "We will be married and settled in our home —"

She lifted her head. "Don't be angry, but I put a deposit on the apartment I told you about." She knew she should have consulted him first, but the apartment would have been gone if they had dallied much longer.

Adam's brows knitted. "I thought we agreed to find a house together — a large house, maybe near your parents."

"I don't want to live in a large house near my parents. I want to live in Brooklyn, near your store. That way, you'll be able to come home for lunch —"

His jaw firmed. "Anna, we are not going to argue today. We are going to be happy. We will decide where we live after the wedding. Until then, we will stay with one of our families."

She jerked her hand away. "No, Adam, we will decide now. Your parents don't have room for us. Besides, have you forgotten the Bible says that 'a man shall leave his father and his mother, and shall cleave unto his wife: and they shall be one flesh'?"

His jaw firmed. "That's unfair, Anna. I'm only trying to please all parties."

"I don't want to live with Mother and Father."

"They wouldn't want their only daughter living like a pauper."

"Adam! It would do them *good* to see how others live."

"And it would do *my* parents good to see how things could be if only they were more industrious!"

She gasped, heartsick. She had *never* heard him speak of his parents in a disrespectful way. What had gotten into him? For that matter, what had gotten into her? They both talked as if they were ashamed of their parents.

She turned her head away. "Adam, I'm afraid we have lost the true meaning of our relationship."

Adam groaned. "Anna, please . . ."

"We have to talk, Adam. Now."

He sighed, shaking his head. "Please don't tell me you're not going to wear Grandmama's dress." His eyes pleaded with her.

"It's not that I don't want to wear it. It's just —" She burst into tears. "It's just so hard, Adam. We can't agree on anything anymore."

"Then let's just *elope*." She could see his patience was clearly at an end.

"We can't do that! Mother would never forgive me!"

"Anna, Genesis 2:24 applies to you as well as to me."

That did it. Wiping her eyes, she took a deep breath. "Maybe we're making a mistake."

"A mistake?" Concern dotted his features.

She couldn't believe she was saying it, but the words came tumbling out. "Maybe we should wait a while before we get married. Maybe we haven't thought it clearly through."

He stared, disbelief written in his eyes. "Anna, you don't mean this."

Tears rolled down her cheeks, and she angrily swiped them away with her mittens. "I do mean this, Adam. If we're still arguing over a silly dress, how will we ever handle anything important?"

"Don't be rash. The dress is the only problem. The church has been reserved, the invitations are out, the cake and flowers are ordered — we'll be married in your parents' church, and you will wear Grandmama's dress." His mouth tightened. "The wedding has turned into a nightmare, Anna. It's so big — we've done everything your mother has asked with the exception of the dress. Is it too much to hope that you observe just one of my family's traditions?"

"No, but you've been too busy working and buying fancy things to realize this isn't *our* wedding anymore. It's our parents'!" She looked away.

He sucked in a deep breath and released it slowly.

She waited, hoping he would beg her to reconsider. She knew she was being childish, that God was bound to be frowning, but she needed reassurance. Reassurance that Adam loved her in spite of everything.

He was silent for a moment, then he said softly, "If you want to delay the wedding, it's your choice."

Her heart sank. He *didn't* love her enough to overlook her past pettiness. She didn't love herself.

"I guess it's the only thing to do at this point." She refused to meet his stoic gaze. "Take me home, Adam. I don't feel much like a picnic."

"Well, it's probably for the best." Anna's mother sank down on the sofa. "I hate to see you so sad, but I must say I believe you could use a little time to think this marriage through more precisely."

Anna could see the relief in her parents' faces, and it hurt. She had wanted them to be happy about her marriage and love Adam as much as she did. Neither had happened.

"Adam is an honorable boy," Father conceded, "but he's not like us. It wouldn't have worked out. You would never be happy with a grocery clerk."

Anna's temper flared. "*You* wouldn't be happy for me to marry a grocery clerk. That's all I wanted, but Adam wanted to be more. He wanted to be like you."

"Now, now," Mother soothed, "you're upset and understandably so. What you need is a long trip to get your mind off this — this misfortune."

Her father cleared his throat. "Perhaps this is a good time for you to attend Mrs. Woodmire's finishing school. Get your mind off Adam Wilhelm —"

Anna's eyes steeled. "I will always be in love with Adam."

"Time heals all wounds, child." Father cleared his throat. "Now, why not buy yourself a new wardrobe? You'll feel better in a few days."

Anna sank down on the side of the bed, staring at the open trunk. Things were just a mess. A big mess. The pressure had been too much; she wasn't marrying Adam on Saturday. She was going to *finishing* school.

Flinging herself across the eyelet spread, she covered her head with a pillow, trying to blot out the world. How could God's children get themselves into such a dilemma? What had gone wrong? Memories of Reverend Lawson's sermon that morning haunted her. He'd spoken from the book of Proverbs about trust, trust that God knew what was best for his children. She'd felt like such an impostor. Where was her trust in God . . . or in Adam, the man she loved? Was she willing to let Adam leave without a fight, when she knew in her heart God had destined them for each other?

She stared at the trunk, willing it to go away. Her hands refused to pack the stack of colorful new dresses and camisoles. Everything inside her rebelled against the idea of attending Elmira Woodmire's stuffy old finishing school. She began to sob. This wasn't what she wanted! But the situation was impossible.

She rolled off the bed and tossed the pillow aside. Her hair stood on end, scrambled from all the wallowing. Stepping to the window, she crossed her arms, studying the gloomy sky. Low clouds promised imminent rain. Red-breasted robins skittered across the lawn. Canada geese honked overhead. Winter was nearly over.

Tears welled behind her eyelids, and she stubbornly quelled them. Where was Adam? She hadn't seen or spoken to him since the day of the picnic. Her heart threatened to split in two when she thought of him. Did he love her so little that he was willing to let her go without a single attempt to reconcile? Not that it would do him any good! Her mind was made up; the wedding was off. So why had she cried for hours when she heard her mother cancel the wedding arrangements?

All she'd ever wanted was the Adam she'd fallen in love with. Not the work-crazed fanatic who talked of nothing but owning a chain of grocery stores and worked two jobs to purchase some ridiculous "motor carriage" whose breakneck speed was going to get him killed!

Burying her face in her hands, she began to weep all over again when she heard a loud ruckus erupt downstairs. Adam's voice, demanding to see her, rumbled up the stairway and caused a quaking to start deep inside her soul. Swiping at her eyes, she quickly opened her bedroom door and stepped into the hallway as Adam ascended the stairs two at a time. Giles hurried behind, trying to detain him.

"Sir! I have to announce you!"

"Don't bother. She'll see me."

"See here, young man!" The disturbance had brought Father out of the study. He stood at the bottom of the stairs, peering up at the commotion. "You *can't* just burst in here —"

Anna stepped to the railing and called down, "It's all right, Father."

Striding toward her, Adam locked his eyes on hers. His face was a dark thundercloud.

Forcing back the lump suddenly crowding her throat, Anna-Marie said softly, "You *don't* have to be so rowdy."

His impatient gaze pinned her to the carpet. "I want to talk to you."

Father started up the flight of stairs. "Shall I summon the authorities, Anna?"

Mother emerged from the parlor, wringing her hands. "Send for the police, Broderick!"

"Mother!" Anna shouted. "Don't anyone *move!*" She grabbed Adam's arm and ushered him onto the small balcony at the end of the upstairs hall. Closing the double doors, she turned to Adam. For a long moment they just looked at each other.

"Anna, I love you," he said.

Her anger dissipated like snowflakes on a warm sidewalk. "I love you, too." Dissolving into tears, she walked into his arms. The scent of soap and masculine cologne washed over her like manna from heaven. She closed her eyes, thanking God that Adam had overlooked her juvenile, petty behavior, even if it had taken him a while. "I'm so sorry."

"No, I should apologize." As he set her gently back from him, his eyes searched hers for understanding and forgiveness. "I don't know what's been happening to us lately, but I don't want to lose you, Anna. I love you with all my heart." He lowered his lips to hers and kissed her tenderly.

When the kiss ended, she still clutched his lapels as he gazed at her solemnly. "I want you to marry me."

She laughed, smiling through tears. "Of course I will. It will take some doing, but if we set our minds to it we can —"

He laid a fingertip across her lips. "Today."

"Adam." The thought rang wildly through her. It was wickedly tempting. Slip off and be married — no fussing over gowns and churches and attendants —

But she couldn't. Mother and Father would be crushed, and so would his parents.

It would be disrespectful. "We can't. Our parents would —"

His kiss stopped her. When he lifted his head, he continued, "You said this was not our wedding anymore. I agree, but I want it to be ours. Don't you see? I've been trying to make us like your parents —"

"And I guess I've been trying to make us like yours."

"We've forgotten that God created us different but equal. Our parents are good, loving people with their own traditions and values. But they're not our traditions."

"Oh, Adam, that's how I've been feeling, and I just didn't know how —"

His anxious kiss stopped her. When their lips parted many long moments later, he whispered, "No disrespect intended to our parents, but I'm not asking them to marry me. I'm asking you, Anna-Marie Martin, to marry me, today."

She wanted to, oh, how she wanted to fling caution to the wind. But would it be right?

He gazed at her expectantly. "We have the marriage license. It's a beautiful spring day, a day for new beginnings." He lightly touched his lips to her forehead. "A day to marry the one you love, and I love you more than words can say."

Was he speaking out of obligation, or were his words coming from the heart? She had to know. "Just because we have a marriage license doesn't mean we *have* to get married," she murmured. She couldn't bear it if he were marrying her out of a sense of duty.

She was warmed by the teasing note in his voice. It had been a long time since she'd heard it. "I understand there's a law that says you must use the license immediately, or they'll lock you up in jail and throw away the key."

She giggled, then sobered. "Oh, Adam . . . I'm so confused. Is this really what God wants for us? Truthfully, I don't want to marry the Adam I've known for the past few weeks. I want the Adam who's content with who and what he is. The gown, the cake, the number of bridesmaids and groomsmen — these issues will pass, but —"

"Anna." He silenced her with a gentle squeeze. "I realize God has been trying to get me to see the importance of contentment. I see so clearly now. I've been wrong in wanting 'things.' It's you I want. If you'll agree to be my wife, I promise I'll be the old Adam. And we can get married on Saturday — or any day you like."

Their mouths drifted back together in another long kiss.

"Listen to me, Anna." His voice softened as he held her near to his heart. She could hear its strong steady beat as she pressed closer. "If I prosper, it will be because of God's grace, not my works. And God doesn't care if you wear Grandmama's wedding gown or your Uncle Murray's. Flowers aren't important, or the number of attendants. I don't think God cares how many guests are served at the reception or if the cake has pink or green rosettes on it. He cares about you and me — two people who love each another. The conflict we've experienced isn't his doing, it's ours — and everyone connected with this wedding. We can't change Mama and Papa, or make your parents any different. But we can have our own wedding."

Sniffling, she wiped her streaming eyes. "Do I have to ride in that awful motor carriage?"

"No." He grinned. "I can't afford that monstrosity. I returned it to the owner before I came over. And you might as well know, I don't have the money to start a chain of Wilhelm groceries — probably never will. But maybe, in time, God will bless us, and Papa and I can build on —"

Her kiss interrupted him this time. When they finally parted, she pinched him on the cheek. "When you talk like that, Adam Wilhelm, how can I refuse to marry you? We can honor, respect, and love our parents, just as the Bible teaches, but we're forming a new and separate union."

His gaze skimmed her affectionately. "A union that will last for an eternity. And I'll even fall in love with that miserable little apartment you've rented." He hugged her tighter, whispering, "The part about coming home for lunch every day persuaded me."

She swatted him playfully. "You're awful."

"You don't know the half of it." He kissed her again. "Now dry your eyes and tell your mother you're getting married Saturday as planned."

Anna-Marie grinned. "I think she'll be relieved. With everything that's happened, she's suffering awful with the vapors."

Chapter Six

The sun was shining late Friday afternoon as Anna slipped into her cloak. It had been a hectic week, but the wedding rehearsal was upon them. Pinpointing Father with her eyes, Anna said, "Don't be such a stick-in-the-mud. If Klaus Wilhelm slaps you on the back, slap him back. It's just his way of being friendly. And Mother, ask Grandmother Wilhelm about her knitting. She makes beautiful sweaters and scarves."

Her mother put her hand to her throat. "I know nothing about *knitting*."

"Just ask — for my sake."

Luellen's shoulders slumped. "Oh, all right, for your sake, I'll ask about scarves and yarn."

Pleased with how smoothly things were going, Anna pulled on her mittens. "Shall we go to the church?"

"Mama, be sure to wear your new coat," Adam warned as they prepared to leave for the rehearsal.

"My old one is varmer," Mama announced. When Adam's eyes pleaded with her, she relented. "Okay, I vill vear new coat," she mumbled. "So who cares if I freeze to death?"

Adam was more nervous about the dinner at the Martins' than he was about the wedding ceremony. He wanted it over so he could be with Anna. The past week had been the loneliest he had ever known. His dreams were filled with Anna. Her smile, her touch, her warmth.

"Papa, Mr. Martin's name is Broderick. I don't think he likes to be called 'Brod.' "

"*Ja,* just being friendly," Papa said, standing in front of a mirror, adjusting his tie. He jerked it off. "I can't get this right. Adam, come help your papa."

Adam stood in front of his father and wrapped the ends over and under into the perfect knot. As he looked into his father's tired eyes, his heart swelled. His parents had sacrificed much for him and his brother — working to give them the education they never had and to provide for them the best they could. He would be proud if he became half the man Klaus Wilhelm was.

Adam helped his grandmother on with her coat and wound the hand-knitted scarf around her neck. "Will you be warm enough, Grandmama?"

She patted his cheek. "I be varm, my pretty boy."

He heard his mother grumble. "Glad someone vill be varm."

Anna was relieved the rehearsal went off without a hitch, if you discounted the fact that the soloist, Ruth Singleton, had come down with a cold and her tone-deaf sister, Gerta, took her place. Luellen was beside herself until they were assured that Ruth would be well enough for the ceremony the following day.

Adam couldn't keep his eyes off Anna through the mock ceremony. He'd whispered in her ear that their days apart had seemed like years, and she'd wholeheartedly agreed. When the "practice" kiss was given, Anna was the first to pull away in embarrassment. The embrace lasted longer than the minister's words leading up to it.

They left the church hand in hand, Anna feeling blessed beyond belief. Their families were together and, for the moment, getting along well. In the flurry of the rehearsal, they hadn't had time to converse beyond a short greeting.

The wedding party was greeted with luxurious sprays of snapdragons and sweet peas dominating the Martins' foyer.

"Darling, the rehearsal was quite touching." Mother, breathtaking in a long, teal blue shimmering gown and classic pearls, reached for Anna's hand, but her eyes were centered on her future son-in-law. "Thank you, Adam. You have made Anna's father and me very happy."

When Adam appeared uncertain with his response, Mother frowned. "Well? Do I have to stand here all night waiting for a kiss?"

Grinning, Adam did the honor.

"Ahh." Mother winked at Anna. "*Now* I see why you find him so irresistible."

Laughing, Adam escorted Grandmother Wilhelm into the parlor. Giles offered to take her wrap, but she refused and clutched tightly to the black purse hanging over her arm.

"Are ve at Valdorf Astoria?" she asked, her eyes wide.

"No, Grandmama, this is Mr. and Mrs. Martin's home."

Her eyes grew wider. "*Ist* home?"

Anna followed behind, accompanied by Adam's mother and father. She helped with their coats and entrusted them to Giles. Elfie and Grandmother Wilhelm walked around the foyer, first examining the vases and tapestries, then the crystal figurines.

Anna's mother smiled pleasantly. "Dinner will be ready shortly. Meanwhile, Giles will be serving hors d'oeuvres." She turned to Mina. "Grandmother Wilhelm, wouldn't you be more comfortable with your coat off?"

The gray-haired lady reluctantly unbuttoned her coat and let it slide off her shoulders.

Mother cleared her throat and glanced toward Anna, then back to the grandmother. "What a lovely scarf. Did you knit it yourself?"

Grandmother's eyes lit up. "You like?" the old lady said. "*Ist* yours. I make more."

Anna bit the sides of her jaws to keep from grinning when Grandmother Wilhelm draped the purple-and-gray scarf around her mother's shoulders. Mother looked as if someone had just slipped a hangman's noose around her neck.

Grandmother peered intently at Mother's necklace. "Are those pearls?"

"Yes, aren't they lovely?" She casually removed the scarf and laid it on the table. "They're a gift from my husband. I'd like Anna to wear them tomorrow."

Grandmother looked horrified as she turned to Anna. "You von't, vill you?"

Anna frowned. "Why do you ask, Grandmother?"

"*Ist* bad luck. For every pearl a bride vears, her husband vill cause her to shed a tear!"

Adam stepped forward. "Grandmama, that's just an old tale —"

"*Nein!* Tears fall ven bride vears pearls!"

"I'm sure it's just a coincidence," Adam said. Mother was groping her necklace as if it were choking her.

Anna quickly diverted the conversation. "If you will permit me, Adam and I have an announcement to make." Slipping her hand into his, she squeezed. "I know you're all wondering what gown I'm going to wear. . . ."

Elfie, Grandmama, and Mother eagerly nodded.

"Adam and I have agreed that a compromise was in order, so, tomorrow, I will wear Uncle Murray's gown and —" she smiled at Adam's grandmother — "and Grandmother Wilhelm's veil. We've also decided to use Grandmother's special ring for the ceremony — if that's all right with her."

"Oh." Mina cupped both her cheeks with her hands. "*Ist* too vonderful. Thank you, my child."

Anna glanced at her mother. "Mother?"

Sighing deeply, Mother gave in. "Of course, dear. It seems quite fitting for the occasion."

A sense of relief enveloped the room.

"Papa," Adam said, nodding toward Anna's father as they started into dinner, "tell Mr. Martin about the . . . the new sign you're planning to put up."

"Oh, he's not interested in some old sign —" Adam frowned, and Klaus picked up the conversation. "*Ist* great big sign that says, 'Vilhelm's Grocery Store' — vat else can I say?" Adam's eyes prodded him to go on. "And how's your campaign coming, Brod-erick?" Klaus asked.

Anna motioned her father to answer. He fumbled with his hands as if he didn't know what to do with them, then with a shrug slapped Klaus heartily on the back. "Couldn't be better, . . . uh . . . Klau."

Adam leaned toward Anna and whispered, *"Klau?"*

"Be grateful for small favors," she whispered back.

"Son." Anna's father clasped Adam on the shoulder, moving him away from all the commotion. "We need to talk about my financing those new grocery stores you're wanting to start. Now —"

"Sir," Adam respectfully interrupted.

"Yes?"

"Thank you, but I've changed my mind." Adam's eyes traveled to his bride. Anna's heart swelled. It was as if she could read his thoughts: *Thank you, God, for making me see what's really important in my life.*

"Anna and I have talked it over, and we won't be opening any new stores — at least not anytime soon."

Anna's father frowned. "How's that, Son?"

Adam's wink brought a blush to Anna, who was being seated by Klaus. "Anna and I think a family will be more satisfying than money in the bank."

Tears misted Broderick's eyes as he fumbled in his back pocket for a handkerchief. "Well . . . perhaps you're right, Son. Perhaps you're right."

~~~

"Exquisite! Utterly exquisite!" Saturday afternoon, Murray Jacobs arranged Grandmama Wilhelm's simple wreath of dried red and white roses entwined with myrtle on Anna's head, then stepped back to inspect his godchild. He fairly glowed with pride.

Smoothing her hand over the delicate layers of satin and lace, Anna smiled nervously. "Do I look all right?"

Uncle Murray's face crumpled with emotion. "Simply perfect, as I knew you would."

"Come now, no more time for fussing." Mother hurried Anna into the hallway where the wedding party had assembled. Strains of organ music were already filling St. Luke's foyer. Anna's best friend, Betsy, and Jena Parker, a bridesmaid, followed close behind, carrying Anna's train with devoted care.

Arranging the whisper-soft fabric in a pool on the floor, her maid of honor reached for her bouquet of red and white roses. Giving Anna a brief hug, Betsy whispered, "I'll pray that you and Adam will always love each other as much as you do this day."

"Thanks, Bets." Anna blew her a kiss. "I love you."

On cue, Betsy opened the two heavy oak doors leading to the sanctuary and motioned the giggling bridesmaids inside.

The organ music suddenly swelled, rattling the rafters as the double doors swung wide, signaling Anna's descent down the long, carpeted aisle on her father's right arm.

Smiling through a veil of tears, she held tightly to Father's arm, aware of Adam's family seated on the right front pews. Mama, Papa, and Grandmama all nodded their approval. On the left, Mother stood in the bride's pew, alone, a tear rolling from the corner of her eye as she watched her daughter walking slowly down the aisle.

Her family forever, as it should be.

A knot crowded the back of Anna's throat when she saw Adam standing straight and tall, flanked by his brother, George, and six groomsmen, resplendent in double-breasted black suits, white shirts, and black ties. Adam's sheer handsomeness took her breath away. *Thank you, God, a hundred times thank you,* her heart sang, proclaiming God's never-ending love.

As she reached the altar, her father gently patted her hand, and she sensed his reluctance to let go. Emotion welled in his eyes. She knew he longed to speak but couldn't find the words. She didn't need words. She knew that he and her mother would always be there, offering unconditional love. Today's ceremony would never change that.

Breaking tradition, she gently lifted her veil and kissed him softly on the cheek. "Thanks for loving me, for raising me, and most of all, for letting go," she whispered.

Father hugged her gruffly. "Hardest thing a parent ever has to do."

Stepping to her left, she reached for her mother's hand. Words weren't necessary. The bond of mother and daughter fell away, and, for a brief moment, two women shared a common bond. Best friends. Women in love. Mother blinked back tears, squeezed Anna's hand, then carefully readjusted the veil.

Moving to take her place beside Adam, Anna smiled, holding tightly to his hand. She belonged to him now.

What God hath joined together, let no man put asunder.

Author's Note

Traditionally, among Germany's upper classes, the woman, rather than the man, held the power to make the matrimonial choice. In a family able to provide a generous dowry, a daughter consulted with her mother as to whom she should marry and chose accordingly. Acceptable prospects frequently included military officers, government officials, professional men, or merchants. A young woman with a bit more imagination might even contemplate marrying an artist or a man of literary ability.

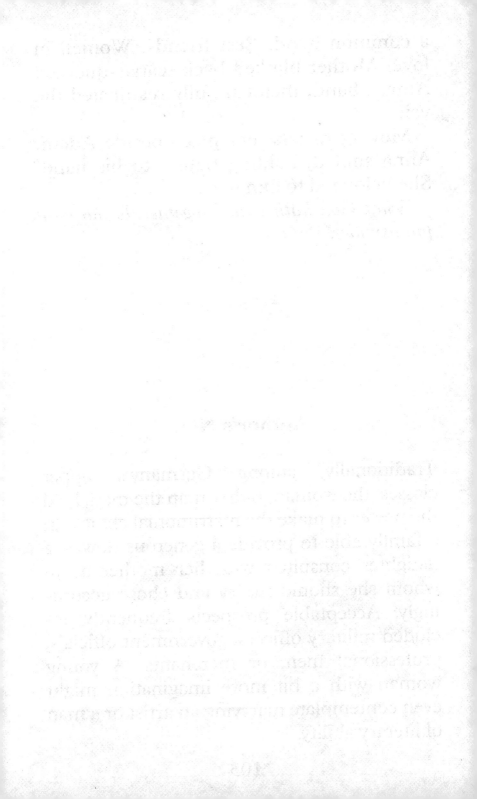

Something New

Dianna Crawford

Be ye not unequally yoked together with unbelievers: for what fellowship hath righteousness with unrighteouness? and what communion hath light with darkness?

2 CORINTHIANS 6:14

Chapter One

San Francisco, California, August 1895

The ship slid out of the mist and into brilliant sunlight, leaving behind the vast Pacific. Rachel Rabinovich clutched the railing to still her trembling hands. A huge bay lay before her. To her right, the long-awaited hills of San Francisco jutted up from a shimmer of blue water — emerald hills, covered with an amazing array of buildings and sliced by tidy straight streets.

On one of those streets lived her betrothed, a man she had never seen, a stranger to whom she had been promised since she was twelve years old. Now, after her family's many sacrifices to purchase her fare, not to mention her endless months of travel from Russia, she would come face-to-face with him — only to tell him she could not be his bride.

Miss Wilkinson, a Christian missionary who had befriended her on the long voyage since leaving New York, wrapped a bony yet comforting arm around Rachel's shoulder.

"Lean on the Lord, my dear. He'll see you through your time of trial."

In response to the woman's kindness, Rachel managed little more than a nod as her insides shrank into a tight, painful ball. Having decided not to marry David Mikhols, Rachel knew the kind missionary's Jesus surely would be her only friend when she stepped off the ship. Once she told her fiancé and his parents that she had become a Christian, they would shun her, declare her dead. Worse, her own dear family back in Russia would have no choice but to do the same. Jewish law could be very harsh. Very harsh indeed.

But not even for her family could she deny the new light of understanding and the over-flowing love that had become a part of her from the moment she had accepted Jesus as the fulfillment of all she'd ever been taught in the synagogue.

The deck beneath her feet shuddered. A portent of this dreaded day?

Miss Wilkinson gave her a reassuring squeeze. "Just the engines slowing."

Rachel glanced at the gaunt lady whose face was almost swallowed by her floppy hat and attempted a smile. "I know. But this fear I cannot put away. I pray I am strong woman. To marry with man who is not

Christian is wrong thing for me. Two oxen pulling one cart in different directions. No place it would get us. And the Lord knows this better than I do. I hope so, anyway."

The missionary turned Rachel toward her. Her sharp eyes searched Rachel's. "I'll pray that God strengthens your faith with each passing day."

"Pray he will take from me this hurt in the heart when I am thinking of my mama and my papa. So hard they work to send me to this new land. To give me chance my papa never had. He is great violinist. Everything I know, he teach me."

"You have a wonderful gift with the violin, but you are so much more than your ability to play. You are a lovely, giving person with the warmest, most honest smile I've ever seen. Promise me you'll remember that."

These things were easy enough to promise aboard ship. Rachel wondered, though, if her smile would be so friendly and truthful once she disembarked and left her mentor behind. How much easier it would be to remain aboard ship and travel on to the Hawaiian Islands with Miss Wilkinson. But that would require additional funds for passage neither woman had.

Rachel glanced across the azure water to the many piers thrusting from the shoreline and to the ships docked alongside them. Soon the *Pacific Maiden* would join the others, and she would be obliged to walk down the gangplank and into a strange and uncertain world. And meet the man who expected her to be his wife.

Hank Weldon, driving the two-seater surrey, nudged David Michaels with his elbow as he began an enthusiastic imitation of a tuba, his freckled cheeks puffing with each note.

David's mood was equally festive. On a burst of laughter, he joined his carrot-topped chum in a spirited rendition of John Philip Sousa's march *Semper Fidelis*. If the neighbors thought them a touch daft as Hank drove David up Ellis Street to his home, so be it. The Sunday afternoon concert at Golden Gate Park had been rousing. Stupendous.

"Makes a fellow almost want to join the marines, doesn't it?" David said at the end of the number.

Hank's hazel eyes widened. "And leave the Parker twins behind? Hardly, old man. They've promised to meet us at the park again next Sunday. And with picnic baskets this time. Which one of the girls do you want to eat with, Penny or Pris?"

"Does it matter? I can't tell them apart. They even giggle alike."

"I'll bet if I could get one of those cute gals alone, I could kiss her silly laughter away."

"I doubt it. Those titters and giggles seem built in, like in a wind-up toy."

Hank drew the bay Hackney to the side of the street in front of David's narrow-fronted Victorian house. "Are you saying you wouldn't court one of the darlings if you had the chance? Their father is one of the biggest importers on the West Coast."

The conversation was taking an unpleasant turn for David. He exhaled. "I'm afraid that option isn't open to me. You forget, not only am I Jewish, but . . . I might as well tell you before it's too late. Several years ago, my parents arranged a marriage for me with some Russian peasant girl, my mother's cousin's daughter. And nothing I've said since I was old enough to understand how unsuitable she would be has swayed them in the least. Needless to say, with such an unsophisticated creature on my arm, social invitations will quickly come to an end."

"Not from me, good buddy."

Only half-believing his lifelong friend, David merely shrugged. "We'll see. Anyway, a letter arrived from the girl's parents a couple months back. She's on her way."

"I can't believe you never told me this."

"What difference would it have made?"

"You're a grown man, David. Refuse to marry her. You can't let them saddle you *for life* with some foreign frump."

"That's easy for you to say. But I can't imagine you defying your father on such an important family matter any more than I can. To my parents it would be a betrayal to them and everything they hold sacred. And the embarrassment they'd suffer, sending the girl back to my mother's relatives in the Old Country. And don't forget, my father and I work together in the shop every day — I simply couldn't do it."

"They should've at least allowed you to marry one of the local Jewish girls."

"It seems there's been a lot of trouble for the Jews in Russia the past few years, and this one's family thinks she's special — a gifted violinist. With us being violin makers, they figured my parents would have a soft spot where she was concerned. And they were right."

"But this will affect the rest of your life."

"I know," David said with a grim nod. "I know all too well." But there was nothing left to say. He extended his hand. "Thanks for the ride. Till next week — and our picnic with the giggling Parkers — hopefully not our last."

His red-haired friend broke into a quick boyish grin. "Yes, here's to making hay while the sun still shines."

"Yoo-hoo, mister," a youthful voice sounded from down the street.

David swung around to see a skinny lad of about twelve hailing him. A familiar lad . . . the one he had hired to watch for the *Pacific Maiden*'s arrival. He swallowed down a sudden surge of dismay. "Yes?"

"Your ship's come in," the boy called up to him out of breath. It was a steady climb from the Embarcadero. "She's docking at Pier Seven right now."

"Pier Seven," David repeated numbly as he continued to stare at the bearer of this fateful news. "The *sending* has arrived."

"Thanks, kid," Hank said and flipped the lad a coin.

Catching it midair, the boy took off at a dead run.

"Pier Seven," Hank chuckled. "I thought the number seven was supposed to be lucky."

David sagged back onto the surrey's brown leather seat. "So did I. Well," he sighed, "I guess I'd better go in and tell my folks. They'll want to go down and fetch her straightaway."

"No need." Hank snapped the reins over the bay's back. "I'll take you. I don't believe I've ever met a *sending*."

"Don't call her that in front of my parents. It's just something I dubbed her once I knew she was coming."

Hank guided the high-stepping horse to Market Street, then down to the east side of the peninsula and the expansive commercial wharf. Although Hank casually commented on any sight along the way that caught his interest, David remained silent. This trip was anything but casual to him.

When he noticed his knuckles turning white from gripping the side bar of the fringed surrey, he released his hold and found something less telling for his hands to do. He resettled his tweed billed cap squarely on his head. Its prior jaunty tilt no longer matched his mood.

Too soon the brick-paved streets gave way to the planked wharf of the Embarcadero with its gigantic warehouses, lengthy piers, and briny breezes. Because this was the Christian Sabbath, the traffic was light, and Hank had no problem guiding the surrey down to Pier Seven, its wheels rumbling loudly, fatefully, across every board.

As Hank reined the Hackney horse onto the correct pier, David tensed. In the slip alongside, a large white steamship gently rocked against its mooring. Trimmed in black, she sported two red smokestacks and the name *Pacific Maiden*. Passengers were already coming down the gangplank.

Hank gave David's knee a slap. "Buck up. We'll take a peek at the girl before we present ourselves. If she's too much of a dog, I'll simply turn this rig around, and we'll leave her here."

David gave his childhood pal a weary glance. This was not the first time Hank's mouth had run ahead of his brain . . . nor would it be the last. "Tempting as that sounds, she's supposed to know English — my mother sent books. Enough English at any rate to ask directions to our house. Besides, I'd never leave anyone, no matter what she looked like, standing on a dock after she's traveled halfway around the world to get here. Think of it — she had to take a train from Polotsk to Riga on the Baltic, then secure passage across it and the Atlantic to reach America. Then, because her family couldn't afford train fare from New York, the poor thing had to take another ship down to South America and around the Horn. Five months . . . it's taken her five months to get here."

"That kind of thinking is going to be your downfall."

Just then, David saw her. Though she was one of several women disembarking, he had no doubt. Standing at the top of the gangplank in a drab, unfashionable dress and a head scarf tied beneath her chin, the young woman searched the crowd with a bewildered expression.

He pointed. "There she is. The one just starting down."

"You're joking. It can't be. Surely, she'll be one of the other passengers."

No matter how David wanted to agree, he knew this was his fiancée. Dressed exactly as he'd expected. Exactly as he'd dreaded. He grimaced.

Rachel looked out over the crowd of departing passengers. They mingled with those who had come to fetch them. Greetings and happy embraces abounded. But there was not a Jew to be seen on the long pier. No one waited for her in the traditional black hat and frock coat with a fringed prayer shawl peeking out from beneath. She saw no full beards or ringlets hanging down on either side of any man's face.

Most likely, the Mikholses had yet to

learn of the *Pacific Maiden*'s arrival. Wanting desperately to retreat to the ship, Rachel glanced longingly back at Miss Wilkinson standing on the upper deck. The skeletal woman flashed a sympathetic smile and waved good-bye with a lace handkerchief.

And good-bye it would have to be. With only a few coins in her pocket, Rachel could not afford the coward's way out. Clutching the carpetbag containing the precious English Bible, Miss Wilkinson's parting gift to her, she started down the gangplank. In her other hand, she gripped the handle of her other prized possession — her violin in its case.

Then a thought occurred to her. This ship could easily come and go without the Mikhols family ever knowing. Instead of asking directions to their house, she could simply walk into the city and ask the way to the nearest church. Hadn't Miss Wilkinson encouraged her to seek out a Christian minister if she needed help with lodging or a job?

Yes, that's what she would do. The mere thought straightened her slumping shoulders and quickened her pace. The minister could help her find work, and, who knew, maybe her lifelong wish still might come true — the chance to play with a symphony orchestra. After all, she was about to set foot in the New World. In America anything was possible. It was said a man here was judged not by who he was, but by what he did. So why couldn't it be so for a woman, too?

"Miss Rabinovich?"

Rachel's fantasies evaporated. With dismay, she scanned the thinning crowd for the source of the male voice. But still she saw no one in traditional Jewish attire.

A young, clean-shaven man who appeared to be a Gentile raised his hand and called her name again. Perhaps he'd been hired to fetch her. Rachel felt a measure of relief at this temporary reprieve from facing her betrothed and the rest of the Mikhols family. She started in his direction.

As he and a shorter companion approached, they both removed their caps. The second man had the reddest hair she'd ever seen.

The one who had spoken her name stepped forward, presenting himself in a buff suit that complemented his tall, lean frame and dark hair. His eyes, though, were his most outstanding feature. The lightest of blues, they made a striking contrast to his tanned face.

"How do you do?" he said in a smooth baritone, while taking her overstuffed carpetbag from her. "I'm David, your betrothed. I've come to fetch you."

"*David Mikhols?*" Her mouth fell open. She clamped it shut. "This cannot be. The clothes . . . you are dressed as Gen—"

"As a San Francisco gentleman," he finished in a firm voice. "And in America my name is pronounced *Da*-vid *Mi*-chaels."

"And I'm his friend Hank Weldon," the one with flaming-red hair said. A friendly smile dimpled both cheeks of his square, freckled face as he took her violin case, then her elbow, and began escorting her. "My surrey is right over here. Do you have many trunks?"

"Only two." One steamer trunk held her clothing. The other contained, along with a few parting household gifts, the table linens, sheets, and a counterpane upon which she'd been tatting and embroidering since she was twelve in preparation for the day when she would wed. So many years she had waited to become David Mikhols's bride.

At the thought, she glanced at her betrothed again and noted the lack of humor on his otherwise pleasing face — a face far more manly than his mother's letters had described. On his arm she could have been the envy of every young maiden. Suddenly, she wished he would smile at her as his friend had.

But this he did not do.

And it hurt.

She knew she should be relieved he found her unworthy of a smile, since her intent was to cancel the wedding. Yet, as unstylish as she looked compared to all these worldly people, how could this David not be disappointed?

The ship to New York had been packed with emigrants dressed like Rachel. But only one such young couple had boarded the ship going around the Horn, and they had disembarked at Los Angeles. Of the women surrounding her now, she alone wore no fashionable bonnet, merely a plain woolen scarf. And there was nothing favorable that could be said for the coarse weave of her simple, unadorned dress. Her poverty was as glaringly obvious as her Old World appearance. Even her hair. No other woman present wore hers in a single braid down her back. All had upswept and swirling tresses tucked beneath headgear of every shape, decoration, and color.

To her betrothed, she was most assuredly unacceptable. So why couldn't she count it as a blessing? The Lord seemed to be helping her with her dilemma. Yet, her foremost urge was to hide behind something big, like a stack of barrels.

The redheaded gentleman led her to a carriage with a fringed yellow canopy — a carriage more richly appointed than any she'd ever ridden in. He helped her up onto the cushioned front bench and again favored her with a bright cheery smile. Or was it one of amusement? Was he making sport at his friend's expense?

"I suppose you're eager," he said with a carefree lilt, "to meet the rest of the family. From what David says, they've been waiting for you for a very long time."

"Yes," was all she managed to mumble. Glancing down at her betrothed and his stiff expression, she wondered if David's parents would be as disappointed in her as their son was. She sighed, wishing their opinion didn't matter so much. Still, the outcome of the meeting was inevitable. Grim.

Chapter Two

After asking the Lord to quiet her nerves, Rachel almost forgot her anxieties on the ride up the main street of the city. But she couldn't be sure if her calmness was due to prayer or to all the sights and sounds and smells she'd been missing these past months. The aroma of the bakery they passed, the scents from a huge flower market, even the smell of a horse were welcome changes.

So many new things to see and hear. Red-and-gold trainlike cars, with clanging bells, were most amazing, since they had neither horses nor a steam engine drawing them. They ran unaided down the middle of the busy street edged by buildings several stories high, yet no one gave them any notice.

"Electricity," the affable Mr. Weldon said as he sat on the front seat beside her. Shifting the reins to one freckled hand, he pointed to wires strung above them. "The power comes through those lines and down to the cable cars."

It was hard not to like the driver. He said everything with a winning smile, unlike Rachel's fiancé, who sat somberly on the bench seat behind her with the luggage. She counted herself lucky he was not in front, marring her calm respite.

"But the wires, they go everywhere. See? To the buildings."

"We're a very modern city," the flame-haired fellow continued. "The lines bring electricity. All the stores have electric lights."

Mr. Weldon then began pointing out various shops with women's fashions displayed in their windows, causing Rachel to become uncomfortable again. There was a false airiness to his voice, and she couldn't be sure if his remarks about the quality of each establishment's merchandise was merely innocent chatter or aimed at David. Both men surely knew the cost of turning David's betrothed into a proper San Francisco lady would be considerable. And undoubtedly necessary. Every person strolling up and down the boulevard was impeccably attired. Not a poor person could be found — not one like her. *Oy vay,* what a conspicuous sight she must make.

Shaking off the thought, she centered her attention on several two-wheeled contraptions going past with people astride them, mostly young men and women. They laughed and talked together as gaily as Mr. Weldon did.

But then, he, no doubt, was a wealthy Gentile. What could he possibly have to worry about? From his appearance, he seemed to lack for nothing, from the dapper cap on top of his head down to his highly polished shoes, and out to his elegant bobtailed carriage horse. He had never known the travails of living in a Jewish ghetto, never cringed at the sound of thundering horse hooves, nor feared the sight of Russian soldiers galloping through the ghetto with clubs and torches, pillaging and destroying just for the sport.

"Those are bicycles they're riding," David surprised her by offering softly from behind.

He'd obviously been watching her every move. But somehow the gentleness in his voice was like a soothing balm. Perhaps she'd judged David too harshly. When they reached San Francisco's ghetto gates, she might see another reason for his somber behavior, one that had nothing to do with her. In the meantime, she was determined to enjoy the neat buildings, the trim lawns, and shade trees.

They turned off Market Street, and the horse strained to take them up a steep hill toward the blue, blue sky where two soaring seagulls cavorted on the cool breezes. A few moments later they turned left onto another street, then another, this last one lined with narrow two-story homes of brick and clapboard with lacelike trim and neat flower gardens. So many turns — they must be getting close to the ghetto gates. "How far to the Mikhols' house — pardon my error — the Michaels' house?"

Mr. Weldon grinned at her. "Don't worry about your English. You speak it much better than I would have ever dreamed, considering . . ."

From the manner in which his last word trailed off, Rachel caught the double meaning. Swallowing down a retort, she pretended not to notice. "For five years I am studying the language, but to properly pronounce all the words I did not learn, until I am aboard ship with this American lady. She also teach me how to read better." She tipped her hand back and forth. "So-so, I think. How far is to go?"

"We're here," David said from behind as Hank reined the horse to the side of the brick-paved road.

She glanced around, puzzled. They had passed through no gates that would lock the Jews in at night. And where were the walls?

"This is truly where the Jews live?"

"I don't know." Mr. Weldon braked the carriage to a stop and swung around. "Are there other Jews living on your block, David?"

"No," he said, as humorless as he'd been earlier. "Please help Miss Rabinovich to the ground, then I'd appreciate a hand with these trunks."

Her fiancé had actually relegated the task of assisting her person to another. Any kind thoughts she'd had about him evaporated. Trying to keep her mind off yet another affront, Rachel occupied herself by studying the house before her. It was two-storied and snugged close to the other houses on the street, but with a major difference. Aside from the etched glass in the front door, there were only two high, round windows on the lower floor facing the street.

Was that for the family's safety?

Still, the two shades of muted green covering the wood siding and the intricate trim of the exterior was not only charming but rich-looking. And the front yard abounded with lush foliage and flowers that edged the walk and two small patches of grass.

A flower garden.

A sudden wave of homesickness washed over Rachel as she remembered her mother tending their own flowers on a summer day, doing what she could to beautify the front of their drab little dwelling.

"Miss Rabinovich, would you please get the door for us?"

Turning at David Michaels's voice, she saw that each man had an end of the largest, heaviest trunk. She snatched her carpetbag and violin case from the floorboards and ran ahead of them. Opening the door wide, she walked into an entry wallpapered in flocked gold and green that looked even richer than the exterior. In one corner stood a beautiful carved clock, its pendulum swinging back and forth behind a glass door. Next to it stood a fine chair and a table with a gilt-framed mirror above.

Remembering the men behind her, she stepped aside as they toted the trunk past her and down a long carpeted hall that stretched to the back door. Halting about halfway, David hollered up an adjacent stairwell, "Mom, Pops, come down. We've got company."

Hearing footsteps overhead, Rachel felt a tremor shoot through her. *Help me, Lord, to see this through,* she cried silently as she glanced heavenward . . . only to see one more reminder of the grand life she would be relinquishing when she confessed to the

Michaels family. Suspended from the ceiling was a lovely amber glass and brass lantern with crystal teardrops and strange rounded white globes sitting where the wicks should have been.

A tall, elegant lady appeared on the stairs. As she swept downward, there was something remarkably familiar about her. Beneath all the rich cream-colored lace and linen was a woman who bore a striking resemblance to Rachel's own mother, . . . and suddenly she didn't feel quite so alone.

Behind Magda Michaels, a short, rather stout man followed on her heels. Like David, he was beardless, without a *yamulke*, the traditional skullcap, and attired in the clothing of a Gentile gentleman. Rachel could only assume he was Magda's husband, Sol.

David intercepted his mother and drew her toward the entry. Tall and fit, he, too, now resembled family. "Mother," he said, "may I introduce you to our guest? Your cousin's daughter from Opochka has arrived. Rachel Rabinovich."

A gasp was followed instantly by a huge grin and wide-open arms as the frilled and ruffled woman plunged forward. "Rachel!"

Rachel managed to put down her satchel and violin case just before Magda engulfed her in a wonderful welcoming hug. Rachel couldn't help reveling in the enthusiastic greeting, any more than she could help enjoying the heady fragrance of her second cousin's cologne.

In the next instant, Sol had Rachel, catching her tight against the many buttons of his brown tweed vest. "You're here. You're finally here."

"Let me get a good look at her." Magda pulled Rachel away, as if she were a ball being tossed between two happy children. "Yes, yes," Magda crooned, her gaze skimming up and down, a pleased expression glowing from eyes a shade grayer than David's light blue — eyes framed with laugh lines. "Just as Yenta wrote. Like your mother you look. Exactly like her at your age."

"And you, my rose," Sol added, bestowing a loving smile on his wife. "She's the image of you when you were her age."

"Do you think so?" She returned her husband's smile. Then her attention chased back to Rachel, and she became all business as she disposed of Rachel's scarf and brought her heavy braid over her shoulder. "Such wonderful thick hair you have, my dear. We'll be able to do so many clever things with it. Yes, with a shopping trip or two and a new hairstyle . . . I'm telling you, wherever you go, heads, they'll be turning."

"You're absolutely right, Mrs. Michaels," Hank chimed in. "With the proper clothes, she'll be positively —"

"You should know, Hank," David cut in, "since wearing your father's fashions to advertise them is your one and only job." His words had an edge to them.

Hank either did not notice or did not mind. That easy smile dented his cheeks while his attention remained on Rachel. "I know; I'm cursed. This business of being utterly dashing every single day." His smile widening, he pushed back his tan suede cap. "But somebody has to do it."

Glancing at David, Rachel saw his mood hadn't lightened in the least.

He took Hank by the arm and started toward the door. "Then I think it's time you got back to your business."

Laughing out loud, Hank waved back at them as David herded him past the door. "Nice meeting you, Miss Rabinovich. See you later."

Both the older Michaelses stared after the departing twosome with puzzled expressions, then Sol turned to Rachel. "It's so *good* to have you here — *at long last.*"

Rachel loved his comfortably heavy,

lived-in sort of face. "Thank you. Everyone at home sends greetings and many messages."

"I can hardly wait to hear them."

"And I must say, my dear," Magda interjected, "your English, it's perfection. You've almost no accent at all. Oh, yes, you'll do very well. Very well, indeed."

Not really, Rachel knew, but she couldn't bring herself to dash their moment of pleasure. After she satisfied their hunger for word from Russia, then would be time enough for the fateful news of her conversion.

"Of course she will," Sol said, "but now I want to hear about all our old friends. Tell me, Rachel, does old Seymour Levin still take his milk cow for a walk through town every morning? And does he still whisper sweet nothings in her ear?"

"Forgive me, sir. I'm thinking I do not know this person."

Magda caught her hand and squeezed. "Of course you don't. That crazy old man probably died twenty years ago. Come along, dear. We need to get you settled. David," she called to her son returning from outside, "you and your father need to take Rachel's things up to your sister's room."

As David strode toward them, his expression seemed even more dour than before.

And Rachel again felt the sting of rejection. Reaching down for her smaller cases, she reminded herself that his disappointment in her would only make her refusal of him less difficult.

The door banged open, rattling the gilded mirror frames and sconces lining the hallway. A young girl about sixteen rushed in, her blue-striped taffeta skirt rustling loudly. "Is it true?" She halted, her large brown eyes growing wider. "It is! I passed Hank on the way in, but I thought he was jesting. David has to marry *her?*" Even if her words hadn't betrayed her shock, her tone would have. "She's so — so —"

"*Judy!*" her parents scolded in unison.

Magda planted fists on her hips. "Mind your manners, young lady, if you know what's good for you." Then, lacing her fingers together in a display of composing herself, she turned to Rachel. "This, my dear, is our daughter, Judy, whose deportment quite often does not match her age. Allowances I hope you can make for her. You'll be sharing a room until the wedding." Then Magda's long fingers flew to her slim cheeks. "*Oy vay, the wedding!* So much to do."

Everything said after the word *wedding* bypassed Rachel's ears, and she eventually found herself numbly going up the stairs with Judy to settle in before supper. At the dinner hour or, at the very latest, tomorrow morning, she would have to inform them she would not become a part of this family. And the saddest part was that already she knew she would miss both huggable Sol and generous, gracious Magda immensely — if not their offspring. It mattered little how nicely David's smooth tan went with his silver-blue eyes, or the white of his starched collar . . . or how his dark hair brushed away from his temples with just the right amount of curl. . . .

If only he would smile. Just once.

Upstairs, Rachel scarcely had time for a perusal of Judy's room with its rosebud carpet, crocheted bedspread and scarves, the many pieces of furniture, and scatterings of pictures on the floral wallpaper. Judy immediately relieved Rachel of her cases, then stepped directly in front of her.

"Is it really true that all the Jewish men where you come from wear only black clothes? And do they all have great long beards and silly-looking ringlets in place of sideburns?"

"Yes," Rachel replied evenly, though she didn't appreciate the impertinent girl's poverty of manners.

"Thank goodness Mama and Papa aren't making *me* marry someone from the Old Country," Judy gushed. In a whirl, she pulled the pins from her beribboned straw hat and tossed the lot onto her dressing table, its surface already cluttered with all manner of fancy bottles. "I'd simply die of embarrassment. I know I would."

And that David shared his sister's sentiments, Rachel had no doubt.

She watched Judy fumble with the buttons on her blue-striped jacket — one that molded perfectly to the girl. Not too tall or too thin as Rachel was, Judy had inherited an attractively rounded figure from her father's side, as well as his big brown eyes. But, Rachel reminded herself, Cousin Sol didn't seem to mind that his slender wife stood as tall as him. He seemed thoroughly taken with her, even after decades of marriage.

"Not that I think your countrymen wouldn't be perfectly pleasant fellows," Judy continued, draping her jacket over a spiraled bedpost. "It's just — it's — I want to choose my *own* husband, not some clod Mama would pick. And I'm going to do it too. Just you watch me."

Rachel decided there was nothing to lose in being equally blunt. "I think your brother is not pleased with an Old World match any more than you are."

Judy's gaze wavered, and her round face, fringed with black curls, looked quite guilty. "Ah, but the relatives all said . . ." Avoiding Rachel's eyes, she glanced out between her swagged brocade curtains. "They said you were too gifted not to be given an opportunity for a better life. That you have a special talent for the violin."

Rachel was almost relieved by the turn of topic. "My father thinks so. And we hear in America anything is possible. So I am wishing to play for your new symphony orchestra. The one Cousin Sol and David make the stringed instruments for."

Judy's straight brows dipped in question.

"You do have a symphony orchestra — do you not?" Rachel asked.

"Oh, yes." An exuberant smile replaced Judy's frown. "Just this year one started up again. The Baldwin Hotel built an absolutely gorgeous hall for them. It's all in red velvet and gold." Then, in another abrupt change of expression, she stepped back, her thick-lashed eyes narrowing, and cocked her head. "My, but you do have grand plans for yourself . . . a poor girl just off the boat."

Judy's rudeness was back. Nonetheless, the girl was a willing source of information.

Rachel pressed on. "I do *if* the musicians are paid a living wage. Are they?"

"If by some miracle you were hired, I'm sure your salary would be more than enough for your . . . simple tastes." With the last words, the girl's pug nose crinkled slightly as she eyed Rachel's plain dress.

Rachel certainly would have no problem declining sisterhood to this girl. Still she refrained from raising her voice. "From your words, I think David is not upset if I stop the marriage."

Judy's pouty lips fell slack. "You would turn down my brother? You're just saying that to save face. Every girl I know positively drools over him."

After Judy's uppity behavior, Rachel enjoyed bringing the girl down a bit, even if just for a moment. "I have good reason for not to marry with your brother."

Judy shot forward and grabbed Rachel's shoulders. "Oh, Rachel, David would be so relieved. He's been in such a state since he knew you were coming. I thought he might leave home or something."

Rachel blanched. Before he even met her, he hated the prospect.

Releasing Rachel, the younger girl went on. "You see, in America, things are done differently. No matchmakers or parents to get

Chapter Three

er *what?*" Standing within the
the bathroom into which Judy
agged him, David knew he must
derstood his sister's words.
ard me," she whispered with ur-

crazy. *You're* crazy."
on't think so when I tell you why
getting Rachel an audition with
Gustoff. If you help her secure a
th the symphony, she can start
her own money, and she'll tell
nd Papa that she can't marry you."
marry me?" Nonsense. What was
to? He let her rattle on. Eventually,
me out with it.
n't you just thrilled? You won't have
y some poor Russian peasant after
u'll be free to marry whomever you
. And then maybe . . ." She broke into
those grins that always meant she was
g something up.
ow is it you know all this, Miss Smart
h? You weren't alone with Rachel for

140

in the way. Here a man meets a girl he likes and comes calling. Then after they've fallen madly, passionately in love, on a *very special night,* he asks for her hand in marriage." Judy smiled wistfully. "It's all so romantic."

Rachel pondered this revelation. "Young Jewish men do this too?"

Judy's expression hardened. "My Benny will. You wait and see. He will." Then, like quicksilver, her face crumpled. "But Mama and Papa will say no. Just because his father is a cannery worker. I know they will, *unless* . . . If David breaks with tradition by picking his own bride, I know I can use that in my favor." She caught her breath. "Are you turning David down because you, too, have found someone else? Will you break with tradition and marry without the blessing?"

"My reason I tell when the time is right. For now, my most need is to earn money by playing the violin with the symphony. To become independent woman."

"The symphony again?" Judy wailed and fell back onto the bed. "Women don't play in the symphony, you ninny. Just men."

"This is true even in America? *Oy vay!* What will I do?"

Judy leapt to her feet again and was back in Rachel's face. "Don't you worry about a thing. We know everyone in the orchestra, even the maestro. If anyone can get you an audition, David can —" Her words halted — the girl was a virtual kaleidoscope of emotions. Now her eyes became suspicious slits. "That is, *if* you really can play." Dropping down before Rachel's violin case, Judy opened it and ripped out the instrument and bow. "Show me."

Despite Judy's willingness to help, this audacious questioning of Rachel's one true ability infuriated her. She collected her beloved instrument and bow from the upstart. Sweeping the violin up to her chin, she strode closer to the girl and slammed the taut horsehair across the strings in a burst of sound.

Judy retreated a step.

Rachel filled the space. And she kept filling any Judy vacated, as she let her nimble fingers fly up and down the violin's neck while she whipped the bow back and forth. It felt marvelous, unleashing the storm that had been brewing since she met her betrothed and his sister.

Then the music took over, and Rachel let it have its way . . . wild, furious, free. Thunder and lightning on a whirlwind . . . until her anger at the cornered girl dissipated. She swung away toward the window and let the music lift her up on its great wings, then down past birds singing among

rustling le
the flush o1

A colorec
rocks above
of music . . . 1
and swirling,
became but a

As she pluck
turned back to
family standing
dumbfounded.
Mute.

Magda recover
dear, your playing
Most inappropria
never to play like
people think?" The
gift for sudden moo
came all smiles. "N
much too busy prepar
think about such non
two weeks, you know."

Two weeks? Rachel sho
found that both he and hi
stunned. Despite herself
pity the two pampered you

But she had little time to
prehensions. Magda had
"Come along, dear. I need
for some new clothes."

"You told h
confines of
had just dr
have misun
"You hea

gency.
"That's
"You w
you'll be
Maestro
place wi
earning
Mama a
"Not
Judy up
she'd co
"Are
to mar
all. Yo
choose
one of
cooki
"H
Mou

more than ten minutes."

"Long enough for her to tell me she doesn't want you any more than you want her." Judy flipped her nose in a taunt. The brat enjoyed trying to knock him down a peg or two.

Which she had, though he'd never admit it to her.

"All that raggedy girl wants," Judy continued, "is to play her beat-up old violin."

In spite of himself, David was starting to believe his sister. "But the symphony. I've never heard of such a thing — a woman playing in a serious orchestra. At social gatherings, maybe, but —"

Judy stiffened. "You men are all alike. You think you can do everything better than we can. You heard Rachel play. She was absolutely brilliant, and you know it."

"It doesn't matter what I think. The maestro is not going to have a lone woman in the midst of all his musicians. It would be . . . never mind. You wouldn't understand."

"And you're sounding more like Papa every day."

"Good. I'm glad you think so." He started for the door.

"But this is the rest of our lives we're talking about," Judy entreated. "If we don't stop Mama now, I'll be next."

He stopped. "You're right." As much as he hated discussing this with his trouble-making little sister, he felt compelled to turn back. "Tell you what. I'll post a sign at the shop, offering Rachel's services as a music teacher. If she gets enough students, she could make a modest living. Eventually."

His sister's jaw practically unhinged. "Post a sign? That's all?"

"I could run an advertisement in the *Examiner*, too, I guess."

"But that would take too long. She needs to be earning money within the next two weeks. If you want Rachel to refuse you, you'd better start thinking seriously about it. She won't feel comfortable staying here after she tells Mama and Papa she doesn't want you — *if* she tells them — whether she's Mama's second cousin or not. She has to have her own money *starting now*."

That trapped feeling was coming back as strong as when David first heard the ship had arrived. "Only two weeks till the wedding." He raked fingers through his cropped hair. "You're asking the impossible."

"Judy." Their mother's muffled call came from down the hall. A number of footsteps followed, then knocking on the door. "Are you in there, Judy?"

"Yes, Mama. I'll be out in a minute." She

placed her finger to her lips as if they were in the midst of a great conspiracy.

And perhaps they were.

"Hurry," Magda's voice again came from the other side. "I want to see if a couple of your dresses might be altered for Rachel until we can find some new ones."

Judy's eyes sprang wide. "*My* dresses?"

"Yes, dear. Something pretty for her first evening with us."

Something pretty? Judy mouthed with the exaggerated gestures of a distraught street mime.

Hearing his mother's retreat down the stairs, David started out the door.

Judy pulled him back. "We haven't settled on a plan yet. I'm telling you, a job for her with the symphony would solve everything in short order."

"And I told you, that's out of the question."

"For you, maybe." Judy shoved past him and left.

David slumped against the doorjamb. The brat was impossible. But a wedding to a total stranger in two short weeks was even more impossible.

Even if Magda hadn't told her she was gorgeous, Rachel had no doubt her clothes at least were. She smoothed her hand over the swagged watered silk skirt. Magda had selflessly retrieved it from her own closet and had taken in the waistband.

Real silk.

Never in her life had she felt fabric so pleasing to the touch, let alone worn it . . . or heard its fluid whisper as she moved down the stairs behind her generous second cousin. Nor had she ever worn such a vibrant hue of pink. The lacy blouse with hugely puffed sleeves was several shades lighter, but the two were brought together by a wide sash, its pink somewhere in between. Adding even more elegance, Magda had adorned with ribbons the upswept and topknotted hairstyle she'd created for Rachel. She'd even tied another ribbon at the base of the stand-up collar. The dear woman had fussed over her like a hen with one chick.

And all the time Magda had been preparing Rachel for the dinner hour, she hadn't stopped talking about the materials she already had bought for Rachel's wedding gown — purchases she'd made the moment she heard her new daughter was on the way from Russia.

At that moment, Rachel had come so close to telling Magda the truth. But if Judy could convince David to get her an audition with the symphony's maestro, then surely, one night of good fellowship with Sol and Magda would be worth a little guilt.

Spicy aromas floated on the air, and Rachel's stomach reacted impatiently. "Smells delicious, the food," she said as they reached the bottom of the stairs.

"Come with me to the kitchen, and we'll see how the meal is coming."

Rachel followed Magda down the long hall to a doorway near the rear of the house and into a large kitchen twice the size of the one at home. Painted a sunny yellow, it had ever so many cupboards and drawers and a very large stove. An Oriental woman stood at a long counter. A pot in her hand, she rinsed it in water running from a pipe above a built-in sink. *Steaming hot water!* Oh, these were indeed rich people. Earlier, upstairs, she'd been shown something called a toilet. It had flushed water from its large bowl, then refilled like magic. And now, hot water at the touch of a finger.

"Rachel, dear. This is Su Lin. She's been doing the cooking here for nine years now. What I'd do without her, I don't want to think."

The tiny woman bowed low. "Me cook only kosher for you. Food no touchy this, no touchy that. Tonight ever'thing plenty ko-sher." She wore her hair in the same braided fashion Rachel had worn before this evening but over a loose-fitting shirt and baggy cotton trousers.

Magda chuckled. "I'm afraid you'll find we follow few of the old traditions, but this evening Su Lin is making the special meal in honor of your long-awaited arrival."

Across the room, Judy charged through a swinging door. Seeing Rachel, she broke into a smile. "Oh, Rachel, you look really nice. I can't believe the change. And I love what Mama did with your hair. Now, come help me set the table. We're using our best china tonight. You'd think the rabbi was coming for *Shabbes* or something." Without waiting for an answer, Judy caught Rachel's hand and started back the way she'd come.

The dining room took Rachel's breath away. Beneath a crystal chandelier, the table was spread with a lace-trimmed tablecloth, flowers, and jade candlesticks. And dishes . . . so thin and delicate. The cups were fluted, and every piece was trimmed with silver. Absolutely everything, from the fragile-looking chairs to the china cabinet and the buffet, showed grace and flair. A room fit for royalty.

It must be true. Everyone in America was

rich. She could hardly wait to explore the parlor just beyond the velvet-swagged archway.

"I've told David," Judy announced out of the blue.

"*What?*" Rachel's heart stopped. Then started pounding. She swung her gaze to the girl. "You told him? What did he say?"

"We'll both do all we can to get you an audition," Judy said, opening a wide buffet drawer and retrieving pieces of silverware. "Don't worry. Just leave David and everything else to me."

Rachel certainly wanted more of an explanation than that. As she was about to ask, the hall clock chimed, Magda came through the door, and footsteps sounded from above. The six o'clock dinner hour had begun.

Judy thrust several forks into Rachel's hand. "Help, please. I'm not finished."

As Rachel placed the last piece of silver flatware on its white linen napkin, she glanced up to see David and Sol coming through the parlor archway. Both stopped and stared.

Suddenly nervous at seeing David now that she knew Judy had spoken with him, Rachel fixed her gaze on Sol.

"An angel," the gregarious older man pronounced. "An angel from heaven. A mere woman should look so good." He took Rachel's hands and led her toward David. "Such a miracle my Magda has made with the clothes."

Rachel had no choice, now, but to look up at her betrothed.

He was smiling! Actually smiling!

Her heart lurched.

A bright smile. A sincere one. And in his eyes there was more. Interest, the kind a man reserves for a favored miss. "You're absolutely right, Pops," he said, stepping closer. The smile turned scampish. "Close the drapes. Lock the doors, or every bachelor in town will be descending on us."

Rachel would have enjoyed his words more if she hadn't known that these first compliments came only after he knew he would not have to marry her. But, still, the admiration in his eyes was enough to start a flush creeping up to her cheeks.

From the hall came a banging. The door knocker.

David lost his smile. "Company at supper time?"

"I'll get it!" With expectant excitement, Judy skipped through the parlor and out to the entrance.

Probably hoping her Benjamin had come

148

calling. Rachel couldn't help but be amused
—until she felt David's intent gaze return to
her.

His eyes, she realized, had settled on her
mouth, and for some unaccountable reason,
her heart started thumping again. And
those same lips suddenly felt extremely dry,
but she dared not wet them with her tongue.

Judy returned at that moment with Mr.
Weldon in tow. "It's just Hank," she announced with none of her previous gusto.

The redhead had changed his attire since
Rachel had seen him last. He now wore a
navy-blue suit with a green-and-blue bow
tie along with his usual grin. Catching sight
of Rachel, he did a double take, then dem-
onstrated his approval with two long whistles.

"Hank, how nice to see you," Magda
called as she walked in from the kitchen
with a plate of *k'tzetzot,* chopped-beef pat-
ties. "For supper you're just in time."

"No, thank you, ma'am," he said. "I don't
want to intrude. I just stopped by to give the
most lovely Miss Rabinovich a proper welcome to our fair city." From behind his back
he withdrew a white box tied with a bright
red bow. "Nothing says San Francisco like
Ghirardelli's Chocolates." He stepped between Rachel and David and handed her the

149

gift with a gallant bow. "To make your first day here all the sweeter."

"How thoughtful," Magda answered rather stiffly for Rachel. "Such a lot of trouble you went to for a total stranger."

"Yes," Judy said. But unlike Magda, she was again bursting with energy. "And we insist you stay for supper. I'll set another place."

"Yes, stay." Sol slapped Hank on the back. "It's been a while."

Rachel felt a hand at her elbow. David's.

"May I escort you to the table?" His smile was gone.

Could David be jealous? Despite herself, Rachel hoped so.

He seated her next to him, relegating Hank to the opposite side.

Hank chose the chair directly across from her.

Rachel had never had so much male attention before. A shyness overtook her. Not knowing how to respond — considering the confession she soon would be making — she hung on to the candy box as if she were clinging to a limb.

"Dear, let me get that out of your way." Magda came from behind and took the chocolates, placing the candy on the buffet. "I'll tell Su Lin to serve now, if no one minds."

Feeling all the remaining eyes at the table on her, Rachel snatched up her napkin and spent an inordinate amount of time arranging it over the silk skirt. She was going to have to tell these good people the truth soon. With each passing moment, their acts of kindness made the prospect of the dreaded task more wrenching.

Food began circulating around the table, and Rachel was grateful the others had something besides her to occupy themselves. That is, until the blessing, when Sol thanked God for bringing her safely to their home. All eyes returned to her, heaping yet more guilt upon her head for delaying her confession. She was dishonoring these kind people as well as her Lord. Soon. She would tell them soon.

At last, people started concentrating on the meal. Everyone except Rachel. She sat much too close to David. So near she couldn't help noticing his every move, the spicy scent of his cologne. So near and so attractive. For just a moment, she decided, she would allow herself to dwell on what it might have been like had she not become a Christian. The two of them did make a striking couple. That was fact, not vanity. Both were blue eyed, tall, his hair and skin only a shade darker than hers. And the mere remembrance of that smile she'd waited for all afternoon sent a wave of warmth through her.

"Judy," Magda said, breaking the silence, "Rachel and I are going shopping in the morning. While we're out, I want you to write in the date on the wedding invitations. Sunday after next. They're all made out except for that. You'll find them in the top drawer of the desk."

Judy shot a glance at David, then looked over at Rachel. "But, Mama, I want to go shopping too."

Rachel had no doubt sending out invitations was the last thing Judy wished to do.

"Please do as I say. There are so many details. And this is something you're much better at than I." Magda then addressed Rachel. "Such beautiful handwriting our Judy has, you wouldn't believe. And, Rachel, wait till you see where the wedding is going to be held. This place you're going to love. The Palace Hotel."

"That's the big building that I pointed out to you on the ride from the wharf, Miss Rabinovich," Hank said, taking over. "It's spectacular inside. One of *the* premier hotels of the world. If you'd like, we could drop by in a day or two. I'd love to show you the Grand Court."

"From what Mother says," David inserted, cutting Hank off, "she'll be keeping Rachel very busy for the next couple of weeks."

For a man who supposedly didn't plan to wed her himself, David certainly was blocking Hank's every effort to spend time close to her. Pleased far more than she should be, Rachel hid a smile behind her napkin.

"Papa," Judy said, toying with a matzo ball, "it's not fair."

"What, my little *halvah?*"

"That men get to do all the fun stuff. And all we ever get to do is stand back and tell them how good they are at it."

"Judith, we have guests," Magda scolded.

With a wink at David, Judy softened her next words. "It's just that someone with Rachel's talent should get a chance to play with the symphony. If she were a man, you'd be pushing her to do it, hailing her as a prodigy, a genius. A Mozart. Instead, Mama would rather Rachel pretend she can't play at all."

"I said no such thing. It was merely that particular selection I minded." A bit flustered, Magda smoothed her silver-threaded dark hair back from her brow. "A matter of preference."

"I take it that Miss Rabinovich favored

you with a piece," Hank inserted. "I wish I'd been here. Beautiful *and* talented. She really is quite a catch." His last words were directed to David along with what seemed like a challenge.

David's fingers tightened around his fork. "Yes, our little Jewish community will be very pleased to have her among our number."

Rachel felt as if she'd fallen from her limb and into a hole she was digging for herself, particularly when she saw Sol and Magda's pleased expressions at David's comment. She quickly changed the subject. "Sol, my father, he says your family make the finest violins west of Moscow before you leave for America. He wants to know if they are still sounding this full of soul."

"You should hear a more soulful violin than the one we just finished for Mr. Baur, the concertmaster." The heaviness disappeared from Sol's face as he explained the minute changes in depth and shape that created the difference. "David and I are very proud of this one. In fact," he said, tossing his napkin onto his plate, "I brought it over from the shop. We wanted you should play it. Tell us what you think." Without further ado, he rose from his seat.

"But, Sol," Magda chided, "we haven't

had our dessert yet."

"After she plays, *bubele*," he placated with a Yiddish endearment. "Our Rachel plays like her papa. And homesick I am for the sound. Reminds me of when Moshe and I were out serenading you and your cousin, Yenta."

Rachel caught their exchange of private glances just as Judy complained, "But you said marriages were always arranged between parents with the help of matchmakers."

Sol chuckled. "And with the help of some very strong hints by me, you can be sure. Come, Rachel, the violin is in the music alcove."

Stepping through a parlor decorated mostly in shades of cream, green, and dark wood tones, Rachel observed a room richly appointed with lamps, bric-a-brac, and overlays of pillows, scarves, and wall hangings. Despite the clutter, it remained very homey.

Sol turned a small knob beside a second archway, and, instantly, an equally well-appointed music alcove filled with light. An intricately carved organ sat against the back wall between two circled windows, the ones she'd noticed when she first arrived. Flanking the organ were a harp on one side and two chairs with music stands on the other. Behind the chairs stood a music cabinet, and on top lay a brand-new violin case.

Sol opened it and lifted out a highly polished instrument and its gleaming bow. With a pleased smile, he offered them to Rachel. "It's already tuned."

Eager to test the new design, she wasted no time, playing up and down the scale, double stringing, plucking, and thumping the body. Sol had not exaggerated. The sound virtually resonated within the alcove. She desperately wished to play something powerful, something moving.

Rachel looked beyond the violin to Magda. "I beg you, just this once, let me play a piece that would do it justice."

With a good-natured shrug, Magda sighed and waved her off. "So, play it in good health."

David watched Rachel close her eyes and slide the bow across the strings with swift sure strokes, losing herself in the sweeping strains. As she played, the glow on her face transfigured her into the angel his father had lightly proclaimed her to be. A beautiful angel sent to him by . . . God?

And Hank — had his friend seen past her Old World clothes, seen the beauty beneath, as his parents had? Why else would he have brought the chocolates? Had David alone been too blinded by his shallowness to see? But Hank, he rationalized, hadn't been saddled with an enforced betrothal to a total stranger. He, David, had been the only one with everything to lose. . . . Or gain?

A melody he vaguely recalled began emerging from Rachel's music . . . a Schubert piece . . . the gypsylike Allegro from his *Fantasy in C*. But she played it faster and with more drama than he'd ever heard. His little sister had been right. Rachel was a prodigy, a genius. A miracle.

What a tragic waste. No symphony would ever consider including a woman.

Rachel finished with a climactic crescendo. After an awestruck moment, David and the others began to applaud. He clapped so hard and long his hands stung. Then he started toward her, but his father beat him there and wrapped her in one of his bear hugs.

"Just like our Moshe you sound. Just like our Moshe," Pops said over and over, with tears in his eyes. "If only Moshe could've come to America, had his chance."

David felt a tug on his sleeve. It was Judy, with Hank beside her.

"Come out into the hall," she said with that I've-got-a-secret roll of the eyes.

As David followed them, he was almost

certain she'd told Hank about Rachel's willingness to walk away from the marriage. The very idea that Judy would blab about a private family matter, plus the fact that Hank was trying to take advantage of the situation, turned David rigid with rage. He and Hank were supposed to be buddies.

"See? What did I tell you," Judy whispered to the interloper, confirming David's suspicions. "Now, all we have to do is figure out a way to get Maestro Gustoff to grant her an audition."

"The maestro will never break with tradition," David returned, eyeing Hank, daring him to disagree. "No matter how talented she is."

Judy stepped between them. "We have to get him to grant one, so Mama's plans will fail. This marriage tradition is one that must come to an end. I'm *not* letting it happen to me."

"All you ever think about is yourself, Judy. This is none of your business. Stay out of it." Before he lost all his manners and insulted their dinner guest as well, David turned on his heel and started back to join Rachel and his parents. But when the other two didn't follow, his skin began to prickle at the nape of his neck. Hank had no more sense than Judy.

Chapter Four

Early the next morning, Rachel eased the bedroom door shut behind her and stepped softly down the hall. Sleeping — or rather, not sleeping — with the restless Judy had been a rough and tumble tug-of-war. She'd struggled to hang on to even a corner of blanket — an experience she did not want to repeat. Even praying had given her no comfort since she had taken the coward's way out by not telling her hosts about her becoming a Christian.

This morning, symphony or no symphony, she would tell the family. The rest would have to be left to the Lord. She already felt far too deeply indebted to these kind people.

Yesterday, when Judy's clothing had proven to be too short for Rachel, Magda had taken in the waist of two of her own skirts and had insisted — no, demanded — that they, along with their matching blouses, now belonged to her. Though grateful to be given attire in the style of the San Franciscans, she simply couldn't accept another thing under false colors.

At the top of the stairs, Rachel lifted the hem of the newly acquired navy linen skirt and started down. As she did, she heard voices.

Her breath caught. She wasn't the first one up as she'd thought. She would be facing the elder Michaels, *telling them,* sooner than she'd anticipated. With trepidation, Rachel walked into the sunny kitchen. But she spotted Sol with not Magda, but David. They sat at the simple white table, their morning coffee in front of them.

Both greeted her with surprised but happy smiles.

"Pour yourself some coffee and join us," Sol said, patting the table. "I see you're an early riser, like David and me. My Magda, she likes to sleep in, so Su Lin always has some kind of nut bread here waiting for us."

Rachel felt David's eyes on her as she turned away, and the very thought of him taking such an interest sent prickles of anticipation up her spine.

While she served herself, Sol shifted the conversation to his son. "David, I'll get started on the order from Los Angeles. You, I want to go down to the warehouse at Pier Eighteen. Our shipment of rosin has come in."

Earthenware cup in hand, Rachel sat between the men at the square table, wishing David had grown less attractive during the night. But he remained as handsome as ever — more so, if anything — with his sleeves rolled up to his elbows and his shirt open at the collar. And the sincerity in his smile . . . Yesterday's wish was a *very* big mistake.

"Did you rest well?" Sol asked, lifting a morsel of spicy bread to his mouth.

"I doubt it," David chuckled. "She was sleeping with the thrashing machine."

"Coffee smells good." Rachel changed the subject, not wanting to evoke any further solicitude. "I developed a taste for it aboard ship."

Sol shoved back his chair and eased to his feet. "Sorry, but I need to get to work. David, you keep our Rachel company till after breakfast. Get her anything she wants to eat." With a satisfied expression — one that conveyed his pleasure in giving the two young people time alone to get acquainted — he walked out the door.

If only he knew.

"What would you like?" David asked, starting to rise. "Milk? We have some fresh peaches from the valley."

"No, please, only coffee, I think." *And a compassionate ear,* she prayed silently. She took a much-needed sip as he resettled into his chair and leaned forward.

His expression turned serious. "I've been hoping for the chance to speak to you privately since I heard about your conversation with my sister. Judy is not the most tactful person in the world. Fact is, she can be a real brat, and it's very important for you to understand that my not wanting to marry has nothing to do with you personally."

"That's what I want —"

"Please." He held up his hand. "Let me finish — around this house, any scrap of privacy is hard to come by. What I wanted to say is —" he took a breath and shifted uneasily in his seat — "I very much wish to be in love with the person I marry *before* I marry her. I know Mom and Pops say that love comes later. But that's not always true. And I want her to feel the same about me, too. It's for *life*, you know."

When David finished, he glanced around uncomfortably. He obviously was not accustomed to speaking of such things.

Rachel rested her hand over his much larger one. "I understand. Truly, I do. My sister, Leah, is given in marriage to older man she has no feelings for. To my parents it is enough that he loves her. When Yossi Shumaker sends the matchmaker to say he will take her even without dowry, my parents think this is good thing for Leah. And for me. He is kind man with good business to support her, and her dowry helps pay for me to come to America. But Leah must be with this man she does not love. I hate she is the sacrifice. This gives me much pain."

David placed his other hand over hers. Her skin tingled from his mere touch as he gazed upon her with utmost empathy. "Then you know what I mean. You understand. I see now why you were so willing to free me, even though you have no other family here, nowhere to go."

Rachel withdrew her hand. He was giving her far more credit than she deserved. "You are most kind, but this is not the reason. I make the decision not to marry with you before I reach San Francisco. This thing I should tell to you when you first meet me at the dock. For this I am sorry. I am coward."

The change in David's face was sad to see. He reverted to his closed expression of the day before.

"Please. This is not what you think. But when I tell the reason, I fear you will declare me dead. That you will cast me from your house, from your sight. Your memory."

"For heaven's sake, Rachel, what have you done?"

"I —" She swallowed. "I am converted to Christianity on the voyage here. I am believing now that Jesus is the Son of God, the Messiah."

"*What?*" He stared at her.

Her palms went clammy.

"You — you've converted?"

"Yes." She answered softly, hoping to calm him. "And I learn Christian is not supposed to marry outside the faith any more than Jew is. The Bible says it is not good, this being unequally yoked. Marriage should not be made when the husband and wife are pulling in different directions. So, you see, when Judy says you do not want to marry me, I think this is answer to my prayer."

"An answer to prayer?" he blurted angrily. "We may seldom celebrate the *Shabbes* meal in our home or go to the synagogue but we . . ." He paused, his eyes searching her soul. "Rachel, you're a Jew, one of the Chosen People. How could you think to do such a thing?"

His reaction was exactly what she'd dreaded. "I could never, *would* never. Accident, it was just accident. Or, maybe, God is smiling down on me? To read and write the English, this I have need to learn. The kind lady says she will teach me. For reading all she has is the Christian Bible. The Torah, the Prophets, *and* the writings about Jesus all in one book. And, David, this most wonderful thing happens. My mind is made open, and I see everything clear. Everything I ever learn about Moses and King David and the prophets, it has more meaning. Amazing meaning. And now I have such joy here in my heart," she added as she experienced, even now, a resurgence of that fruit of the Spirit.

"You think you know more than our rabbis and scholars? More than what they've learned over the past two thousand years?" His reply was more of a challenge than a question.

Rachel sent a plea heavenward for the right words. "So many things I now see. Remember in the Torah when God tells Moses all firstborn of Egypt are to die in the night, except for people who sacrifice the lamb and smear its blood over the door?"

"Of course; that's *Pesach,* Passover."

"This thing God does to make picture — picture for when he sends to us the final sacrifice. The one for all time. Jesus is the lamb with no spots and more. He is firstborn son who dies. And remember when Abraham takes Isaac to the altar?"

David, his face of stone, said nothing but nodded slightly.

Rachel could hardly believe it. He was still listening. She dared to say more. "Isaac is spared, but God does not spare his own begotten son. Jesus dies just as King David says hundreds of years before in Twenty-second Psalm, 'Dogs have compassed me: the assembly of the wicked have inclosed me: they pierced my hands and my feet.' I memorize this so I do not become weak when my people say different. Everyone knows it is the hands and feet of Jesus that are nailed to a cross, not King David."

David's expression was still unreadable, but he hadn't stopped her, so she pressed on. "I now know that all who look up to him are saved, just like the wandering Israelites when poison snakes come to their camp, killing the people. Remember?"

He said, "Yes," but his expression was no longer flat. He now had the harried look of a trapped fox.

Nonetheless, she was compelled to continue. "If the people look up to the dead snake Moses nails to the pole, they do not die. Oh, what faith it must take to look up, when crawling at your feet are killer snakes. Look up to the pole where snake has been killed and live; look down where the snakes live and die." She took a quick breath. "That is what I am trying to do. Keep my eyes on heaven and believe our Messiah will take care of me — even here, alone in this strange land. This scares me, but I am trying very hard."

"But, Rachel, to give up your heritage, to forget the centuries of struggle."

"No. This is the thing of most wonder. I feel more part of my people now than ever. With us, Jesus is like hand in glove. Hand in glove."

David's gaze softened. He laced his fingers through hers. After studying them a few seconds, he looked up to her eyes. "Sweet Rachel, you are such an innocent. Promise me you won't tell anyone else about this until I've found another place for you. Judy is so desperate to keep us from marrying for her own reasons that she'd use it against you. Too, I'm not sure how Mom will react."

"And your papa?"

David chuckled. "Pops makes violins. The rest he leaves to his Magda. Promise me."

"But Magda and Sol are so good to me. I do not like to take advantage."

"At the moment, it's more important that you're not sent packing. Give me a couple of days to locate suitable lodging for you. Then if the worst happens . . ." He took both her hands now and squeezed. "Promise."

"It is hard promise. But, very well. Two days."

Watching him leave, Rachel was amazed at how well he had taken the news after the initial shock. Not only had he not declared her dead, he had listened, and he even planned to help her.

"Thank you, heavenly Father," she sighed as she attempted to pray aloud in her new language for the first time. "But, you know, this trust is a fearful thing. This walking through a strange place, not knowing what I stumble over while I am trying to keep my eyes up there on you. And one more thing, since we're already talking, Lord. Did you take a good look at this David Michaels? A man like him, a girl shouldn't have to give up."

⤳⤲

Horribly guilty, that's how Rachel felt as she followed Magda into the house that afternoon, her arms loaded with packages. Magda was not a woman to be stopped when she was on a shopping spree. Judy, looking fresh in lavender dimity, came from the parlor to greet them.

"This Rachel," Magda told her daughter, "she is the exact opposite of you." The older woman reached up and plucked the pins from her flower-bedecked teal bonnet. "I must force her to take every little thing we buy. *Oy vay,* but I'm tired."

Judy took her mother's hat and hung it on a hook above the entry table. "You do look exhausted, Mama. Why don't you go up and take a nap. I'll help Su Lin with supper."

A moist smile brightened Magda's slim face. "Thank you, dear. How thoughtful. You truly are growing up — and into such a considerate daughter, too." She ambled up the hall, mumbling as she went. "Just a little nap. An hour or so."

Rachel started to follow.

Blocking her path, Judy frantically motioned her into the parlor. She led Rachel toward the marble fireplace at the far end, then she grabbed the packages from her and tossed them onto a green velvet armchair. "I thought you'd never get back," she whispered quickly, excited.

What could possibly be so urgent? Rachel wondered, but she kept her silence, since Judy was absolutely bursting to tell her.

Judy glanced back at the hallway, then relaxed slightly. "At noon, when Papa came across the alley for lunch, he said Mr. Baur, the symphony's concertmaster, is coming to the shop to pick up his new violin. At *three.* That's only a few minutes from now."

"Yes, Sol spoke of him last night after I play his instrument."

"We don't have time for idle chat. Run upstairs and get your violin, then meet me in the backyard. Once Mr. Baur comes out of the shop and hears you playing, he's sure to get you an audition with the maestro."

"But, Judy, when he sees I'm a girl —"

"Who said *see?* You're not to let him *see* you. Only hear you. You'll stand next to the garden shed and play a few bars. Just a few. Some of that gypsy-sounding stuff. Then slip behind the building. I'll take care of the rest."

"But I don't understand the —"

Judy interrupted again, her words snapping with impatience. "Have a little bit of faith, Rachel. Just go get your violin and come on outside. Today we get you that audition. The rest we'll worry about later."

Have a little faith, Rachel repeated in disgusted silence. She'd played a few bars as Judy had insisted, then slipped behind the small shed, where she now hid while knocking away spiderwebs with her horsehair bow. However had she let herself get talked into this childish scheme? Yet here she skulked like a thief, as Judy and Mr. Baur passed close by in their search for the "mysteriously missing" violinist.

"My cousin Ruben, from Russia," she heard Judy say. "I can't imagine where Ruben went. Let's check inside."

Ruben? Judy might be passing her off as a man today, but at any real audition the maestro would insist on seeing as well as hearing.

At least ten more minutes went by before the girl peeked around the corner. "You can come out now. He's gone. And I got you that audition. Tomorrow morning. Eleven o'clock." She whirled around in exuberance, her airy lavender skirt flying out behind her. "Isn't that the grandest?"

"No, this is not. The minute Maestro Gustoff sees I am woman, he will say to me, leave."

"Oh, good!" Apparently Judy had been ignoring her. She grabbed Rachel's arm. "Hank's here to help us out. He came by earlier to take you sightseeing, and I asked him to come back around three-fifteen."

Judy hustled Rachel to the front yard and out to where Hank waited with his surrey. He attempted a pleasant greeting, but Judy cut him off — a habit of hers, it seemed. "We'll have time for small talk later. Right now, we need to get away before Mama notices."

Rachel felt like refusing the rude girl just for principle's sake, but she couldn't make a scene, not in front of David's friend. She let Hank help her up, then she sat crowded between the two.

"How about a turn down to the Palace Hotel? Maybe have a soda in the Court Lounge."

"*No.*" Now Judy was even bossing Hank. "Take us to your house."

Confusion replaced the redhead's usual smile. "You'd rather go there? But that wouldn't be much fun. My mother's home, and so is my kid brother."

"Exactly."

Despite Rachel's own objections, Judy then relayed to Hank what had transpired with the concertmaster. "So you see," she finished, "Rachel has need of one of your brother's better suits of clothes."

"*I beg your pardon.*" Rachel couldn't imagine how Judy had gotten so willfully brazen, considering her tender age. "I cannot pretend to be boy. After audition is finished, I am still girl."

"Yes, but once the maestro hears you, it won't matter. He's not fool enough to pass up such a talent. Isn't that right, Hank?"

"You're asking me? I — uh, I suppose it's worth a shot. The worst he can say is no.

But, just in case, you might think about working up a vaudeville act if you're so set on performing for . . . *pay*." He said the last word as if it were almost an obscenity. "I imagine you could find a trained dog or something. It could dance on its hind legs while you play."

All her years of study and practice merely to accompany a dog? "Thank you, Mr. Weldon, but I think not."

"If she's going to work up an act," Judy said, leaning across Rachel, "she'll do it where it counts. Hank Weldon, meet Ruben Rabinovich, my fourteen-year-old *boy* cousin from Russia."

"Your fashionably dressed boy cousin from Russia," Hank laughed. "If we're going to do this, let's do it with style."

They were talking past Rachel as if she weren't there. She couldn't have that. She leaned forward, blocking their view of one another. "I will not dress as boy."

"Sure you will." Judy pushed Rachel back in her seat. "Hank, see if you can get that dark corduroy suit of your brother's. It's neat but not too pretentious. Wouldn't you say?"

"I am *not* doing this," Rachel repeated with force.

"And shoes. We'll also need a pair of Gordie's shoes, and . . ."

Chapter Five

"Stand still," Judy ordered. She stood before Rachel in their bedroom, her cherubic face in a grimace as she fussed with the bow tie at Rachel's throat. "The miserable thing keeps going crooked."

Rachel had no intention of assisting the stubborn girl. It was more than enough that she had allowed Judy to dress her in boys' clothes. She stared with longing at the drawer of her nightstand. Inside lay her precious Bible — her *unopened* Bible these past two days. If she could only glance through it, she might receive the clear guidance she so urgently needed this morning. David had not exaggerated when he said a private moment was hard to come by here.

Judy stepped back and studied Rachel, then she straightened the scratchy starched collar. After fastening the top button of the jacket, she eyed Rachel again. "Yes, you'll do quite nicely. You're skinny as a boy. As long as you keep that bowler set squarely over your coiled braid . . ."

Rachel let the younger girl's remark about

her being too thin pass. There was not time enough in a day to get angry at every bit of *chutzpa* that came out of that mouth of hers.

"Thank goodness it's Mama's market day." Judy pulled Rachel's carpetbag from beneath the bed and tossed it on top. "Otherwise, we'd never be able to sneak past her. She has the eyes and ears of a cat. Put a change of clothes in here. That way we won't have to sneak back in."

Reaching into the wardrobe, Rachel withdrew the white blouse and navy skirt she had worn the day before. She slowly, deliberately busied herself, precisely folding the garments and placing them with the greatest of care into the bag — anything to stall. Going to the symphony hall dressed as a lad was certainly not her dream for this moment.

"Hurry up." Judy collected Rachel's shoes from beside the bed and carelessly tossed them on top of the blouse. "Hank will be driving up any second."

"Tell me exact words your brother said when you told him about audition," Rachel entreated while whisking the shoes off the blouse and moving them to the bottom of the bag.

"Oh, you know David. He's such a wet blanket, just an old *schlump,* as Mama would say. He said getting one would be impossible. But I proved him wrong, didn't I?"

"Judy, I think you did not tell him everything. *Oy vay,* I wish last night I have chance to speak to him alone. You and Hank, you keep all of us too busy, playing silly 'parlor games,' as you call them. David should be told about this."

"Told, shmold. Get your violin and come on." Judy grabbed the satchel and started out the door. "When my plan works, he'll be right in front, taking credit."

❧❧

On the drive to the Baldwin Hotel where Hank had said the symphony hall was housed, both he and Judy were in high spirits. They laughed and called out to friends they passed on noisy Market Street.

But with Rachel this was not so. Surely someone as learned and wise as the conductor of a symphony would not be fooled so easily by her disguise. She envisioned any number of ways he would expose her, and with each scenario, her stomach felt as if a flock of geese had just taken flight in it.

Hank veered the horse into an alley behind a large, multistoried complex. "The stage entrance is in the back."

Rachel gripped the front rail with both

hands. "I cannot do this."

"Sure you can." Hank halted the high-stepper, and the surrey rolled to a stop. "You're the best violinist I ever heard."

"No. This is wrong." Rachel released the railing and clutched her belly. The geese again.

Judy swung to face her. "I'll tell you what's wrong. Those men thinking they're the only ones worth listening to. Now hold your head up and show them what a woman can do."

Hank hopped down to assist Rachel, his dimpled grin ever present. "Don't fret, pretty one. Judy and I will be right there beside you all the way. Won't we?"

"Sure." Judy nudged Rachel with her elbow. "Now get moving."

After Hank had helped them both down, he opened a door marked *Stage*. Reluctantly, Rachel entered a dark passageway. She'd gotten only a few steps inside when she heard the chaotic strains of musicians tuning their instruments. Scores of them. The entire orchestra would be present for her audition.

She froze.

"What are you waiting for?" Judy hissed. "Keep walking. This will lead us to the stage."

"I am not going." Rachel wheeled around, accidentally slamming her violin case into Hank.

"Whoa, there," he said, steadying her. "No time to get cold feet."

Judy caught Rachel's arm. "Just go in there and play. No one will suspect anything. Just play. Get hired. The rest we'll worry about later."

"Listen to Judy." Hank took Rachel's hand. "The important thing is that they hear you. So go on."

"I am too nervous. My fingers, they are becoming stiff."

Hank lifted her hand and brushed his lips over the back of each one. "There," he said softly, his green eyes teasing as he released her. "I've made them all better."

"Oh, for pity's sake." Judy's disgust was evident as she tugged at Rachel's sleeve. "Let's just go in and get it over with."

Before Rachel knew it, she stood at a wing of the stage, staring at more than fifty men. They were mostly in their shirtsleeves, some seated, tuning or warming up. Others milled about or stood in clusters, chatting. All in all, they seemed quite relaxed.

A thing she definitely was not.

Judy breezed past her and sought out a man carrying a violin. A small, middle-aged fellow, he sported a mustache and goatee, both as neat and trim as the rest of him. Judy pointed toward Rachel, and he looked in her direction. Then Judy motioned for her to join them.

A nudge in the back from Hank propelled Rachel forward.

Oh, God in heaven, give me that peace you speak of. I need it so much now.

The peace Rachel so acutely wanted did not come. She had barely managed to mumble her way through the first introduction when Mr. Baur asked another man to join them.

Maestro Gustoff. The maestro, with his sharp, quick eyes. This man would not be fooled easily. Rachel's throat tightened. Her breaths became short, shallow.

"So, you're the lad Mr. Baur mentioned. Fresh from Russia. With which master did you study?" The instant before she spoke, Rachel remembered to lower her voice. "With my father, Moshe Rabinovich." The pitch hadn't mattered. Every word came out in a croak.

"I don't believe I've heard of him," the bushy-haired, older man said.

Talking about her father helped. Rachel spoke more easily now. "He is great violinist. But, I am sad to say, in Russia the Jew

is rarely lifted up to position of importance."

The maestro nodded thoughtfully while
toying with one side of his long mustache.
"Yes, the curse of being Jewish." Then,
abruptly, he threw back his shoulders. "But
you are in America. No one will stop you
from playing here."

How different his words would have been
had she walked in wearing a skirt!

"Tune your instrument and play something for us."

The moment had come. The one she'd
waited for her whole life. Rachel crouched
down and opened her case. As she did, she
noticed that neither Judy nor Hank was
close by. Then she spotted them going down
steps at the end of the stage, headed out to
the seats of a huge, startlingly plush, red-
and-gold auditorium with private balconies
lining either side. And it had not been five
minutes since Hank had said they would
stay with her "all the way."

Taking a strengthening breath, Rachel
rose to her feet and walked to a man striking
a tuning fork to begin adjusting her violin's
pegs. She was here, she reminded herself,
with a symphony orchestra, its unique
sounds and smells swirling all around her.
Perhaps for the one and only time in her life.

And the maestro had not suspected her gender even for an instant. Why not make the most of it?

On her return to the maestro, she noted for the first time a freedom of movement. In trousers, the constriction of petticoats and skirts was gone. She began striding with renewed confidence.

"What would you like to play for us?" Maestro Gustoff asked with a fatherly smile as she rosined her bow.

"Lalo's *Concerto in F Minor*, if that pleases."

His thick brows rose with surprise, but he nodded his assent. Since the concerto had been written to showcase virtuoso violinists, her ability — or lack thereof — would quickly be determined.

So much the better, Rachel thought as she lifted her violin, her dear old friend, to her chin. This friend would not slip away to a comfortable distance as Hank and Judy had. She raised the bow, its feel and weight as familiar as the piece of music she had chosen. Closing her eyes, she shut out this earthly world, and with Lalo's Spanish-themed concerto, she began creating one of her own.

As her fingers danced across the strings and her bow wrested from her old friend every nuance of flair and passion the piece would surrender, she became aware that all other noise had ceased. Everyone had stopped to listen to her. The thrill of knowing her playing had captured the attention of skilled professionals was one she knew she would carry with her always, no matter the outcome of her masquerade.

Too soon she came to the spirited end of the concerto. Too soon this unforgettable moment was over. Panting heavily from the physical and emotional exertion, she lowered her instrument.

Seconds of silence followed. Then, like an eruption, loud clapping exploded, accompanied by shouts of "Bravo!" and the rapid tapping of bows on music stands. All telling her what she wanted to hear. This was her moment in the sun.

Or was it? No matter how loud or long the ovation lasted, it was tainted. They were not applauding her. They were applauding some nonexistent lad. Rachel looked out to the house seats and saw Hank and Judy on their feet clapping with the enthusiasm of the musicians onstage.

Farther back in the dim lighting, she spotted another person.

David. Hands at his sides, he stared at her, his expression hard, unyielding. Judy had expected he'd be upset by the deception, and he was. But no more than Rachel. Why, why had she allowed the others to think for her? Make her decisions. *And she a professed Christian.*

She ripped away the bowler. Pins flew with it, and her thick braid tumbled down across her shoulder. A sudden hush closed in on her as everyone stared openmouthed.

Rachel turned to the maestro standing a few feet away. "Forgive me, sir. I know I have —"

"Madam!" he roared, his eyes brittle with indignation. "This is an outrage. You are an affront to this orchestra and every musician here. How dare you regard us with so little respect. You are an embarrassment to all womanhood."

"But, sir —"

"Get out! I'll have none of your mealy-mouthed excuses."

He had reacted exactly as she expected. There was nothing left for her but to leave. She replaced the bowler to help hide eyes that stung with unshed tears. Then she stooped, and with trembling fingers, she replaced her violin and bow in their case. Any foolish dream she had ever had of playing with a fine orchestra was over. Dead.

As she flipped the locks closed on the

case, she glanced out to the house seats in search of Hank and Judy. She desperately needed them to return — the idea of walking offstage alone was too chilling to contemplate.

No longer near the front, they were making a hasty retreat toward the foyer. Deserting her. And David? He'd already vanished.

Oh, how she wished she could too. But that was not to be.

Twining her fingers around the handle of her case, she started to rise, hoping the strength in her legs would not desert her as well. She felt a hand at her elbow, firm. Assisting her up. One of the musicians must have taken pity.

"Thank you," she murmured, glancing his way.

David! He had not abandoned her.

He pulled her close and turned to the maestro. "Misguided she may have been. But, ah, what an artist. What an extraordinary, God-given gift you're tossing away. All for the fear of going against tradition."

The maestro bristled. "Mr. Michaels, I would have thought you above this sort of trickery."

David held her all the tighter. "There was no trickery in the music. Now, if you'll excuse us, I'll be seeing my fiancée home." He tipped his hat. "A good day to you all."

As they left the stage and started out the rear of the building, Rachel clung tightly to David. She had felt this grateful only one other time in her life — the day she first realized Jesus had suffered and died for her. Once they were safely away, she would give David her heartfelt thanks.

Emerging into the light of midday, Rachel spotted Hank and Judy standing beside the yellow-fringed surrey. Though Hank was grinning, he seemed embarrassed and avoided Rachel's gaze.

Judy looked furious. She charged forward and shoved the carpetbag at Rachel. "Why? Why did you expose yourself like that? And what about me? All of us. You've ruined everything. *Everything!*" Her voice rose to a wail. "The musicians loved you. The maestro would have hired you then and there. It was all for the taking. All you had to do was pretend to be a boy."

"Only if I live the lie. Forgive me, Judy, but this I cannot do."

"How could you do this to me?" Tears welled up in her big brown eyes. "Me and Benny?"

David stepped in front of his sister. "Your problems are your own. Leave Rachel out of them. And I'll thank you to stop meddling in ours." His angry glower then shifted to Hank. "I thought you were my friend. I guess I was mistaken."

Hank opened his mouth to speak, but nothing came out. His only defense was a sheepish shrug. Slowly shaking his head, David eyed Judy and Hank for several more seconds. The very air was charged with his rage, and Rachel feared what he might say or do next.

"See Judy home, Hank," he finally ordered in a no-nonsense tone. "Rachel and I need to talk. *Alone.*"

Rachel's mouth went dry as she watched Hank and Judy's departure. Despite the fact David had rescued her from the maestro, he had reserved a good measure of his wrath for her. Of that she had no doubt.

She braced herself for the worst.

Chapter Six

With a sweeping perusal, David assessed Rachel — from her bowler hat down to the clumsy boy's shoes. The poor girl looked as if she'd been cast overboard among circling sharks instead of just exiting one of San Francisco's finest hotels. Her expression was both wary and harried, and the men's clothing only made her appear more fragile.

"We haven't given you much of a welcome, have we?" He spoke softly, hoping to wipe away the fear. Stretching out a hand, he brushed it along her cheek. Rachel instantly stiffened, then her shoulders relaxed, and he saw the tender beginnings of trust replace the fear in her deep blue eyes.

He reached up and removed her bowler. "Until we find someplace for you to change, I think it's best if you keep your braid tucked inside."

"Yes," she murmured woodenly and picked up the end of her woven hair. "I make enough scandal for one day."

"Let me." As he took the long plait from her, its weight surprised him. He had a sudden urge to unbraid her hair and see what it looked like loose. To touch its silkiness, feel it tumbling over his hands. Quickly stifling his desires, he coiled the braid on top of her head and snugged the hat securely over it. Then he became aware that her gaze had lifted to his face, and he experienced an uncomfortable moment as he wondered if she'd been able to read his thoughts.

With what he hoped was a disarming smile, he took the satchel from her and offered his arm. "Let's leave this miserable alley."

"Yes. But I am thinking," she said with a surprising flash of a smile, "if two men walk arm in arm, people will not find this odd?"

Though her smile had been fleeting, it had splashed wide and warm, and he intended to see that it made its appearance much more often from now on.

With Rachel beside him, David started out to the street. "Well, as men go," he returned with an appreciative glance, "you make a far better-looking one than Judy. My old castoffs never did fit her right."

"Your sister wears men's clothes?"

"I caught her a time or two. She used to sneak down to the fishermen's wharf with her friends. The second I saw you up on the stage dressed like that, I knew she was responsible."

"But I know better. I should have refused."

"No. It was my family's duty to look after you, and we've done a very poor job. To make up for it, the rest of the day is yours. What's your pleasure? I'm at your disposal," he added with a bow.

They'd reached the end of the narrow alley. Rachel looked in both directions along the busy thoroughfare. "A walk. I think I just like to walk for a while."

"Good idea. This is our third day in a row of sunshine, something every San Franciscan learns to take advantage of. But first, let's stop by the Emporium. You'll be able to change there." He flashed a grin of his own. "Then I can have my lady back. Nothing beats a stroll down Market Street with a lovely girl on my arm."

Rachel chuckled now, a soft, throaty sound.

Not only did he enjoy the fact that he'd made her laugh, but he found himself captivated by the sound. He felt his own tensions melting away. This was turning out to be a really fine day.

Since the giant department store was only a few short blocks away, Rachel soon was dressed in feminine wear again. After he arranged to have her satchel and violin delivered back to the house, they were out strolling as casually as any couple — and better looking together than most, he didn't mind admitting. Some might even consider them a perfect match, as they meandered along — tall, blue eyed, and dark headed. They even sipped identical bottles of Dr. Pepper.

"This is very tasty," Rachel said as they turned onto a tree-shaded grassy square.

And refreshing, too, David thought as he noted the color returning to her cheeks. He noticed the other women in the park, mostly young mothers out with their little ones. In comparison to Rachel, he found them all lacking. Yes, he was beginning to feel very proud indeed, and lucky to be in her company.

"But I am wondering," Rachel said, bypassing a tot pulling a wooden duck. "How is it you come to the symphony hall? Are you not supposed to be at the shop making violins?"

"Yes. But I couldn't get out of my mind all morning what Judy had told me last night. Bragging that she'd gotten you an audition. I found that hard to believe. Something just wasn't right, so I took an early lunch to check it out."

Rachel shuddered. "To say I am ashamed is not enough. To have Maestro Gustoff say such angry words, and to have you hear them."

"I'm just glad I was there." David spotted a vacant bench and steered her toward it. "Forget what the maestro said. However, my sister was right about one thing. No woman should have to hide her true identity. The maestro is wrong."

"I am just as wrong," she said, sitting down on one side of the bench and settling her navy skirt.

He sat beside her, as near as he dared without causing her to feel uneasy. He wanted to be close enough to catch the rose scent of her hair.

"I let others say to me," she continued, seemingly unaware as she shifted her angle slightly toward him, "do this, do that, and I go along. But I cannot any longer. I am telling your parents the truth about me as soon as we return to your home. If I am to believe Jesus is the Way, I cannot go his way only when to me it pleases."

"You must let me find you a suitable place first. I'll ask around as soon as I deliver you home. You did give me two days, remember?"

"But your mother. The wedding."

"Look, I know why my family would be upset, you becoming a Christian and all, but I don't understand your reason. You told me that believing in Jesus made you appreciate your Jewish heritage even more. So, why would you reject me?"

Those intensely blue eyes became pools of compassion. "Oh, David, it is not you. It is me. I need to be with someone who believes Jesus is Messiah. Someone who loves him as I do. I need husband I can talk to about the things of the Bible. Someone to help me understand when my reading the English is not so good."

"I could help you with that."

"You would?"

His words had popped out without forethought. He'd as much as said he would read to her about her Jesus . . . that he was prepared to marry her. Was he? Was he ready to have his family tear their clothes and mourn him as if he were dead if he married a Christian? Whether he was ready or not mattered little when he saw the hope and trust shining from Rachel's eyes. The very sight knotted his insides — she seemed so vulnerable.

He knew he had to be honest. "Hank never talks about his religion, but his cousin Tom has mentioned a few things. And, well, to tell you the truth, they bothered me. For instance, when Moses came down the mountain with ten commandments written in stone by the very finger of God, that was the Law we are meant to live by. But Tom said that your Jesus came along *fifteen hundred years* later and — not to be outdone by the very Creator of the universe — issued two commandments of his own."

Rachel frowned — he must have offended her. Her usually flared brows made a *v* above her nose. She looked away and began fiddling with a splinter on the bench seat. Then, abruptly, she looked up. "You did not read the Bible passage yourself, or you would see the wrong you make. Jesus says if you keep his two commandments — 'Thou shalt love the Lord thy God with all thy heart, and with all thy soul, and with all thy mind; and thou shalt love thy neighbor as thyself. On these two commandments hang all the law and the prophets.' Does this saying not seem true to you?"

"Well, sure, when you put it that way."

"I did not put it this way. Is the Bible, the Word of God." She placed her hand over his.

Her touch set his skin to tingling, making it very hard to think. Not good — she was on the attack with her Jesus.

"But in Russia I know no more than you," Rachel continued. "When *goyim* boys on the street called us 'Christ-killers,' I believe them — until I read in the Bible that our heavenly Father loves us so much, he sent his son to die for us. All of us. The Jew first, then the Gentile. Jesus gave himself as sacrifice. That is why he came. Religious leaders in Jerusalem accuse him, and Roman soldiers, they drive the nails in his hands and feet. Gentile soldiers, they hang him on cross, not Jews. *Goyim* soldiers, like the evil ones who burn our villages today 'in the name of Jesus.' You see, it is all the lie of the devil. To keep us from meeting our Messiah. He loves us all so much — Jew and Gentile. Oh, my." Long, slender fingers went to her lips. "I am talking too much." Offering a weak smile, she looked away and took a sip from her drink.

David did the same. Her fervor for this Jesus was strong. Troubling. But in one thing she was right. He had never opened a Christian Bible. Never proved it true or false for himself. How could he give her a convincing argument if he hadn't? And she would never marry him as long as this Jesus matter stood between them.

Marry? The idea kept popping up. Was she really the woman with whom he wanted to spend the rest of his life? *The rest of his life?* The very thought was like cold water in his face.

He shot her a glance while taking a gulp of Dr. Pepper — then couldn't stop staring. The way she sat, her every move . . . there was such an elegance about her. Even had her features not been attractive, she still would have been beautiful. No finishing school could teach that kind of innate grace.

But her loveliness was only a small part of it. Something — a warmth, an energy — virtually glowed from within. It was like a flame drawing him, the proverbial moth. And this glow was never more evident than now as she tenderly watched a little girl feed crumbs to a few pigeons. Rachel spoke with such guileless purity. And her passion . . . such passion he could not deny. Every time he heard her play her violin, the fierce ardor, the excitement of her music, turned his skin to gooseflesh.

Yes, he wanted her, all right. Enough to fight whatever stood between them. Even her Jesus.

He sprang to his feet and took her hand. "There's a bookstore across the square. Let's go see if they have one of those Bibles. I want to see for myself all the things you've been talking about."

Her eyes widened for an instant, then settled into that irresistible glow as she rose to join him. "Oh, yes, David. There is more I want to show you, so much more."

∽∞∿

The afternoon passed before David realized it was gone. He had never experienced such a stimulating day in his life. No student of a *yeshiva* had ever asked so many questions of the rabbis or argued so many answers. And Rachel had been right. David had never felt more Jewish. Studying the teachings of this Jesus of Nazareth and his disciples made him hungry to know all the more about his own ancient people, the Chosen Ones of God.

Walking home on a rare balmy evening shortly before sunset, he reveled in the firm thickness of the Christian Bible under his arm. So much had been collected within one binding, not scattered about as with the numerous volumes at the synagogue.

Even more thrilling was the feel of Rachel's hand in his. When he'd taken it to steady her progress down a steep incline, he hadn't bothered to let go when they reached the bottom. More important, she hadn't seemed to mind. In companionable silence, they now turned onto his street.

Rachel came to an abrupt stop. She looked up at him, a slight frown making a crease just above her almost dainty nose. "I want to say I have wonderful day with you. I want to say this before we go in."

"I did, too, Rachel. The best," he assured her. Then wisps of her finespun hair caught the fire of the sinking sun, and the day got even better. "We'll do this again tomorrow, though I'm afraid we'll need to wait till I'm through at the shop. Pops and I have more work than we can handle this month."

Her expression remained serious. "You do remember that I am telling Sol and Magda about my faith tonight. As soon as I can get them together. This news of mine, I want to tell only once."

"I wish you would wait. But if you have to, I won't leave you alone to do it. I'll be right there with you."

He really loved what came next. She gazed up at him with what he would swear were adoring eyes. His heart gave a violent kick.

Taking a deep breath, she expelled a nervous laugh. "You and the Lord."

He squeezed her hand and they started walking again. "If Mama insists you leave, I'll take you to one of the better hotels and get you a room there until I can find a nice clean boardinghouse for you."

"A hotel? Is that not most expensive?"

David stopped short and stared up the street. "Money is the least of our worries, Rachel. Look in front of my house. The buggy parked there belongs to Maestro Gustoff." The small one-seater was unmistakable with its brass crest attached to the back — the one with a violin crossing necks with a bassoon.

Rachel retreated a step.

Pulling her close, David tucked her against his side. "Don't be afraid," he whispered against her delicate cheek. "I'll deal with him. *And everyone else.*"

Chapter Seven

The maestro was at the house too? The blood seemed to drain from Rachel's entire body. But for the support of David's arm, her legs would not have carried her another step, let alone the remaining half block.

How much trouble can this day bring? Rachel cried silently to the Lord.

Then she recalled all the saints who had been martyred through the ages, those who had suffered torture and death because of their faith, and she asked forgiveness. Besides, this day had not been all bad. There had been numerous moments of great joy and warm promise. She could still hear the resounding ovation the musicians gave her when she finished playing.

And David.

David's rescue had been absolutely gallant. What girl would not have been impressed? Then he had spent an entire workday afternoon restoring her confidence. His every look, his every touch, had made her feel not only beautiful but desirable.

And what spirited debates they'd had over such things as whether the prophets had written of the coming of two messiahs — one as the sacrifice and the other as king, or, as Christians believed, one Messiah coming twice — first as the sacrifice, then as king.

To Rachel's great joy, David had been no less stimulated by their lengthy discussions than she. It could be heard in the vibrancy of his voice every time he found one of his sought-after Hebrew scriptures — one with which he would start a new challenge.

And the questions. So many questions. He had such a hungry heart. Just as hers had been when Miss Wilkinson first told her about Jesus.

Reaching the Michaels' home, David guided her onto the walkway leading to the house. New dread gripped her.

The likely outcome of the next few minutes — this encounter with the maestro, then with David's parents — would be her permanent banishment from all of their lives.

David gave her shoulder a squeeze and reached for the door. "It'll be OK."

She attempted a brave smile, but she managed only the slightest lift of the corners of her mouth. David might be harboring optimism, but she understood the facts only

too well. Once his family learned about her conversion, he would be forbidden to speak to her ever again. No matter how brave and strong he appeared at the moment, David had been raised to be a good Jewish son — one who would marry a stranger before disobeying his family, before bringing them shame. If that were not enough to take him from her, he still lived in his family's home and worked in his father's shop every day. A breach with his warmhearted parents would be too painful a sacrifice. David opened the door and stepped back for Rachel to precede him. She had no choice but to enter. The time had come.

Once inside, she heard voices in the parlor and approaching footsteps. She froze. David did not. He pulled her with him toward the wide archway. They reached it at the same time as Magda, with the maestro and Sol a few steps behind.

The older woman's face showed the strain of her distress. She did not bother with any greeting whatsoever. Her brittle gaze centered on Rachel. "What Maestro Gustoff says, it is true? Did you actually go to the symphony hall and disgrace yourself? Shame you have brought to the whole family."

"Calm yourself, Mother." David moved

between her and Rachel. "If you're passing out blame, your darling daughter should be at the head of the line. Knowing Judy, though, I'll wager she has yet to show her face around here."

"Judith?"

"Yes, Judith," David confirmed. "She dreamed up the plan, then bullied Rachel into going along — all for her own selfish reasons. So I'd suggest you start with her." He then stepped around his mother to the older men. "As for you, Maestro Gustoff, I would have thought you had far more important matters to attend to than coming here to tattle."

The maestro's face darkened, a stark contrast to his bush of gray hair. He obviously was not accustomed to being upbraided, particularly by one so much his junior. "Mr. Michaels —"

David cut him off. "You had the rare opportunity to bask in the music of a young genius for a few moments. Count it a blessing, and let it go."

Rachel's admiration of David took the bite out of her fear. He was magnificent!

The maestro seemed considerably less impressed. "I cannot do that," he boomed with authority. "And if you'll silence that rash mouth long enough, you'll learn that

I'm not here merely to *tattle*." The man then chuckled — surprising Rachel — before continuing. "Though it *was* too rare a tale to keep to myself. I'm here to offer your fiancée a position with the symphony."

As he switched his attention to Rachel, she questioned her hearing. Everyone had said such a thing was impossible. Or was the maestro jesting?

"Miss Rabinovich, I think one or two solos from you each performance would be most appreciated by our patrons."

This had to be a dream . . . the entire day nothing but a crazy dream.

Maestro Gustoff returned to David. "That does not mean Miss Rabinovich would actually be a member of the orchestra. I'm sure you would agree that I cannot have a lone woman in the company of almost seventy men for several hours every day."

David gave him a curt nod. "Of course not."

"Most of the time I will work with her separately."

David raised a brow. "With a suitable chaperone present." He then swung back to Rachel and took her hand. "Do you still want to play violin for this man?"

She gazed up at her champion, her shield,

and mouthed, *Thank you.* Then she said aloud, "Yes. This thing is the most desire of my father. Is why my family sacrificed so much to send me here."

David nodded his understanding, then he looked beyond her to the orchestra leader. "How much would her pay be?"

Magda gasped. *"David.* It is an honor merely to be given the opportunity."

"What had you planned to offer her, Maestro?" he asked again, as if his mother had not spoken.

Rachel knew why. The *honor* would not pay her rent, put food on her table — needs she knew she would have after tonight.

"I must confess, I hadn't given her salary any thought," the maestro said, his manner now almost too casual. "I thought we could try her out first and see how it goes."

Despite his mother's glare, David continued to press. "I think while you're trying her out, she should receive at least what the newer musicians are paid." He then glanced down at Rachel. "Would that suffice?"

Gratefully, she nodded. "That would be most appreciated."

The maestro stepped up to her. He collected one of her hands and smiled. "Then it's agreed. I'll be looking forward to the beginning of our association. Please be at the hall at nine tomorrow morning, and we'll put in a few hours. Perhaps by Saturday after next, you can give your debut performance." That fatherly feeling she had gotten from him when they first met at the symphony hall returned, twofold.

"Yes, thank you. It will be my pleasure."

"*No!* That's impossible," Magda cried as she nudged past David. "The wedding will be the very next afternoon. Besides, there is so much left to do."

David took her by the shoulders. "Mother, we need to talk about that. First, let me see Maestro Gustoff out." David ushered the distinguished older man to the front door, assuring him, "Miss Rabinovich will be there tomorrow. You can count on it."

Magda chased after them. "Talk, David? Talk about *what?*"

Rachel heard her repeat those words frantically three times before David escorted her back into the parlor.

As for Sol, Rachel was grateful that he had held his tongue since she and David had arrived home.

But that would soon come to an end. Magda rushed to him. "Say something. David has gotten totally out of hand. He'll ruin all my plans."

From Sol's expression, it was obvious he wished he were anywhere else. "Son, you'll learn it's best to let the women have their way when it comes to wedding arrangements."

"Concerning the marriage," David said grimly. "Rachel has been trying to tell you something since she arrived, but we all just took her over. Especially Judy."

A heavy weight of sadness crushed Rachel's chest. These wonderful people, their lovely home . . . David. With her next words, all would be taken from her. "I-I-on the trip here, I-I meet this woman and I-uh —"

"Yes? Yes?" Magda prodded.

"The crux of it is," David said, saving Rachel the agony of saying the words, "Rachel met a missionary on her trip here, and she has become a Christian."

The truth was out. For one very long moment, no one spoke.

Then Magda's mouth fell open. She clutched her bosom. "A *geshmat!* Yenta's girl has become a *geshmat!*"

Sol, though, was disturbingly unreadable as he said, "I see."

Magda's hands moved to her cheeks. "Your mother — have you written her?"

"Not yet."

The older woman wagged her head.

"Yenta's so Old World. She'll declare you dead."

Rachel was more than a little confused by now. Magda should have been attacking, not worrying about Rachel's mama. Her throat clogged with overwhelming sadness. "I know."

"How can you do this to her? to your family?" Magda came toward her, arms open, pleading.

"This I did not do to cause hurt. The English writing — the missionary helped me to read the English with the Christian Bible, and I saw —"

"The *witch*. The *sneaky witch*," Magda railed, her fury returning full force. "This woman, where is she?"

"On her way to Hawaii." *Thank God*, Rachel added silently. Magda looked mad enough to kill.

The distraught woman glanced with narrowed eyes in the direction of the sea. "Gone there, no doubt, to corrupt more helpless innocents."

"No. That is not the way of it," Rachel replied in a placating tone. "You see, when I read the words, everything comes clear. All the words that God gives to his people, generations of generations of words, they fit now like pieces in a great puzzle. I believe.

And I cannot stop this believing, even if I want to." Rachel took Magda's hand, and the older woman did not pull away. A hopeful sign. She continued with more conviction. "So you see why I am not wanting to be part of the wedding plans. No longer am I the acceptable bride for your son." Those last words, she suddenly realized, were her deepest regret.

Magda's pale blue eyes narrowed again. She swung from Rachel to David. "Ha! Now it all comes clear. You knew about her all along. This is why you haggle over money with the good maestro. Money for Rachel to leave us . . . and freedom for you! You think you're too good for a wife from Russia. Too American for the old ways."

That Magda had shifted her rage to her son took Rachel by surprise. But David stood his ground. "You're absolutely right, Mother. I didn't like the idea of spending the rest of my life with someone I'd never met, just for the sake of tradition. For the rest of my life, when I knew nothing about her, or whether or not we would get along."

"*Get along?* What's to get along?" Sol roared, finally joining in. He thrust out his hands, palms up. "You do what you're supposed to. She does what a good Jewish wife does, and you'll get along."

Magda whirled toward the archway. *"Judy!* Where is that girl? You say she's the one who took Rachel to Maestro Gustoff. Such mischief she was making. And what did she hope to gain from this mess?"

"Judy's young and in love — and desperate," David explained, patience returning to his tone. "She's as anxious to rid us of the custom of matchmaking as I am. She's completely smitten with Benjamin Berkowitz."

"The cannery worker's son?" Sol shook his head. "A cannery worker's son for my little princess?"

"We'll deal with Judith later," Magda said, eyeing her son again. "But, David, your way out of the marriage was so simple. All you had to do was speak up, tell us this thing about Rachel."

"I wanted to find a secure situation for her in case you declared her dead and wanted her out of the house."

Standing slightly to the rear of David, Rachel placed her hand on his back in silent thanks. This wrath he was taking was all for her.

"Son." Sol grasped David's shoulder. "You believed we would do that? This is not the Old Country. Many of the old traditions aren't so necessary in America. Here we live and work side by side with the Gentiles. They are not our enemy. But as for family — family will always matter. Very much. Rachel is the daughter of your mother's cousin. We vowed to take care of her as if she were our own." He looked past David to Rachel, wrapping her within the warmth of his gaze. "You are *mishpocheh*, Rachel. Family. Misguided, maybe, but still family. You're welcome to stay here as long as you wish."

His kindness was so unexpected, tears came close to flooding Rachel's eyes.

"Of course, darling," Magda said, pulling her into a hug. "You're Yenta's girl." She returned Rachel to arm's length. "But you should have been honest with us from the start."

These people were so good, so very good. Rachel didn't know how much longer she would be able to keep the tears at bay. "Forgive me. I see now I am very wrong."

Magda's hands flew to her cheeks again. "The wedding invitations! I posted them this morning. *Oy vay!* So much to cancel." She swung away and headed for the hall.

"There's more."

At the seriousness in David's tone, Magda stopped. She slowly turned. Rachel, along with Sol, also eyed him with concern. She thought everything had been resolved.

"This seems as good a time as any to say it," he said evenly. "I, too, am planning to become a follower of Jesus. I believe he is the true Messiah."

Everything stopped. Even breathing. A hush fell upon the room, so complete that the ticking of the hall clock could be heard.

Rachel recovered first. "Oh, David." She rushed to him. "This is such surprise."

"Yes. Like you, I'm beginning to see how everything falls into place. There's no need for us to argue every jot and tittle of the Law when following Jesus answers all the questions."

"My English, it is not good enough to tell you the happiness I am feeling." In the flush of joy, Rachel raised onto her toes and kissed his cheek.

Violently, Rachel was wrenched away from him.

By Magda. The woman shook with rage. "*You* did this. We welcomed you into our home, and this is how you repay us? Seducing my son away from centuries of belief?"

"It's my fault," Sol moaned. "I must accept the blame." Wringing his hands, he rocked back and forth on the balls of his feet. "I should have been a better father.

Should have insisted we celebrate *Shabbes* every Friday night. Should have —"

"No, Pops." David reached out to his father. "Everything I learned of our faith from you and from the rabbi only served to make me understand more clearly that Jesus *is* Messiah."

Sol was not pacified. His burly head began to slowly wag. "So now you will turn your back on everything? *Shabbes?* Being a Jew?"

"No, Pops. Celebrating the Sabbath will have more meaning than ever. Now I *want* to set aside a day for the study and worship of God. More than ever before. I can't tell you how eager I am. And Mom, I don't want you blaming Rachel for this." He took Rachel's hand.

Even now, in the midst of his own crisis, he remained strong, protective. She squeezed his fingers to convey her gratitude, as he continued to explain to his mother what had happened.

"I insisted on hearing what it was that meant so much to her, that she would give up her security, everything, for it."

Then, leaving his mother standing there, speechless for the first time since Rachel met her, he turned to Rachel and blessed her with a lopsided grin. "You see, I had to know what was so important to you that you would choose *it* over me. Being the witty and handsome fellow that I am."

Rachel's heart almost leapt from her chest. He was actually flirting — outrageously! And how she loved it. He was even so confident she would find him irresistible, he'd begun to toy with her. Such a *bonditt!* Laughing, she brushed a lightly curling strand from his brow. Perhaps he needed a bit of a scare of his own. She hiked her chin. "Ah, but now I do not have to choose between you and Jesus. I think maybe you better start running, if you still want your precious freedom."

"What is going on here?" Magda had found her voice. "Sol, what are they saying now?"

David ignored her and stepped within inches of Rachel, his light eyes shimmering with determination . . . and desire.

Suddenly, she knew the chase was on, and it was her David was after. She felt an excited giggle welling up, but she would not back down. She squelched the titter and stared squarely into his eyes.

He leaned closer. "What if I don't want to run? What if I think it's great that Mom sent out the invitations? What if I grabbed you up right here on the spot and kissed you?"

She refused to back off. "What if I kiss you first?"

David's mouth collided with hers.

The shock of his touch, the thrill of it going all the way to her toes . . . Rachel lost all track of who won. There was nothing but him, his faint spicy scent . . . and lips that were at once firm and pliable, cool and electrifyingly hot. With his arms wrapped around her, she had all the love and refuge she would ever need in this strange New World, this wondrous new beginning. She would have Jesus, her music, *and* David. She would have it all.

Somewhere beyond the rapture of David's kiss, beyond the pounding of her heart, Rachel heard a voice . . . a woman's.

"*Oy vay!* Such goings-on! Does this mean I don't have to cancel the wedding?"

Chapter Eight

One bong, then a second, came from the big clock in the entry hall, echoing up the staircase and through the open door of Judy's room. Rachel's heart leapt with excitement. Soon, very soon, it would be time to go.

"Well, you might as well sit down," Judy said glumly, her voice more in tune with a funeral than a wedding, "so I can pin the veil on top of your head."

Judy had not spoken more than three words at any one time to Rachel or the rest of the family since she learned of the wedding. She was that upset. But today Judy had been required to perform sisterly duties for the bride, whose own sister was a continent and an ocean away.

Taking a seat at the dressing table, Rachel looked into the mirror at Judy's morbid expression. The girl's presence threatened to cast a pall on what should be the most festive day of Rachel's life. "Does it make you so unhappy to help me dress for my wedding day? To become my little sister?"

"You know it's not that. I've got nothing

against you personally. It's just — can't you see?" She lifted a length of sheerest chiffon and dropped it over Rachel's French twist and down past her face. "We didn't put a stop to Mama's matchmaking, and now she's getting her way in everything else." Judy grimaced as she fussed with the placement. "Everything, from keeping this a traditional Jewish wedding — even though you and David are now Christians — to —"

"Truly, I do not mind, since she agreed to having a minister come to bless us, as well as the rabbi."

"Well, that's the only thing you've had your way with. Everything else has been her doing, right down to picking the very day and place. Now that you and David have bowed to her every wish, what chance will there be for me and Benny?" she wailed, her voice rising by octaves. "Him with not a single shining prospect for the future. Let me tell you, your debut at the symphony certainly didn't help, everyone fawning over you, telling Mama how lucky she is to have such a gifted daughter-in-law."

With a sigh, Rachel reached for her wreath of roses. As upset as Judy was, the girl would probably slam it down on the veil and ruin her hairstyle beneath. Rachel placed the circlet high, catching the back of it on top of her coiled hair, and let the front dip slightly so every one of the white satin buds could be seen. All the while, she fervently hoped David would think them as beautiful as she did.

Magda had spared no expense in giving her son a bride to be proud of. Rachel felt most elegant, indeed, fitted into a gown of ivory satin, chiffon, and the richest of laces. "Would you secure the crown for me, please?"

Judy scratched around in the drawer for hairpins. If only some sparkle could be put back into her eyes, the younger girl would look quite lovely, too, in white netting over apricot silk. And, as always, her hair was a most becoming riot of black curls, caught by shiny ribbons, but never quite contained — just like the girl herself.

"You know," Rachel said as Judy began pinning the wreath, "the only reason I am the success is because I am here in America . . . the land of opportunity. Why cannot your Benny think of a way to use his talents and become the success too?"

Judy snorted in a most unladylike manner. "There are only so many talented geniuses to go around."

Rachel refused to be baited. She wanted everyone to be as happy as she was on her wedding day. Or as close as they could come, anyway. "Surely your Benny has dreams. What is this thing he wants to do with his life?"

"What he wants is impossible. He wants to go to Stanford College and study medicine. But, of course, his family could never afford that. He's the sixth of eight children."

"That *is* difficult. I know money problems," Rachel said, remembering how many years her father saved for her trip here. "Perhaps I can help. The pay I get for playing the violin, I save back for this school. I think David will not mind. Is always good thing to have doctor in the family."

The remaining hairpins dropped from Judy's fingers as she stared, wide eyed, into the mirror at Rachel. "You would do that? Why? You haven't even met Benny, and I've been absolutely horrid to you."

Rachel reached back, caught the girl around the waist, and gave her a hug. "My happiness, it is so full. I have so much. My Jesus, and now David and the music. If I do not give some of this joy away, I think I am bursting."

A sudden rush of light brightened the room.

"Oh, look!" Rachel rose from the seat and moved to the window, loving the swish and weight of her costly gown as she went. "Look at the sky. After three foggy days, the sun. Is come out to help us celebrate."

As she turned back, Judy stood behind her, tears rolling down her cheeks. "You'd really do this for me? Really?"

Swallowing down her own emotion, Rachel opened her arms, and Judy flew into them. As they embraced, Rachel felt the dampness of Judy's tears on her shoulder. But she cared not the least if they stained the dress. They were treasured tears . . . the tears of her new sister.

After a time, Judy moved away and, swiping at her wet cheeks, looked up at Rachel with the sparkle that had been wanting for so long. "I love you for doing this. David is so lucky to have you."

Rachel thumbed a missed droplet from Judy's jawline. "I love you, too."

"Come along, girls. It's time to go."

To Rachel's surprise, Magda had come to the doorway without them noticing. She looked most attractive in cinnamon lace swagged at the back of her waist with an elaborate satin bow.

"The hired carriage is downstairs waiting." Magda started away, then turned back, her slim hands at her cheeks. "My beautiful daughters. A stick I'll have to carry to beat the men off."

As she spun away again and disappeared down the hall, Rachel and Judy looked at each other and burst into giggles.

Judy contained her mirth first and pulled her face into a serious pose. "Hush, now," she said in a good imitation of her mother. "Don't you know it's serious business, this getting married?" She reached out and straightened the fall of Rachel's veil. As she did, her expression gentled, and her lips slid into a sublime smile. "The beautiful bride," she murmured. "David's beautiful bride."

∽∾∽∾

Hank's father had outdone himself in tailoring David's wedding suit. A little too much, David thought with a grimace. Tails over striped trousers to go with a *yamulke?* But Mr. Weldon had insisted it was the latest thing in formal afternoon wear. And who could argue with him? The man dressed even the wealthiest railroad barons.

But still, David's primary hope was that Rachel wouldn't think he looked as silly as he felt.

Rachel. In a few minutes she would be his. *For life.*

He stood at the far end of the Palace Hotel's banquet hall — a room so large every footstep echoed across the marble, and every called greeting resounded off the paneled walls. Was his cutaway crawling up? He jerked the front down with both hands. Sweaty hands. He reached inside his coat for a kerchief to wipe them.

There had to be two hundred chairs lined up. Most of them already filled. And garlands upon garlands of flowers. He had no idea where the florist had found so many in September.

"Nervous, old boy?" Hank's question dripped with humor as he stood a few feet to David's left.

"You just worry about holding up your canopy pole when the time comes."

"Sure, sure. But I'm telling you, Davy, there's no way any rain is coming through that ceiling." He pointed up to the ornate scrolls and moldings with a smug lift of a brow.

Hank was going to be trouble. David never should have asked him to hold a pole during the ceremony. "I told you before that standing under a white silk canopy is traditional."

"There's got to be more reason than that."

"*Later*," David ground out through clenched teeth. He should have known better than to expect Hank to do anything of a serious nature. Thank heavens, his other friends stood calmly *and* silently by. "Rachel will be here any second. We have to be ready."

In the corner, the hired musicians, along with several volunteers from the symphony, blared out the first note of a tune, and David practically jumped out of his expensive suit. They settled into something soothing that sounded like Brahms.

Maybe that would help calm him.

"Come on, buddy," Hank bellowed louder than a wounded boar. "What's it for?"

"*All right.* Just keep your voice down. The canopy represents the home that will shield the new couple," he explained, hoping Hank wouldn't think the tradition was too corny. "Its having no sides means all our family and friends are welcome."

"Which includes me, of course."

David shot him a warning glance. "That depends."

One of the Goldbergs' small sons raced pell-mell down the center aisle. "They're coming! They're coming!"

David wheeled around. "Men, raise the canopy. Where's the rabbi? the minister?" He looked wildly about. "Where's Pops?"

A hand clamped onto his shoulder. He jumped.

"Such tight muscles you have, my son. Relax."

Relax?

His father led him beneath the canopy that was now being lifted at each corner by those he'd selected to symbolically guard and uphold his household. With the covering of silk and his good friends surrounding him, David felt the tension ease a little. *A little.*

The minister and the rabbi, both in black, rose from the front row to join him — they'd been there all along. Then he spotted a smudge on the toe of his shoe. It laughed up at him and all his efforts.

A hush fell over the room — except for the loud clacking of heels on marble. His mother. She came, hurrying down the aisle, motioning to the musicians. Then she blew him a double-quick kiss and dropped down in a front-row seat, busily straightening her skirt. Flushed and fidgety, she looked as nervous as he.

The musicians began to play a Jewish *hora* at a slow beat. The wedding had started.

David shot a glance up the aisle . . . and all else faded away.

A veiled vision in a cloud of white floated

toward him. She walked between bowers of flowers and good friends. This vision, who had shared with him the mysteries of the ages, now came to share the mystery that was her alone.

He drank in the sight of her as his eyes misted. *Thank you, Jesus. I don't know what I ever did to deserve her.*

As thoughts of all he'd come to know and love this past fortnight filled his being, a peace spread from that deepest part of him, a quieting peace beyond understanding. He would be fine now. Just fine.

Light from one of the huge hanging chandeliers penetrated Rachel's veil, and for a second, David clearly saw her face. Her soul-deep eyes and that sky-wide smile of hers, as she came to him. To *him.*

He started toward her.

A hand stopped him.

Hank's. "Patience, buddy."

Then she was in front of him, her eyes now demurely lowered. Had his brash move frightened her? As he turned to step with her up to the rabbi, she brushed his hand with her fingers, a touch that bespoke her love more than if she'd said the words.

He suddenly felt as if the whole world had been given to him.

From that moment on, David scarcely

heard a word as the rabbi, in his black coat and prayer shawl, recited the wedding ritual. And when David and Rachel sipped from the wedding cup, all he could see were her slender fingers entwining the goblet as she brought it past her veil . . . the goblet touching the full, tender lips of this mystery who would be his wife. For life.

∞∞

David had told Rachel that he loved her any number of times in the past days. But when he'd forgotten himself and started toward her as she came down the aisle, that told her so much more. Nothing was left of the sophisticated, distant stranger who had collected her at the dock that first day. Now all she could see was her sweet enthusiastic David. Her soul mate. Her beloved gift from God.

Now the minister from the Baptist church stepped forward to give his blessing on their union — something she never would have dreamed possible two weeks before. America really was a new world, a place where Jew and Christian could come together in celebration.

The rabbi had been understandably upset. And although he'd argued and pleaded with the young couple for days to return to the faith, in the end, he had reluctantly accepted the arrangement for the sake of Sol and Magda. Rachel hoped in her heart of hearts that during their talks he'd also gotten a glimpse of what she and David now knew. A spark of light, she prayed, that he, along with Sol and Magda, someday would choose to explore.

". . . and may the Lord bless and keep this marriage," Reverend Hollingsworth finished, "until death do you part. In the name of the Father, the Son, and the Holy Ghost."

The words were no sooner out of the minister's mouth than the rabbi placed the napkin-wrapped glass at David's feet to be crushed, a solemn reminder that though this was a day of joy and celebration, the sufferings of Israel must never be forgotten.

Rachel's new husband wasted not a second. He smashed the glass to the guests' resounding cries of *"Mazel tov!"*

He then reached for her.

After a heart-stopping moment of him pausing to behold her, he swept away her veil and possessed her lips with a power and a passion that caught her completely by surprise.

When at last he pulled away, Rachel was breathless. Light-headed. Her knees were weak. He, quite literally, had swept her off her feet.

Cries of congratulations bombarded them from all around as David bent to her ear. And, within their own intimate haven, he whispered, "*L'chayim,* my love . . . To life, for life. Forever."

Gazing up to his eyes of light, she knew he'd never said words more pleasing or more true.

Author's Note

At a traditional Jewish wedding, once the rabbi pronounces his benediction over one glass and after both bride and groom sip from another, the groom breaks a glass by stomping on it. This is to remind the wedding party of the destruction of the temple. It also is a reminder that happiness is transient, and the Jews must never forget the sufferings of Israel.

On a lighter note: It is said that when the groom smashes the glass, it will probably be the last time he's allowed to put his foot down.

Something Borrowed

Ginny Aiken

For where two or three are gathered together in my name, there am I in the
midst of them.

MATTHEW 18:20

Chapter One

"Be careful what you pray for; the Good Lord just might let you have it."

Determined to keep her straw boater in place, Emma Carstairs clapped her palm on its crown and remembered her late mother's frequent warning. Elizabeth Carstairs had instilled her rock-solid faith in her daughter, together with a healthy respect for God's awesome power.

As the buckboard bearing Emma and her worldly possessions jounced across the rutted earth of west central Texas, each bone-jarring lurch drove the desolate reality of the land deeper into her soul. It seemed once again that Mama had been right.

Emma had spent months praying for the Lord to show her how best to serve him. She had always considered dressmaking a fine, respectable occupation, but she'd come to chafe at its lack of opportunity to render meaningful service to the Father. Emma knew in her innermost heart that God had something . . . *more* in store for her.

But when she licked her dry lips and her tongue came up with the dust that eddied from the horse's hooves, she paid heed to her mother's words. That *more* just might surpass what Emma had prayed for.

"Look up ahead," grunted Rattlesnake, the dubiously named foreman she had hired in San Antonio. "That there be Jubal's spread. Won't be long now till we get there."

Squinting, Emma strove to see what had prompted the man's pronouncement. Between two hills on the horizon, a dark dot teetered at the edge of the world. Had Rattlesnake thought his words would reassure her?

They had left San Antonio at the crack of dawn, heading northwest. Now, the sun blazed just past its zenith, its fire relentless as they made their trek toward the Rocking C Ranch — the Carstairs spread.

"My spread," Emma murmured. Papa's only brother, Jubal, had left her all his earthly goods — the ranch, its stock, and a good-sized chunk of Texas prairie. Emma felt certain it was the "more" she had prayed for.

By the time they reached the Rocking C, Emma wasn't so sure. She stared in dismay at the stone house. The door swinging on one hinge, the broken shutters, and the coat of dust on the covered porch did not inspire a feeling of welcome, much less security.

As she stood with Rattlesnake by the wagon, Emma watched a bundle of brown vegetation tumble along the drought-fissured ground. It came to a halt against the rough, unpainted door of what looked like a barn — *if* edifices built to house livestock were called barns in Texas. A few feet away, an empty trough lay on its side.

A corral butted up against the building, and four other structures clustered around the far end of the enclosure. There wasn't an animal in sight; the fallen fence rails probably explained that.

"Right fine ranch you have here," Rattlesnake said. With a monumental heave, he yanked Emma's leather trunk over the side of the wagon and dropped it at her feet. He sighed, and Emma thought she heard yearning in the rough sound. "This here ranch," he said, "has all a body needs. Yessiree, ma'am! You even have a spring on the property. And a pond, too. It's the best land around these parts."

Stunned by his observation, Emma glanced around. "A spring? Where? I see nothing but . . . dirt."

Her companion thumbed his Stetson out

of his line of vision, then gestured grandly. "Look to your left. See all that green?"

Emma stared in the direction Rattlesnake indicated. In the distance she saw what could best be described as brush surrounding massive boulders. "The scrubby stuff over there?"

"Yes, ma'am!"

Emma collapsed onto her trunk. "I have to trudge . . . all that way . . . for *water?*"

"No, ma'am!" Rattlesnake responded. "I told you this here's a right fine ranch. You have the spring and pond, and there's a well to the rear of the house. Jubal even fixed himself a pump inside the kitchen."

Relief rushed through her. "Praise God!"

"Yes, ma'am!" Rattlesnake slapped his hat against his thigh, raising dust from the denim. "The Good Lord provided fine for the Rocking C. Why don't you go inside, take a look whilst I get your things from the wagon?"

For a moment, Emma wondered if she possessed that much courage. The house wore the forlorn look of abandonment.

Squaring her shoulders and firming her spine, Emma stepped forward to survey her new home from its front doorway. The ubiquitous grit littered everything — the plaster floor, the man-sized furniture, the table with its green oilcloth puddled around one leg, the iron cookstove to her left, and the stone fireplace to her right. Feathers were scattered here and there, and she wondered where they might have come from.

Stepping cautiously inside, Emma caught a whiff of noxious fumes. Her stomach lurched.

With a hanky to shield her nose and mouth, she ventured farther into the room. At one end, she noticed a large, white-enameled sink, the three chinks on its rolled edge contrasting darkly. A water pump rose over one side. Rattlesnake had been right.

Emma began to relax, but as she approached the sink, she discovered the source of the stench. Pots filled the basin, molded food stuck to the insides. Flies buzzed around her as she moved closer.

"Close enough," she muttered, backing up.

A door to the right of the fireplace caught her attention. Going to investigate, Emma rounded an enormous chair and heard something crack under her weight. Seconds later, a miasma that made the odor of the rotten food seem like that of rose petals filled the room, making her nose burn, her eyes water.

"Oh, that's bad!" she cried. "Bad, bad, *bad!*"

"Miss Carstairs! Are you all right?" Before she could warn him, Rattlesnake stepped into the house. "*Pheew-eee!* Something stinks near to kill a body in here!" He turned tail and went for his wagon.

Emma followed. From the putrid fumes, she gathered some fowl had abandoned an egg-filled nest. And for a fleeting moment, she considered returning to San Antonio. But, no. San Antonio was too close to this disaster in no-man's-land. Philadelphia's staid structures and paved streets tempted her mightily.

Still, she had prayed for a more meaningful existence, and God had seen fit to give her a ranch. In comparison to her rented room back East, the plastered-stone house boasted palatial proportions. The other buildings looked just as strong and spacious. Surely she could tackle dirt and odor and emerge victorious.

" 'I can do all things through Christ which strengtheneth me,' " Emma whispered, then faced Rattlesnake. "I'm not sure what kind of accommodations I can offer —"

"Never you mind, ma'am. Jubal's bunkhouse is plain, but it has good feather beds. I'll just mosey on over and see what's what."

She sighed in relief. Rattlesnake was most

likely as honest and trustworthy as the next man, but he remained a stranger, and she wasn't ready to invite him to stay inside the house. A house she would have to clean if she intended to sleep there that night, and since the afternoon was partway gone, she had no time to waste.

Gathering her gumption, Emma marched up the porch steps. She opened her trunk, rummaged around, and withdrew a worn petticoat. Cleanliness was next to godliness, her mother had often said. Never before had she been quite so sure of the truth in Mama's dictum.

∽∾

Antonio Mallery Alvarez had killed for the last time. He had claimed his last bounty. And before giving another felon a chance at his own hide, he had put down his gun for good.

It happened after the fateful poker game in Santa Fe three months ago. Lady Luck had perched her lovely self on Tony's shoulder, and poor old Jubal Carstairs hadn't stood a chance. But the pile of money Tony had won from the old man hadn't made him nearly as happy as claiming the crumpled, yellowed deed to the Rocking C Ranch just north and west of San Antone.

He smiled. It seemed sort of fitting, him and the largest town near his new spread sharing the same name.

Impatience dogged him. He slapped the reins on the dun mare's back before he could stop himself. She couldn't go any faster, and he knew it. Not while pulling the wagon loaded with everything he and his mother had deemed indispensable for their new home. Certainly not under this deucedly hot August sun.

"Now, Son, was that *really* necessary?" his mother asked in her sweet-as-syrup, firm-as-steel voice.

"No, Mother, of course it wasn't," he answered patiently, then thought it wise to ask the horse's forgiveness. "*Perdóname*, Matilda."

At the ripe old age of thirty-three, Tony found it nigh unto impossible to endure his mother's instructions, warnings, and gentle scolding. He'd been on his own for more years than he cared to count, overcoming greater risks than she would care to imagine, and thriving on the rush of danger for many of those years.

Thinking back, Tony frowned. When had it all begun to weigh on him?

He had worked just this side of the law. And although killing his prey had never been pleasant, the last time he'd been forced to shoot had sickened him. Rotten through and through, the vermin he caught had held up a stage, killed an entire family and their driver, then gone on to enjoy the fruits of their crime, mindless of the lives they'd snuffed out.

As he lined up his sights, however, Tony's conscience had nudged to the forefront of his thoughts, altering the angle at which he held his gun.

Thou shalt not kill.

Although half his lifetime had passed since he set foot inside a church, some of his mother's lessons had obviously taken root. Yes, he wounded the two robbers — enough to get them back to town and the jail where they rightly belonged — but he spared their lives.

Tony counted himself lucky. He'd had to kill on few occasions, and then, only when his own life or another's had been at stake.

But killing never felt right. It left a bitter taste in a man's mouth. So he was starting over. A brand-new life awaited him at the Rocking C Ranch. From the details on his deed, Tony knew he owned a prime piece of Texas prairie that came with two treasures. In a vast plain where water was man's most valuable resource, the Rocking C had not only a spring and a pond, but if he pictured it right, a well had been dug behind the house.

Right about now, a long, cool drink of water from that well would put him on the right side of bliss.

Althea Alvarez's lush voice broke into Tony's thoughts. "Do you think it will be much farther, Son?"

Tony started to respond with his usual curse, but a maternal glare cut short the offending expression. He grinned sheepishly. If he didn't watch himself, she would be after him with one of those nasty cakes of lye soap she had used to wash his mouth out with when he was a kid!

With a sniff, his mother continued. "Well, Antonio, we've been ridin' *forever* across this . . . this brushland, and the sun's starting to reach for the earth. Where *is* this new ranch of yours?"

Tony tipped up his black hat and squinted. He couldn't be sure, but he thought he could just make out a cluster of buildings a few miles ahead. "See those black specks above the ground? If I'm not mistaken —" and he sure hoped he wasn't — "that's the Rocking C Ranch."

"Oh, mercy!" Mother exclaimed. "Praised be the Lord!"

A twinge of guilt jabbed Tony. The trip had been rough on her — rougher than he had expected before leaving Santa Fe. He hadn't known what else to do but bring her with him.

His Spanish father had died when Tony was seventeen. Bitter, and raging against the God who had turned a deaf ear to his prayers for his father, Tony left home not long after the funeral on a mission to exact justice.

But last month he had walked his beaming sister Amaryllis up the aisle and handed her into François de Michaud's keeping. The newlyweds promptly departed for the bridegroom's home in Bordeaux, France. Tony hadn't had the heart to leave his mother behind when he claimed his new ranch — not to mention the funds. Amaryllis's wedding and dowry had wiped out the last of his father's money. There was nothing left for Mother to live on in Santa Fe.

Tony couldn't afford to keep two residences. True, he'd collected on a number of bounties over the years, but that hadn't added up to a fortune. He had enough to get his new ranch up and running, but he had to be careful, since his cash did have a limit.

Besides, he would need his mother's help around the house, since he expected to be busy tending stock.

A self-satisfied grin crossed his face. Just the thought of the sweet deal he'd struck at that poker table made the heat, the dust, the emptiness of west central Texas mighty appealing. He had thought to chase outlaws for another couple of years until he had enough to buy himself a spread, even though he'd tired of the chase and feared losing the edge of his instincts with age. Lady Luck had kindly moved his plans up a bit, giving him the chance to retire his gun as he wished.

Two hours later, as the western sky began to display bands of scarlet, purple, and deepest blue, Tony pulled on Matilda's reins and called, *"Alto, niña!"*

The homely mare stopped all at once. Tony grabbed the wooden seat to avoid flying over the nag's back and bit off an epithet.

"Antonio!" his mother warned, clutching his arm.

He clenched his teeth. "Sorry, Mother. I'll try to be more respectful of your sensibilities."

"It's not *my* sensibilities you need worry about! As God's children, we are called to bless and curse not, even those who persecute us."

Tony studied the low stone house before him to avoid the disapproval he knew he would see in his mother's gray eyes. It seemed deserted, as if no one had looked after the place since old Jubal left for Santa Fe. The door had fallen off a couple of hinges, and some shutters lay in pieces below one of the windows. Apart from those minor details, the house appeared sturdy, of a good size, and awaiting its new owner.

With a grin on his lips and excitement in his belly, he vaulted over the side of the buckboard. Bowing in courtly fashion, he extended his hand to his mother. "Allow me to welcome you to your new abode."

As he tucked her hand in the crook of his arm, Tony strode toward the house. Narrowing his gaze against the shadows on the porch, he spotted a flash of white rhythmically rocking from side to side in the darkened doorway. He paused.

His mother's fingers bit into his arm. "Wh— what's that?"

"I have no idea. Maybe some animal's wandered inside. That door's wide open."

As they stared, the flash of white took shape. Inch by inch, a woman backed out of the doorway and onto the porch. Moments later, he realized the swaying motion came from the vigorous scrubbing she was giving the floor just inside the house.

"Hello, there!" he called. "I didn't realize Jubal had left a housekeeper in charge."

All movement stopped. Slowly, warily, a pair of sapphire blue eyes peered at Tony and his mother from a face so filthy he couldn't even take a stab at guessing the woman's age.

"He didn't," she said in a no-nonsense Yankee voice.

"Oh. I see." But he didn't. Not really. "Then introductions are in order. I'm Antonio Mallery Alvarez, the new owner of the Rocking C Ranch. This is my mother, *Doña* Althea Alvarez."

Abruptly, the woman stood and faced them. A golden ringlet fell on her grimy forehead, and she blew it out of her way. "Says who?"

Tony frowned. Although she seemed young, Jubal's housekeeper didn't look stupid. "What do you mean, says who? Says me. I'm Tony Alvarez, and this is my mother."

"Not that. Who says you're the new owner of the Rocking C?"

He reached into his pocket. "This deed says so."

Blue eyes narrowed. Every feature blazed suspicion. "Let me see that deed."

Now it was Tony's turn to frown. "Why?"

"Because *I'm* the new owner of the Rocking C."

After extricating his arm from his mother's death grip, he advanced. "Says who?"

"You hold it right there, mister."

"Oh?"

"No 'oh.' I meant what I said. You'd better not come any closer. Not before I read that fraudulent deed."

Tony snorted. "There's nothing fraudulent about it. I had it authenticated in San Antone yesterday."

She laughed. "You couldn't have. I inherited the Rocking C three months ago when my uncle passed away."

"Sorry, *querida*," Tony countered in his best lady-killer voice, "I obtained this deed from old Jubal Carstairs two days before he left Santa Fe — very much alive and kicking. I'd say you're at the wrong Rocking C Ranch."

"And I would say you have the wrong Jubal. Jubal Carstairs died in San Antonio three months ago."

"Three months ago — give or take a coupla days — old Jubal bellied up to the poker table where I was playing. After losing every cent he had, he anted up the deed. My

245

straight flush beat his four of a kind."

Tony winced at his mother's gasp. "You never mentioned the *gambling,* Antonio," she rebuked softly.

He shot her a beseeching look. "Not now, Mother! Can't you see I have to deal with this woman?" Donning his finest smile, Tony took another step toward the porch.

The filthy female raised a hand, palm out. "Don't come closer!"

"I won't hurt you," he wheedled. "I only want to show you Jubal's signature."

"Uh-uh." She shook her head so hard a long hank of dusty golden hair tumbled down over one shoulder. "Not another step."

"But —"

"No buts!" she spat, then whirled toward the house.

Taking advantage of her retreat, Tony started forward, then stopped short. There was a lot to be said for exercising caution when faced by a woman with a shotgun aimed at your heart.

"I mean it, Mr. Alvarez," the woman warned. "You stay where you are. This is *my* ranch. My uncle left it to *me* in his duly executed will. Besides, I have possession of *my* property. It is up to you to prove the legitimacy of your claim."

"Oh, for heaven's sake — sorry, Mother — I have the stronger claim. Can't you see? Jubal signed over the deed while he was alive. The ranch is mine!"

She nibbled at her bottom lip. Then, laying her cheek on the gun's stock and cocking the hammer, she smiled in triumph. "I guess there's truth to that saying about possession being nine-tenths of the law. I'm here, and you're *there*." She jabbed her chin in his direction. "Besides," he heard her mutter, "the Rocking C's the answer to all my prayers."

Tony chuckled wryly. "Lady, if a will made no good by a poker game is what you call the answer to your prayers, I'd hate to see what you call trouble."

Chapter Two

"I suggest you avoid mirrors, then," Emma answered, praying her shaking hands wouldn't betray her fear. "And stay off my property. Unless you want to get familiar with my bullets."

Mr. Alvarez — all six feet plus, black hair, cat-yellow eyes, and dimpled chin — took another step toward her. "But, *querida* —"

"Look, I don't know what you keep calling me, but unless it means 'Lady Ranch Owner,' I suggest you stop."

At his frown, Emma breathed easier. He clearly used the foreign word to get his way with women, but she wasn't so foolish as to fall for sweet words in a velvet-rough voice. The time when a man's charm might have swayed her was long past. She wouldn't be coaxed now when her ranch hung in the balance.

The lovely woman at his side again laid slender fingers on his forearm. "Antonio," she said in a drawling voice, "perhaps we ought to return to San Antone and look into this matter there."

Emma envied the feminine power in that voice. Mr. Alvarez sucked in a breath and backed two steps away from the house. The woman — as elegant and exquisite as any in Philadelphia — didn't look old enough to be the mother of this handsome, strapping man. Emma wondered what underhanded scheme the pair might have in mind. In any case, she would have to think twice as hard as usual to outwit their devious intentions.

Mr. Alvarez again eluded the woman's hold and stepped closer to Emma, a dangerous gleam in his cat eyes. "Look, lady —"

"Miss Carstairs," she cut in, using her name to press her advantage.

He waved dismissively. "Fine. Miss Carstairs, we've come a long way. I can't impose the hardship of the ride back to San Antonio on my mother, and I do have the deed to the ranch. I suggest you put down the gun and help us solve this matter reasonably."

The male arrogance in his stance, his firm tone, and his unwavering gaze immediately raised Emma's dander. "Or else?"

The yellow eyes narrowed. The lean jaw clenched. The finely drawn lips tightened. Emma gulped when he took another swaggering step closer.

"Allow me to mention, Miss Carstairs, that I've made my living hunting men for the bounty on their heads." His voice deepened a notch. "A slip of a woman like you isn't going to keep me from claiming the Rocking C's bounty."

"Antonio!" cried the woman at his side, color leaching from her cheeks. "How could you *ever* say such a thing? I raised you better than that! Now beg the lady's pardon and ask for the Father's forgiveness. To think you would threaten her for protecting what she believes is hers . . . why, I *never* . . ."

To Emma's amazement, Mr. Alvarez turned a most fascinating shade of red. He scuffed a booted toe in the loose Texas grit, and sheepish sounds escaped his mouth. Emma smiled.

Until his defiant gaze met hers again.

"Beggin' pardon, ma'am," he said with no trace of remorse.

Beware, Emma thought. This man was used to getting his way. And he had no qualms how he went about it.

Suddenly she felt sympathy for his mother. She *was* his mother; a lady friend wouldn't care if he bullied Emma. Mrs. Alvarez said she had raised him better than to intimidate a woman. She even invoked the Father's name. And her son's outrageous behavior had horrified her to the point of paling. Understanding inspired

Emma's next words.

"Mrs. Alvarez, I would be honored if you stayed here tonight. We can discuss the ranch and decide what must be done to remedy your son's mistaken notion. Now, we haven't a lot of supplies —"

"Don't you fret a moment about that," said Mrs. Alvarez, a winsome smile on her lips. "We brought enough to feed an army for a year!"

Emma returned the smile. "Well, praise the Lord!"

"Amen!" chimed Mrs. Alvarez as she approached the porch. "We'll just be needing a place to rest. And sensible talk about this sorry misunderstanding."

"Of course," Emma concurred. "It's a pleasure to find someone with a reasonable grasp of the situation."

Stepping aside to allow Mrs. Alvarez inside, Emma felt much comforted and nowhere near as lonely as she had before. Then the gunman's foot hit the bottom porch step. "Hold it!" she cried.

The sound that accompanied his frown came close to a snarl. But he heeded her command. "Now what?"

Cradling Uncle Jubal's shotgun in her arms, Emma used her chin to point. "You can spend the night in the bunkhouse with

Rattlesnake. I invited only your weary mother inside."

"You want me to bunk with a snake?" His eyebrows rose to meet the shiny black hair that tumbled over his forehead. "I've done *you* no harm."

"I intend to keep it that way."

"By killing me?"

Rattlesnake, who'd watched the exchange from the far side of the house, stepped forward, harrumphing loudly. "I'm the snake, boy. Ain't never kilt no one, ain't about to start now. Come along with me like the missy said. 'Fraid I wouldn't trust you, neither."

Mr. Alvarez shot Rattlesnake one of his venomous glares. Emma shuddered, remembering the impact of that yellow gaze.

"Just who might this rattler be?" Mr. Alvarez asked in his deadly voice.

Rattlesnake stood taller. "I'm the new foreman of the Rocking C, and you look like nothing better'n trouble."

When Mr. Alvarez sent an appraising look Emma's way, she braced Uncle Jubal's gun on her shoulder. He then frowned at Rattlesnake. Finally, muttering to himself, he stalked to the wagon. He pulled down a black leather satchel from the stack of trunks and crates and boxes, dropped it at

Emma's feet. "Mother's overnight bag," he growled, then followed Rattlesnake.

For the first time since she set eyes on the man, Emma took an easy breath. Whispering a prayer of thanksgiving, she went inside to prepare a meal for her first guests at the Rocking C Ranch.

Supper went as well as could be expected. After saying grace — something Mr. Alvarez clearly resented as much as his mother relished — Althea took the reins of the conversation, chatting amiably with Rattlesnake. Which was just as well, Emma thought, for if the task had been left up to her and Mr. Alvarez, few words would have been exchanged during the entire meal.

Later, after having gained access to the house, Mr. Alvarez showed surprise when, once the dishes were cleared, Emma took up her shotgun and ushered him off the porch.

Having set the pattern, Emma repeated it the next morning at breakfast. Despite the words spoken, she and Mr. Alvarez resolved nothing about the ownership of the ranch. Finally, when Rattlesnake mentioned the missing stock, Mr. Alvarez latched onto that subject, dropping the other, to Emma's relief.

"What do you mean, the stock's missing?"

he asked, his eyes razor sharp. "Where'd it go?"

Rattlesnake rubbed his shiny pate. "Can't rightly say, Son. But I know Jubal had a coupla hundred head of cattle, and a passel of horses, too. Ain't nothing here now."

Feline eyes narrowed. "Any ideas?"

Rattlesnake eyed him just as shrewdly. "Some. Care to hear 'em?"

"And act on them, if they have merit."

"Oh, they do. But it ain't gonna be easy."

"Nothing worthwhile ever is."

Emma followed their conversation with a sinking feeling in her stomach. "Ahem!" When the two men turned her way, she leveled a glare at them. "Aren't you forgetting something? Like the owner of the ranch? Me?"

Mr. Alvarez scoffed.

Rattlesnake smiled sheepishly. "Sorry, Miss Carstairs. But this here's a matter for men. We'll take care of it for you. Don't you worry your pretty little head over this."

Althea said, "Oh, dear."

Mr. Alvarez snickered.

Emma saw red. "Could we get one thing straight? Unless you want to return to San Antonio, Rattlesnake, you will stop that 'pretty little head' nonsense. I own this spread —" the usual thrill chased up her spine — "and *everything* about it concerns me. You will not act without consulting me."

Mr. Alvarez stood, obviously ready to object. Despite the thumping of her heart, Emma grabbed her shotgun. From her place at the table, she took aim. "Seems to me, Mr. Alvarez, your manhunting ways have taught you to respect a gun more than a woman. I meant what I said. If you and Rattlesnake intend to do something about the missing stock, you will do well to discuss it with me first."

Rattlesnake's red cheeks swelled and shrank like a fireplace bellows. "Fine, Miss Carstairs. We'll do that — soon's we have something to discuss. Come on, Tony. Can't find a steer while jawing."

Emma noticed that the men's relationship had progressed to a first-name basis. And she momentarily noted how well the name *Tony* suited the man. Direct and masculine, it suggested a no-nonsense nature, one that kept him focused on his goal. Unfortunately, his current goal ran counter to hers.

Emma brought her wayward thoughts back to the matter at hand. "When will you let me know what you are up to?"

Rattlesnake refused to meet her gaze. "When *we* know what we're up against."

She stared. "Up against? That does *not* sound good."

Rattlesnake picked up his Stetson. Holding the brim, he turned it in a circle. "It don't *look* good, neither."

Emma's heart skipped a beat. "What does that mean?"

Cramming the hat onto his bald head, Rattlesnake strode to the door. "It means someone stole the Rocking C stock."

For the rest of the day, Rattlesnake's words stayed with Emma. As she unpacked her belongings and decided where to store what, all she could think about was that someone already had done her harm. And it hadn't even been Tony Alvarez.

The Rocking C had another enemy, one she didn't yet know. Tony might be unpleasant, but at least she knew him. She also knew his mother's presence would likely temper the damage he would wreak. This other threat, the one already carried out by an unknown foe, worried her more than the swaggering male with bold yellow eyes.

God is our refuge and strength, a very present help in trouble. Therefore will not we fear. . . . She had always found comfort in the words of the psalmist. Today, facing an unknown enemy, Emma found herself unable to yield her burden to the Lord — even though he had brought her to Texas for a purpose, in answer to her prayers.

A soft hand landed on her shoulder. "Faith," said Althea Alvarez. "You must have faith, Emma."

Mustering a smile, Emma asked, "How did you know what was on my mind?"

"I'm a mother, dear. Not yours, but a mother. I've had years of practice reading my children's cryptic expressions. You're wondering who stole from you and if you can trust my son — and me. You're even wondering if it was such a fine idea to come to Texas."

Impressed, Emma covered the other woman's hand with hers. "No, Mrs. Alvarez, the Lord led me here in answer to my prayers. But you are quite right on the rest."

Althea nodded. "Well, then, have faith. In God's infinite wisdom and in my son."

When Emma opened her lips to object, Althea shook her head. "Listen to me. He has many faults, as I'm the first to admit, but Antonio is a good man with a streak of honesty as wide as the blue sky. If someone's wronged you, why, he won't stop until he sees justice done. That sense of right and wrong is what leads Antonio to danger, and taking it to a misguided extreme is what led him away from the Lord."

Emma eyed Althea dubiously. "He is your son," she said, wondering how much of the sterling description was due to motherly love. "While I suppose you know him well, I see no evidence of him ever knowing God."

Althea gasped.

Emma winced, regretting her candid words. "I *am* sorry. I didn't mean to criticize you. I only describe the hard man I see."

Pain in her gray eyes, Althea nodded. "I understand, dear. Still, it never stops hurting. You see, Antonio wasn't always as you see him. His faith was once rock firm."

Curiosity nipped at Emma. "What happened?"

"His daddy died."

Emma frowned. "And . . . ?"

"And my son couldn't forgive his heavenly Father for letting our Lorenzo die. Anger changed Antonio. It hardened him."

Emma sniffed. "I would think hunting men did it."

Althea sighed deeply. "What do you think set him to chasing bounties in the first place?"

"His father's death?"

"Precisely."

Emma didn't understand. "I know people mourn in different ways, but this is the first I've heard of someone turning to killing after a death in the family."

Misery twisted Althea's features. "Antonio rejected God's will. He simply refused to accept it. Lorenzo was shot when he surprised rustlers stealing his prized Spanish stallion. He died a few days later. Since Antonio felt the Lord did such a poor job with Lorenzo, he took the decision of who would live and who would die into his own hands. He went after my husband's killers."

"How awful! Such sinful pride."

Again, Althea winced. "Think of his pain, child. It's all I've thought of — prayed for — over the years. My son is hurting, and he won't reach out for the Father's comfort and love. He only sees that God allowed him to suffer."

Emma nodded slowly. "He does need prayer. But I cannot see how that makes him someone I can trust."

"Don't worry so much that he'll take your ranch away, dear. He's already out there fighting for what's yours."

This time, Emma didn't keep the disdain from her voice. "Hardly. He is after what he believes is *his*, what someone took from *him*."

Resignation darkened Althea's eyes. "Either way, he won't stop until justice is served, until the Rocking C's stock is back where it belongs. And he won't waste a thought on his own safety. That's why I count on trust and faith. Trust in the terrifying skills Antonio developed over the years, and faith in my heavenly Father to protect my son."

"He would *kill* whoever took the Rocking C stock?"

"That's what I'm afraid of," murmured Althea, a frown pleating her smooth brow.

Emma's stomach turned. "Oh, dear. I can't have that. The ranch needs animals, but . . . cows and horses aren't worth even one human life."

Althea only nodded.

"Besides," Emma added, "it isn't Tony's — Antonio's — *Mr. Alvarez's* duty to resolve the situation. It is my ranch."

Althea studied Emma. "My dear," she finally said, "I understand you've come a long way, and I can see what the ranch means to you, but I must say, I do believe you're mistaken. Antonio's deed is legal. He holds the rightful title to the Rockin' C."

Emma pushed her chin out. "I have Uncle Jubal's duly executed will. It says I own the ranch."

"Not without the title, you don't. And if I understand correctly, Jubal Carstairs signed the deed over to Antonio voluntarily. You couldn't inherit what Jubal no longer owned."

"Then Tony will have to prove Uncle Jubal signed over the deed. He will have to prove the will worthless. He'll have to prove his claim."

Turning so that Althea didn't see her fear, Emma caught her bottom lip between her teeth. It couldn't be. It simply could not be true. The Rocking C was the answer to her prayers. She would never let Antonio Alvarez take it away. Even if she had to use Uncle Jubal's shotgun to protect her rights . . .

Uncle Jubal's shotgun.

Was she ready to shoot Tony to keep the ranch? To do what she had just criticized him for?

Hours later, Rattlesnake and Tony returned. Emma watched out the kitchen window as they washed up at the pump behind the house. Shortly after, heavy boots sounded on the back steps. The men came inside. Catching sight of Althea, Rattlesnake blushed and ripped off his hat. "Evening, ma'am."

To Emma's amazement, Althea's cheeks colored, too. "Good evenin', Mr. Rattlesnake," she murmured, smiling.

The man puffed out his chest, reminding Emma of a bantam rooster. "Don't need the 'mister.' Rattlesnake'll do."

"Then you may call me Althea."

Emma bit back a chuckle when Rattlesnake's Adam's apple bobbed. "Much obliged, ma'am — er, Miz Althea." At the table, he held out a chair. Althea covered his hand with hers on the backrest and smiled into his admiring eyes.

"How kind of you," she said. Sitting, they continued to chat.

A whistle came from near the door. Emma turned and saw Tony's bemused expression. He opened his mouth as if to comment, and she glared at him. "Don't you dare! Unless you are about to greet them nicely, just keep your mouth shut."

The cat eyes scoured her face. Emma felt his gaze as if it were flesh and blood. How a look could so rattle a sensible woman, she'd never know. Opting for the safe and sane, she said, "Supper is ready."

Tony joined the pair at the table. "Good evening, Mother," he said, still staring at Emma.

Though his hard, handsome face bore no smile, Emma knew he was mocking her. Laughing inside, at the very least.

Chin held high, Emma sat.

Althea clasped her hands, preparing to say grace.

Tony ground his teeth audibly.

Rattlesnake beamed at the devout woman.

Closing her eyes for the prayer, Emma silently added thanks for Althea's exquisite manners and conversational ease, since they relieved her of having to make small talk — especially with Tony.

Soon, the discussion turned toward ranch matters. From what the men said, both were sure the Rocking C herd had been led off intentionally, but they had found no clues to the identity of the perpetrator.

Emma's unease continued after seeing the men leave the house and while waiting for Althea to retire. Then, taking the lantern, she led the way to the bedroom wing.

"You know, Emma," murmured Althea after they said their good-nights, "there is one way to settle the claim where neither you nor Antonio would have to give up the ranch."

Emma frowned. "I don't understand."

"Think, dear. You're alone in the world and at the mercy of a rustler. Antonio is alone, too, and needs the gentling of a godly woman. Why, I believe this was God's plan when he brought you both here."

Horror swam through Emma's head. "You couldn't possibly mean . . . what I think you mean. . . ."

"Of course I do. I can't think of a better solution than marriage. You'd make a perfect daughter, you know."

Emma's throat worked, but no sound came out.

Althea hugged her, then added, "And the perfect wife for Antonio."

Chapter Three

Late the next afternoon, after Tony and Rattlesnake spent the better part of the day looking for clues — anything that might lead them to the Rocking C stock — they called it quits, no further ahead than when they'd started.

Obviously, Jubal Carstairs hadn't planned on dying three months ago. And according to Rattlesnake, the man hadn't abandoned the ranch. But his men must have fled after learning of their boss's death, some maybe taking with them more than their personal belongings. Tony could see where a man might think he was owed compensation.

Still, there had to be something to show what had happened to the cattle and horses. The lack of clues made Tony wary. Someone had gone to mighty great lengths to leave no trace of the Rocking C stock. Tony knew of only one reason a man might cover his tracks so thoroughly — a reason he wouldn't easily let pass.

As they approached the ranch house, he noticed a big black stallion tethered to a still-standing portion of the corral fence. Coming closer, he spotted a stranger on the porch with Emma. Tall as the horse, the beefy man had dingy-blond hair and a florid complexion. When he and Rattlesnake were only a few paces away, Tony also saw the visitor's mealy smile and bootlicking manner.

And Emma's simpering response.

Tony frowned. How could she stomach the cowpuncher's act? Funny, he hadn't thought her gullible. Misguided as to who owned the Rocking C, yes, but not stupid or easy to dupe.

"Ah, Miss Carstairs," said the blond *hombre*, "if I'da known you were coming, I'da made sure one of my boys met you in San Antone. It just ain't right for a pretty lady like you to travel all by your lonesome. I'm plumb sorry, ma'am."

A flush brightened Emma's face. "Oh, Mr. Pierce —"

"Now, I toldja to call me Luther. You'll hurt my feelings if you don't."

As Emma's flush deepened, her blue eyes appeared brighter. Tony grimaced at the evidence of female foolishness.

"All right, Luther," she said in a softer tone than he'd heard from her yet. "I hired a foreman for the Rocking C in San Antonio, and he drove the wagon here. I wasn't alone."

Sparse eyebrows rose. "A foreman, you say? You spent all that time with a stranger?"

Emma chuckled. "Your man would have been as much a stranger as Rattlesnake."

Pierce's lips tightened. "You hired that crazy ol' coot?"

A frown lined Emma's forehead. "Rattlesnake doesn't strike me as crazy, Mr. Pierce — er, Luther. I don't know what I would do without him."

Reacting to the strength in Emma's words, Pierce straightened his shoulders. Tony smiled. That was more like his Emma.

His Emma? Since when did he think of that ornery female as his? Heaven forbid! He liked his women agreeable and accommodating, not prickly and armed to the teeth.

"Well, ma'am," said Pierce, obviously trying to regain lost territory, "now that you know how close I am, I'm hoping you'll call on me for whatever your heart desires. I'm fairly aching to help you out."

Out of what? wondered Tony, leery of the man's oily words.

"How kind of you, Luther!" Emma exclaimed. "I can't think of anything, but if I do, I'll let you know."

"Can't tell you, Miss Emma — may I call you Emma? — what a *pleasure* it is to find a blossom in the desert. I'm smitten with your beauty, ma'am."

At Tony's side, Rattlesnake snickered. "Pheweeee! He's sure laying it on thick-like."

"I'll say," Tony muttered. "Question is, why?"

Rattlesnake jabbed an elbow into Tony's side. "Ain't many good-looking women out here, boy. Miss Emma's likely to get more men calling on her than a carcass gets buzzards."

Tony gave Rattlesnake a disgusted look. "Not an image the lady would appreciate," he said, "but I get the picture. I hope she's not so stupid as to buy what this one's selling."

Rattlesnake's humor evaporated. "Miss Emma ain't stupid, but Luther Pierce *is* trouble. Almost as bad as you."

Tony glared at the man at his side before turning his attention back to the fellow bending over Emma's hand. When full lips touched her fingers, Tony's stomach rebelled. With narrowed gaze, he approached. "Afternoon!" he called. "Didn't know we were expecting callers, Emma."

Her eyebrows rose. "Nor did I. Luther

was a lovely surprise."

"And would Luther have a last name?"

Their guest nodded. "Pierce. Luther Pierce."

Tony held out his hand. "Alvarez. Antonio Alvarez."

A superior smile bowed Pierce's thick lips. "Mexican?"

"My father was Spanish," Tony answered, "with business in Mexico. He settled near Santa Fe after meeting and marrying my mother in Texas."

"I see." Pierce turned back to Emma. "Well, Miss Emma, I must be going, but you best be ready. Luther Pierce's gonna come call on you regular. I'm giving you fair warning. When I see something I like, I make sure I get it." He ran an admiring gaze over Emma's face and figure. "Today, I found plenty to like."

To Tony's relief, Emma looked shocked. The man's arrogance rubbed him wrong. He'd come across it while tracking wanted men. "Where's your spread, Pierce?" he asked.

With an expression that spoke resentment, Pierce nodded toward the west. "A coupla miles yonder."

"A neighbor, then."

Impatience flared on Pierce's face. "*Miss*

269

Carstairs's neighbor. What're you to the Rockin' C, since the ranch is hers?"

Tony smiled without humor. "Funny you should ask. You see, there's some confusion as to who owns the Rocking C."

That caught Pierce's full attention. "Oh?"

"Um-hmmm." Tony took note of Pierce's alarm. "I have Jubal's deed. Won it in a poker game. Emma has his will. We're figuring out who owns the place."

Pierce's gaze turned speculative. "Interesting."

Playing a hunch, Tony asked, "You wouldn't know what happened to Jubal's stock?"

A muscle twitched at Pierce's jaw. "How could I?"

"Oh," Tony drawled, "being neighbors and all, I would think you might have kept an eye out for each other. Like to see when someone stole Jubal blind."

"What're you insinuating, Mex?"

Tony ground his teeth at the insult. "I'm not insinuating anything. Just asking if you've seen the Rocking C stock lately. Because I'm going to find it. When I do, I'll feel mighty sorry for the dirty —"

"Antonio!" cried Althea from the doorway behind Emma.

"Sorry, Mother," he said automatically.

"As I was saying, Pierce, when I find the stock, I'll deal with the fool who messed with what's mine."

"I ain't got time for this," Pierce said. "Good day, Miss Emma. I'll come back when this . . . *furriner* ain't around. If he bothers you, ma'am, you just let me know. Luther Pierce'll be proud to take care of the Rocking C — and you, of course." Stomping off the porch, Pierce mounted the massive black horse and dug his spurs into the animal's sides.

Watching in silence, Tony reckoned he was done tracking. The instinct that served him so well while hunting outlaws told him he'd soon find the Rocking C stock.

For supper, Tony was served his mother's tongue-lashing and Emma's cold shoulder. Sick to death of their attitude, he threw down his napkin and shoved his chair back as he stood. "I don't care how rude I was to that 'nice' Mr. Pierce. He's as crooked as they come, and if I'm not mistaken, he has the Rocking C stock. What he wants with Emma, I don't know, but I figure he's not above marrying her for the ranch."

Emma stood too. "You, Mr. Alvarez, could learn some of Mr. Pierce's nice manners. Your words are most offensive. As is

271

your presence on my property."

As she turned to retrieve her ever-present shotgun, Tony crossed his arms over his chest. Time he called her bluff. "So what are you going to do? Shoot me off the ranch?"

"If need be," she answered, propping the stock on her shoulder.

Tony opened his arms wide. "Be my guest."

His mother gasped.

Rattlesnake guffawed.

Emma's eyes widened.

Tony smiled. "Can we put it away now?"

She glared at him. "Fine. I can't shoot you. More's the pity. Remember, you are only here because I suffer your presence. For your mother's sake, you understand."

Tony chuckled. "Whatever you say, darlin'."

"Don't call me that!"

"Very well, *querida*."

"Or that, either."

"As you wish, Miss Carstairs." The flush on her cheeks made her prettier, and when riled, the sparkle in her eyes made them look like gems. Tony had always appreciated beauty, even when partnered with a prickly temper.

"My conscience is clear," he said, "since you know what I want. I'll bet Pierce has your stock, and he wants still more from you. What exactly, I don't know. Maybe your pretty face and fine figure, but I doubt it. I think he's after the ranch."

Her chin leapt up with pricked pride. "Your arrogance knows no bounds. You think nothing of offending a lady, even the one whose hospitality you abuse. How dare you insinuate that a man wouldn't want me for myself!"

"I didn't say that!"

"Just about."

"Well, you *are* a spinster."

"Antonio!" his mother cried.

"Now what?"

Red circles blazed on his mother's cheeks. "Mercy, Son, you owe Emma an apology. That was uncalled for. If you don't like Mr. Pierce's suit, then *you* should pay her more attention — of the pleasant sort, of course." She gave him a pointed look. "You know, if anyone *was* to marry Emma for the ranch, I would think you'd be the one most interested."

Tony's eyes bulged. He should consider hog-tying himself to a gun-toting she-wolf for the sake of the ranch? *His* ranch?

"Althea!" Emma objected. "That's an appalling notion."

Tony jumped on the opening. "*Appalling,*

Miss Carstairs? *Now* who's being offensive?"

"Children, children," his mother scolded in her Texas drawl, "there's no reason for name-callin'. Why, Antonio, I cannot believe the thought hasn't occurred to you. I am certain the Good Lord brought you and Emma together for a purpose. And I can't believe it was to fight. Perhaps you are to learn to live in peace, harmony, respect, and yes, even love someday."

Emma's jaw dropped. She snapped it shut again, her lips nearly disappearing. Tony didn't blame her. His mother's suggestion was ridiculous.

But she wasn't done. "God's will is infallible. He knows what our future holds and what will best serve us in that future. And I know, Son — to my eternal regret — how far you've wandered from what your father and I taught you when you were young. Perhaps, in his infinite wisdom, Jesus brought a godly woman into your life to help you get back on the right path."

His mother's words raked to life the coals of loss. Despite the years, Tony still felt the pain of his father's death.

Why? Why had his mother's God forsaken the prayers of a seventeen-year-old? Why had God let a good man like Lorenzo

Alvarez die while vermin like Luther Pierce still prospered off the misery of others?

Tony had never reconciled those two facts, even after years of chasing down crooks, outlaws, and killers to deliver justice — the justice God had failed to mete. But no matter how many he killed or brought to trial, his father remained dead. The pain and anger of unforgiveness lived on in his heart — as it raged right now.

"While on that right path — as you choose to call it, Mother — I lost my father. Others on it are also wronged with no one to protect or defend them. Where is God then? Where was he when you prayed for your husband? When I prayed for my father? Why won't he listen to those on that 'right path' of his?"

Unable to stop them, the accusations rolled off his tongue. "How could you accept Father's death? Did you just think, 'Oh, fine, God wants him dead'? Didn't you love him? I did, and I never forget God let him die."

Tears bathing her face, his mother whispered, "I loved him, Son. You know I did."

"Then how could you accept your God's supposedly infallible will?"

"Because God loved your father even more than I did. Just as he loves you and me."

"I don't buy that. Not then, not now. If God had loved Father, he would have spared his life."

"Oh, Son, I don't know why your father had to die. I'll never know in this life, and neither will you. But the Lord does, and I trust him. In spite of the pain, God has always been with me. Verse 5 in Isaiah 54 says, 'For thy Maker is thine husband,' and I assure you he has been that since your father died."

Tony made a scoffing sound.

"Listen to me, Antonio. Jesus has walked with me every day of my life. His presence sustained me through your father's death. He sheltered me, comforted me, loved me when I most needed his love. He even held my hand all the years you were gone."

Tony sucked in a breath, but she shook her head to avert his outburst. She went on. "My heavenly Father has never forsaken me, and I daresay, he hasn't forsaken you, despite your efforts to walk away from him."

"Bah!" Having heard enough, Tony stalked to the door. "God forsook me when he ignored my prayers. That was enough for me. I won't give him another chance to devastate me."

The slamming door punctuated Tony's words.

Tears welled in Emma's eyes. Although she feared what he might do to her future, she had just felt his pain.

When she faced Althea, she saw Rattlesnake wrap an arm around her friend's shaking shoulders. "Almighty Father," he said in a rough voice, "that there boy needs to meet up with you again soon. For his mama's sake, I pray the meetin' ain't too hard on him. If I can help, well then, use me to your glory. Amen."

Opening her eyes, Emma read gratitude in Althea's smile and heard her echo Rattlesnake's earthy but sincere petition with a soft amen.

She realized then that the Father awaited her own prayers for Tony, for the wretched state of his heart. Even if in the end, it meant giving up the ranch.

Had she mistaken God's leading? Was the ranch not the answer to her prayers?

That thought brought more tears to her eyes and an ache to her throat. What would become of her if the ranch was not to be hers?

Or, as Althea suggested, did the Father want Emma and Tony to . . . to marry? To learn to love, honor, cherish each other?

Surely not.

Emma couldn't see how she could love a man who had turned his back on God. A killer. A man who solved problems with a gun.

What did you do when he threatened your claim?

Her cheeks burned. With embarrassment. With guilt. With shame. She knew what she had to do, despite her pride's violent objections.

"If you'll excuse me," she murmured as she left the room, although she doubted Althea or Rattlesnake would hear.

From the porch, Emma saw light at the bunkhouse window. She headed that way. Approaching, she called out, "Tony?"

Silence greeted her.

"Tony? I know you're in there. Please come out. I-I need to speak with you. There's something I must say."

When she still heard no response, her temper began to simmer. Abruptly, the door opened, and Tony stood in the opening, the light from behind outlining his lean frame.

She swallowed. Hard. "Ah . . ."

Oh, dear. This was harder than she had thought. "I . . . owe you an apology."

His sudden stiffening revealed his surprise. "Oh?"

He wasn't about to make it easy for her. Emma squared her shoulders. "I . . . shouldn't have threatened you with Uncle

Jubal's shotgun. I was scared and didn't think past keeping you away from what I wanted so badly. I refused to consider your claim to the ranch, because . . . well, because I had persuaded myself it was mine. I thought I deserved it."

To her chagrin, he crossed his arms and donned his cocky grin. "Mm-hmmm."

She refused to let his insufferable attitude stop her. "It's difficult enough to do what is right in God's sight, so please, don't rile me."

That wiped the smirk right off his face.

"You see," she said, "I stopped seeking his will when I decided the ranch was it. I hardened myself against his leading and tried to take matters into my own hands."

Tony's expression turned thundercloud dark.

She rushed on to keep him from interrupting. "I had no right to turn a gun on you. Please forgive me. If God wants me to leave the Rocking C, well, then . . . I will go."

Swallowing against the thickness in her throat, Emma feared she might break down. *Dear God, no! Not right now. Later.* Later she could cry all she wanted. Right then she had to make herself clear. "If we are meant to share this land, well, you can count on me to do what is right."

"Why?"

"Why what?"

"Why are you saying all this?"

"Because your mother spoke the truth tonight. The Father's will is infallible, but mine fails at times. Even if I'm called to face hardship as a result, I much prefer his will to mine. If he brought me into your life to lead you back to him, then I won't be an obstacle in his plan."

Bemusement filled his face. "You mean that, don't you?"

"I wouldn't be out here otherwise."

Tony chuckled. "Oh, I believe that."

"So . . . do you?"

"Do I what?"

"You know, forgive me."

He didn't answer right away. Then a wry grin kicked up a corner of his mouth. "Guess I'd better. Who knows when you'll change your mind and go for that shotgun again. Since I laid down my gun for good, I'm at your mercy."

Anger roared through her. "You didn't listen to a word I said! I *won't* use the gun, no matter how well you earn a seatful of shot!"

He laughed, slapping his hands against his rear. Emma's gaze followed, then darted to his lips, and finally to his dancing eyes. Her cheeks burned, and she faltered for words.

He didn't. "I only made a joke. I understood what you said — not that I agree with your religious reasons — but I do accept your apology. If you feel you need it, you have my forgiveness."

"Thank you," she said, eyes averted.

"You're welcome."

Still uncomfortable, Emma stepped back. "I'll say good night."

"Good night."

Although he didn't smile, she again felt he was laughing at her. She ran back to the ranch house fuming at her foolishness.

How could that man scramble her brains every time he came near? Why couldn't she just brace herself against his charm? his good looks? his appeal?

Why had his pain affected her so?

Emma forced herself to think of something else. Anything. The missing stock. Althea's friendship. Anything to keep from thinking of Tony as a part of her future, as God's answer to her prayers.

Hours later, the stirring notes of a guitar slipped into Emma's sleep. At first, she thought the music was part of her convoluted dreams, but as she listened more carefully, she realized it was real indeed.

Who could be playing at this hour? The

moon, full and bright, cast a puddle of silver on the bare wooden floor of her room, and the peace of the Texas prairie extended beyond the soulful sound.

Rising, she approached the window. What she saw made her catch her breath. Sitting on a chair tipped against the bunkhouse wall, Tony embraced a guitar as his fingers wrought a lament from its strings. His rich baritone rose and fell with the notes.

She would never have thought a former gunman might hide such a talent behind his tough exterior. Despite herself, Emma felt his charm surround her once again.

With her elbows on the window frame and her chin in her hands, Emma listened, his music captivating her, reminding her of the questions that had buzzed through her mind since she first met Tony Alvarez.

He is my child too.

Emma straightened with a snap. Where had that thought come from? Was it perhaps the still, silent voice of God?

Perhaps.

She listened to the man outside, trying to make out the words of his song, but they were in Spanish, and she didn't understand.

Tony glanced at the moon. Sorrow clouded his face. For a second, something sparkled on his cheek. A tear?

Then his gaze found hers, and Emma couldn't turn away. His fingers faltered on the strings, but he continued to play.

Although she wasn't sure how or why, Emma suddenly knew her life would never be the same. Not now that she had been shown the other side of the man.

Chapter Four

After the stirring exchange in the night, Emma feared seeing Tony again, but when she rose, he was nowhere to be found. Neither was Rattlesnake.

Althea was up and dressed unusually early. "Weren't you able to sleep?" Emma asked, concerned by the dark smudges under her friend's eyes.

Althea shrugged. "I had a lot on my mind. Even more to pray about."

"And you haven't found peace."

Again, Althea lifted a shoulder. "The men came in early," she said. "They made the most awful ruckus with the coffeepot and said they were headed toward San Antonio. Of course, my son would never leave without a bracing cup."

"They left? Why?"

"Something about the stock." A frown on her smooth face, she shook her head. "I can't fathom why they'd go east to look for the missing herd, since Antonio and Rattlesnake suspect Mr. Pierce has it. The Leaning P is west of us. I don't know what they're up to. I *am* sure they didn't want to give me details."

"I suspect they didn't want you to give *me* those details."

Althea chuckled. "Perhaps. You and Antonio do seem to raise each other's hackles."

Not always, piped a mischievous part of Emma's mind. She remembered the sympathy and warm feelings Tony's music had evoked. "It's to be expected. We both want the ranch."

Althea's gaze turned shrewd. "I daresay there is more to it than the ranch, but neither of you can accept it yet."

"Don't you start that marrying nonsense again," Emma warned, her cheeks stinging. "Nothing could be more ludicrous than that."

"As you wish," said Althea, her tone conciliatory, the twinkle in her eyes undiminished.

No matter how hard Emma tried, she couldn't forget that middle-of-the-night serenade. Tony Alvarez was more than a cocky, heartless outlaw hunter. She now had abundant evidence of that.

If so, was Althea's notion that far-fetched?

Had the Lord brought her into Tony's life for a purpose? Was it only to lead the man back to the fold? Or did God have a reason for bringing Tony into *her* life as well?

Was Tony the *more* she once yearned for? Did he bring the meaning and fullness her life had lacked for so long? Did the Lord have love in mind for her future?

With no answers to her questions, Emma found them clinging to the forefront of her thoughts with unexpected tenacity. Even though it frightened her, the depth of emotion she had seen in Tony's eyes stirred her more than anything she'd ever known.

∞∞

After days with no word of Tony or Rattlesnake, Emma and Althea sat down to yet another quiet supper, their concern growing. But before they had finished praying, the sound of milling animals brought them running to the porch.

The two women stared, open mouthed, as they took in the astounding scene. Big, shaggy, noisy cattle stomped around outside the corral, bleating and snorting and lowing. Dogs barked over the rumble, and a number of riders circled the beeves, whooping and cheering and laughing despite the dust.

Bewildered, Emma glanced from stranger to stranger, from cow to cow. What was going on here? Then she heard a familiar voice. Tony's voice.

286

Moments later, he rode into sight, his cocky grin catching her eye. "Hello there, *querida!*" he called out. "Miss me?"

She had and was irrationally elated — not to mention relieved he was in one piece — to see him again. But nothing would make her admit it. "How could a woman miss a pesky fly?"

"Oh, she could miss its tickling — her fancy, that is."

Emma's cheeks grew hot. "You're certainly in a fine mood, Mr. Alvarez. What has brought it on?"

"We're celebrating! We rode hard and are home safe and sound." He waved toward the herd. "Besides, we now have us a *real* ranch."

"We? *I've* had a ranch all along. And where did the cattle come from? Is this my missing stock?"

Tony clenched his jaw, smile fading, eyes growing grim. "No, it's not the Rocking C's missing stock. But a man can't have much of a ranch without a herd, so I went to San Antone, hired six hands, and nearly bankrupted myself buying livestock for the Rocking C. *My* livestock." He fell silent again, and a muscle in his cheek tightened. "Since it doesn't look like I can chase you off, and since I aim to keep Rattlesnake as my ramrod, I guess we're stuck sharing the ranch."

Emma tapped a toe. "Fine. But what about the missing stock? Will you continue looking for it now that you have your own? Or are you giving up on finding what's rightfully mine simply because it's not *yours?*"

Tony's distinctive yellow eyes narrowed. "It *is* mine. I won *everything* on the Rocking C. That includes Jubal's herd. And I'm sure Pierce has it. I just need proof. I can't ride over and check the brands. He's not dumb enough to let me within miles of those beeves. But you can bank on my finding that stock. I don't give up easily. Even if it means having to share the ranch with you."

Although Emma should have felt relief, disquiet filled her. She would indeed have to share the ranch with Tony. With the man who disturbed her sleep, who made her knees weak when he smiled, who enraged her with the least provocation.

The man Althea thought the Lord meant for Emma.

That prospect brought her no peace at all. "Well, Mr. Alvarez, as long as you don't even consider sharing the ranch *house,* I suppose I can use the additional help around the spread."

Tony brought his dun mare closer. "You mean you want me to keep on sleeping in that stinkin' bunkhouse?"

"With your ranch hands, of course. It would be most unseemly for you to stay in the house. After all, we are both unmarried."

He rolled his eyes. "But Mother's there, too. How much more propriety could you ask for?"

"I don't trust you, sir. And since, as we said when you first appeared, possession is nine-tenths of the law, I will lay down the law since I have possession of the house."

Althea chuckled behind her. "Mercy! He is hardly back five minutes, and you are both bristlin' already. Mark my words. . . ."

Spotting Althea, Tony sobered immediately. "Hello, Mother."

"Son," she answered, "I am so glad to see you again. You couldn't know how much I missed you." Descending the porch steps, she went to his side.

Tony studied the dusty ground, his hands holding the reins, clearly avoiding her gaze. "I'm sorry, Mother. I should never have said what I did that night. I thought long and hard about my accusations, and I realized I had no right. I know you, and I know how much you loved —"

"Hush, now," Althea said, laying her hand on his thigh. "I knew you were hurting, Son.

I forgave you then, as I did when you left all those years ago. I love you, and I always will. No matter how difficult you make it for me."

When Tony raised his head, Emma spied a mistiness in his eyes. "What if I promise to make it easier from now on?"

"You'd make me a very happy woman, Antonio."

He smiled ruefully. "I could stand to see you happy."

Hoofbeats accompanied an approaching cloud of dust. "Happy?" asked Rattlesnake as he reined in his horse. "I should say she is! Now she's the mama of a real red-blooded rancher."

Althea smiled in delight. "And what does that make you, Rattlesnake?"

"A cowboy ready to serve the Good Lord as a full-fledged ramrod, ma'am." As an aside, he said, "Beggin' pardon, Miss Emma, but you had no herd before. Tony here got me some cattle to work."

Rattlesnake seemed to have eyes only for Althea, and she for him. Emma suspected God had brought this unlikely pair together for more than friendship and support. Despite their visible differences, their obvious love for their heavenly Father made that possibility far more plausible than an understanding between Tony and herself.

Emma experienced a pang of sadness. It seemed unlikely she and Tony would ever stop fighting long enough to learn to like each other, much less embark upon a courtship or romance. And she couldn't help but wonder what that might have been like.

Would Tony's eyes have lit up at the sight of her? Would he have reached out to hold her when she cried? Would he have tried to spare her trouble? pain? Would he perhaps have looked at her as if the sun rose and set upon her?

As if from a distance, she heard him say, "Sure could use a hot supper. I'm half starved from chasing the cattle home all day."

Emma blinked, ending her foolish daydream. "Supper is ready, Mr. Alvarez, as it has been every night you've been gone. Since we didn't know when you would return, your mother didn't want you to go hungry just because we weren't prepared."

"Thank you, Mother," he said automatically, his gaze on Emma. "What about you? Surely you didn't plan to starve me to death? By now you must know you can't get rid of me — not so long as you stay at the Rocking C."

"Mr. Alvarez —"

"You've called me Tony before."

"A slip of the tongue."

"One you should allow more often."

"A lady doesn't indulge in frequent lapses into familiarity."

When he rolled his eyes again, Emma nudged her chin up. "As I said the night before you left, Mr. Alvarez, I will do everything possible to make this odd arrangement succeed. I plan to work with you — as long as what you expect is reasonable and decent."

Tony chuckled. "Supper sounds decent enough. To start."

She ignored his remark. "Please wash up, since it looks as if you brought back the road you traveled."

"Yes, ma'am," he countered, tapping two fingers to the brim of his hat. Turning his mount, he headed toward the barn.

"Wait!" she called. "What about the animals? They can't just wander around the house."

Tipping up his Stetson, Tony winked. "Don't you worry your pretty little head. The ranch hands will see to the cattle."

Emma's temper reared itself predictably, but she refused to let his taunt goad her into losing control. "Fine, Mr. Alvarez. Just don't track half of Texas into the house."

"Yes, ma'am."

Fuming, Emma stormed into the kitchen. She stirred the beans. Checked the bread. She smacked plates, utensils, glasses, napkins at the appropriate places. "Pretty little head," she muttered. "I'll show him a pretty little head. . . ."

In her pique, she grew careless and reached barehanded for the cast-iron skillet of browned potatoes. Pain bit her fingers, and she cried out.

Tony ran in, concern on his face. "Are you all right?"

Trying both to pump water and cradle her seared hand, Emma fought back tears. "I'm sure I will be. I just burned myself."

He pried her unscathed fingers from the throbbing ones. When she trembled, he braced her against himself. "Let me see."

She let him examine the burn, surprised that his touch soothed her rattled nerves. "It's nothing," she murmured. "I should have used a towel."

He didn't say a word, just pumped more water. As its coolness sluiced over her singed skin, Emma began to feel relief. At the same time, she grew increasingly aware of Tony's nearness and his tender ministrations.

As he continued to support her, Emma felt a strange current run through her, a foreign excitement, the thrill of being near this handsome, intriguing man.

"I'm sorry, Emma," he murmured. "I'll wager you were still irked with me and didn't watch what you were doing. It's a mighty lame thing to say, but I do enjoy teasing you. Your cheeks turn rosy and your eyes shine like stars. You look even prettier than usual when you get mad."

Emma's jaw dropped. "You think I'm pretty?"

A slow smile curved his mouth. "Yep, I do that."

"Oh. I-I didn't know."

His grin turned mischievous. "Hmmm ... know what? Your cheeks are just as pink now as when you get angry, and your eyes are all wide open and sparkly. Maybe I've gone about this all wrong — as Mother would say. Maybe compliments become you even more than teasing does."

Emma tore her gaze away. She didn't want him to see how his words affected her. Could she handle more of his compliments? This one had virtually turned her knees to mush.

He let go of the pump and cupped her cheek in his hand. With gentle pressure, he made her face him again. "No response?" he asked. "How unlike you."

She couldn't help smiling. "I thought you said you would stop teasing."

Counterfeit surprise overtook his features. He stepped back, jabbing his chest with his thumb. "Who, me? You must be mistaken, Miss Carstairs. I only said I might try compliments as well. I could never give up the pleasure of teasing a rise out of you."

Emma chuckled and tried to reclaim her hand, but Tony seemed to have no intention of letting her succeed. "Where are you going?"

"I must finish fixing supper."

"I don't see a crowd waiting."

"Your mother and Rattlesnake will be here any minute."

"Hmmm . . . I doubt it. I've a feeling Rattlesnake's keeping Mother to himself a while longer. He talked an awful lot about her while we were gone."

"Yes, well. It would be wrong for them to find us alone like this. Most inappropriate. They might get the wrong idea."

"And what wrong idea would that be?" he asked, his rogue's grin in place.

Emma's cheeks warmed up again. *Oh, dear.* She had talked herself into quite a corner. If she told him what she feared Althea would think, he would know she had given his mother's suggestion undue consideration.

But their intimacy shouldn't continue. And he showed no sign of releasing her.

What to do?

Footsteps sounded on the porch. Although she tried to move away, Tony refused to relinquish her hand. To Emma's dismay, Althea and Rattlesnake walked in to find her hand in his.

"Mercy, Son!" exclaimed Althea in a delighted voice. "I'm so proud of you. You've decided to see reason. Now isn't it better to court Emma than bicker with her?"

Tony chuckled and gave her wrist a gentle squeeze before letting go. "Shall we say I have seen the error in some of my ways?"

Rattlesnake laughed. "I told you, Miz Althea, the boy ain't dumb. Time alone together works wonders."

Emma glowered all around. "It seems I'm the victim of a conspiracy. I will *not* give up my claim to the ranch no matter how many honeyed words Ton — *Mr. Alvarez* pours on me or how much matchmaking you two do."

Althea smiled knowingly. "Hmmm . . . fightin' over the ranch again. Somehow, I don't think it's your chief worry anymore. Why, I wonder if you're not just using it now to guard your heart."

Emma blinked, shocked by Althea's comment.

Tony swaggered to the table, smug grin in place.

Rattlesnake guffawed, then drew out Althea's chair.

Althea smiled benevolently, encouraging everyone to sit.

The next morning when Emma went to call Tony and Rattlesnake for breakfast, she found only a handful of horses in the corral and none of the cattle. "Oh, no!" she wailed, then ran toward the barn, calling Tony.

When she got no response, she yelled again. "Tony!"

Moments later, the barn door flew open and he ran out. "Emma! What happened?"

She twisted her hands. "Oh, Tony. Rustlers took off with the new stock." She pointed to the corral. "They're gone."

To her astonishment, he laughed — as did Rattlesnake, who'd emerged from the barn behind Tony, and the two cowhands who followed. Emma sobered immediately.

"All right, gentlemen," she said, tapping her toe. "You've had your fun. Now please tell me what is so amusing."

"Why, *querida*," said Tony between peals of mirth, "we don't want you to stop making us laugh. It's a mighty fine way to start the day."

"At least tell me what's so funny."

Tony approached. "Where did you expect me to put that many beeves? Our little barn couldn't house more than about a dozen of them."

"You mean, I worried about those stupid cows for nothing?"

"They're stupid, all right," he said, grinning. "All of 'em. They're also just fine. The other four hands took them out to graze. They belong on the prairie, not at the ranch. There's nothing here for them to eat."

"Oh. I didn't know."

"Of course you didn't."

"Don't you dare patronize me, Mr. Alvarez —"

"Tony."

"*Mr. Alvarez.* I merely came out to tell you breakfast is ready. I didn't think about this before," she said, hoping to change the embarrassing subject, "but am I to cook for the hands — I'm new to ranching, remember? How many should I plan to serve today?"

Tony slipped an arm around her waist, but Emma scooted away like a scalded cat. "Mr. Alvarez! Mind yourself."

Cocking an eyebrow, he let her know her skittishness amused him as much as her lack of ranching knowledge. "I'd be much obliged if you could serve two more, *Miss Carstairs.*"

Although she should have been pleased by his formal address, Emma was piqued. She hadn't realized how much she enjoyed hearing her name in his rich baritone.

Hurrying back to the safety of her kitchen, she called out, "We can feed two more. It will only take a moment."

As she ran inside, she heard his chuckle.

A shiver tripped down her spine. Why did that rogue's voice, his laughter, have to thrill her so?

A few days later Emma found herself entertaining company again. Shortly after placing that evening's beans in the oven, she decided to do some mending. As she stitched the torn hem of a work dress, Luther Pierce arrived.

When she heard his booming voice outside, she stuck her needle into the fabric, patted her hair into place, doffed her apron, and smoothed her skirt over her hips. He had, after all, said he would call on her.

Not wishing to appear unduly eager, she counted off seconds after he rapped on the door before answering. Then, feigning surprise at finding him at her doorstep, she ushered him inside. "Mrs. Alvarez," she called, "we have company."

"How come you did that?" Luther chided. "I didn't come callin' on Missus Alvarez. I came for your sweet smile."

"I always consider propriety, sir."

Pierce gestured dismissively. "We have a different code out here, Miss Emma. We don't put much stock in that twaddle."

"Ah," she said, "but I'm not a Texan."

"Yet," he countered.

While Emma supposed Luther's obvious intentions should flatter her, something about him didn't sit right with her. Which bothered her. Although his boldness was at times embarrassing, a polite, settled rancher seemed a far better choice for suitor than Tony Alvarez, yet his smile did nothing to her insides, as Tony's so often did. Emma decided to try harder to like the man, since he was such a better prospect than the flirtatious former gunman.

When Althea joined them, Emma led Pierce to the sofa, and they spent an agreeable hour chatting about life on the west central Texas plain. Emma had much to learn.

Finally, when she hinted at work awaiting her, Luther stood, slapped his Stetson against his palm, and cleared his throat. "Miss Emma. I find I must be asking a favor of you. I'd be in your debt if you could see your way clear to letting me water some of my herd at your pond."

"Your animals need my water?"

"Well, ma'am, we've had ourselves a coupla dry years running, and the Leaning P ain't blessed with as much water as your spread. Some of my animals are faring poorly, and I might lose 'em if they don't get enough to drink."

"Oh." Emma wondered if the Rocking C herd would have enough with the one pond on the ranch. She would have to ask that night at supper.

"I suppose . . ." Emma glanced at Althea, who frowned and mouthed her son's name. So Tony wouldn't like Luther's animals drinking from *her* pond? "I don't object to you watering animals at the Rocking C pond. I wouldn't want them to suffer. . . ."

"Ah, Miss Emma. I'm much obliged. You're just as kind as you are beautiful."

Emma waved aside his praise. "I'm glad I can help. Now, Mr. Pierce, if you will excuse me, I have supper to see to."

"Then I'll be on my way." Smiling broadly, he winked. "But I'll be back. You have no idea how much a look from your pretty eyes means to me."

Emma walked the man to the door and held out her hand. As before, he bent at the waist and kissed it soundly. Again, Emma experienced a wriggle of distaste when she should have felt charmed. "Good day, Mr. Pierce."

"Luther, remember? And I'll be countin' the days until I see you again." Setting his Stetson at a jaunty angle on straw brown hair, Pierce opened the door and left.

Emma frowned, trying to figure out why he bothered her when she felt he really shouldn't.

"My dear," said Althea, shaking her head, "I'm afraid you made a mistake about the water. Antonio must know right away that you gave Luther Pierce permission to use the pond for his herd. My son isn't going to like this. Mark my words, you'll have trouble with him over the water hole. And . . . something else. I can't quite put my finger on it, but something about that man, that Luther Pierce, strikes me wrong."

Reluctantly, Emma said, "I agree. Although he does have a way with words."

"Perhaps that's it," Althea offered. "He's *too* much the soft-soaper for comfort."

And for me, Emma thought, unwilling to admit it out loud. Althea would surely see it as reason to celebrate.

Tony spent the day trying to get close to

the Leaning P herd, but it was clear Luther's men had instructions to keep their animals away from Rocking C land. And although he considered riding right up and demanding a look at the brands, each time he approached, Pierce's men brandished their rifles.

As he rode by the pond on the western end of the Rocking C, his frustration ebbed, and he began to anticipate the moment he would see Emma again. Yes, the lady was pretty enough, but there was more to her than looks, much more that appealed to him.

Surprisingly.

For one thing, she got along remarkably well with his mother. The two clearly had based their friendship on their many similarities.

Neither made a secret of her faith in Christ. Emma's plea for forgiveness had given him much to think about. As did her demands for propriety, despite the color on her cheeks that said she liked his attention. He smiled, remembering how flustered she grew when he said he found her pretty.

And he did. Her blonde curls bounced with the same energy she used to fight him, and her blue eyes filled with sympathy as easily as anger. He'd seen both emotions reflected there. For him.

She had kept her distance that night when he poured out his pain with the help of his guitar. But the moon had gilded her with its silver light, and the compassion in her gaze had been impossible to miss.

That night she'd known how deeply he hurt. And if his suspicions were right, her love of God had led her to pray for him. More than once.

That knowledge warmed a formerly cold spot in his heart.

True, his mother always prayed for him, but he knew her prayers sprang from maternal love. Emma's prayers were different. She had no reason to pray for him unless she felt something. Then again, maybe she prayed for him just as she would for any rotten sinner.

Tony frowned. He didn't much like *that* possibility. He hoped she had come to care a little for him. If not care, at least not hate him. Then he chuckled. Emma Carstairs didn't hate him. Her concern when she thought his new herd was missing had revealed plenty. She'd been distressed at the thought of him suffering a loss. If she'd hated him, she would likely have celebrated. "What's so funny, Son?" asked Rattlesnake, riding at his side.

"Emma's worrying about my herd."

"Now don't you make fun of her. Be proud she cares enough to worry."

Tony shot him a glare. "Been reading my thoughts?"

A smile split Rattlesnake's leathery face. "Aha! So you *were* tickled."

"A man can stand a woman's quibbling only so long."

Rattlesnake's eyebrow arched. "And hers has nothing to do with your mischief?"

Tony chuckled. "Nothing at all."

"Liar," the older man countered without rancor.

Both laughed, then fell silent when they heard horses coming. They saw Pierce and one of his men at the same time, but the rancher didn't spot them as quickly, since he was turned to the man riding at his side. They caught the tail end of his conversation.

"Yessir. Easy like all spinsters. Soon's a man feeds her pretty words, she gives him what he wants. Lucky for her, all I want is her water."

His companion laughed salaciously. "For now, Boss."

"Yeah, Smitty. Lady's toothsome enough. Has a fine spread. A body could do worse —"

"He certainly could," said Tony, having

heard more than enough. "As you will, if you continue to bother Miss Carstairs."

"Well, if it ain't the Mex."

Tony ignored the slight. "You mentioned the Rocking C's water. What about it?"

"None of *your* business." Pierce gave his horse a brutal stab with his spurs and rode off, Smitty hot at his heels.

Rattlesnake harrumphed. "He bears watching, boy."

"No need to tell me."

"He's a passel of trouble."

"And aiming for Emma," Tony added, vowing silently to keep trouble away from her. Even if it was the last thing he did.

Chapter Five

"Are you mad, woman?" Tony roared as Emma joined him and Althea on the verandah later that afternoon. "How could you tell Pierce to bring his mangy beasts to my pond?"

Althea gave her a sympathetic smile and went inside.

"Well?" he asked again, looming closer.

Emma tipped her chin up. "I saw no reason to refuse those poor animals water. Besides, Mr. Pierce asked for permission — politely, I might add. You could learn from him —"

"I know all I need to know about that snake —"

"He's not a snake!" Emma refused to give an inch, even though she had her own doubts about Luther Pierce. Tony's attitude left a lot to be desired. "He's a nice man who treats me like a lady."

Yellow cat eyes narrowed, and a muscle twitched in Tony's lean cheek. "I suppose you don't think I do."

Emma arched an eyebrow but kept silent.

Tony sighed, then ran a hand through his hair. "Look, Emma, I'm sorry I yelled." At her smile, he took a step closer, his frown deepening. "That doesn't mean what you did was right. Or that I shouldn't be steamin' mad. Have you noticed how dry this land is?"

At her nod, he went on. "We barely have enough water for our herd, never mind Pierce's. And water is the one thing that keeps a rancher from disaster. It's worth more than gold out here. Men *kill* for water in this part of Texas."

It was Emma's turn to frown. "But it's only *water*. Not worth killing for."

"It is when you don't have enough — not that I'm saying anyone *should* kill for water, just that they do. Pierce wants ours. Without paying for it, either." Tony went to the porch railing, leaned a hip against the top board, and crossed his arms over his chest. His chin jutted out. "He can't have it. We need every drop. You can write him a letter telling him he can just forget it."

"And if I don't agree with you about his intentions?"

"You don't have to agree. You just have to tell him to keep his beeves away from our pond. Or ours won't have enough to drink. They'll die, Emma. Every last one I bought will die if we can't keep them watered."

"What about Luther's cattle?"

"That's his problem."

"But you said he had the Rocking C herd."

Tony shot her a sharp look. "I intend to get our cattle back where we can take care of it. And I doubt Pierce is dumb enough to bring *our* beeves to *our* pond. He knows I'd be on him in no time."

"I see." She'd made a mistake. And she had to rectify it. "I'll write the letter."

"One of the hands can ride it over after supper." He ran down the porch steps and headed for the bunkhouse.

"Tony," she called.

He stopped and turned. "Yes?"

"I-I'm sorry. I didn't know."

He nodded. "Next time, ask me before making a decision about the ranch. I know what I'm doing, and you *can* trust me." Then he gave her his roguish grin. "Even if you don't want to."

As usual, his smile affected her, and Emma grew flustered. He was no longer trying to run her off the ranch, and he certainly seemed determined to do his best for the Rocking C, but could she trust a man who turned her knees to mush? a scoundrel with an easy way with words? a charmer who had strayed far from the Lord?

That night, after she finished in the kitchen, Emma sat on the porch steps. The sky overhead spread forever black, a million stars winking against its velvet nap. The scent of dry earth had become familiar by now. Occasionally she heard a horse nicker, and behind her, Tony's and Althea's voices blended into a pleasant murmur.

Emma felt at peace. Despite her blunders, she felt certain this was where God meant her to be. She only wished she felt less uncertain about Tony.

Althea, she loved. Despite the difference in their ages, they had become fast friends, and Emma often thanked the Father for the precious gift of that friendship.

A salt-of-the-earth sort, Rattlesnake had struck her as responsible, reliable, and resourceful from the moment they met. Emma's instincts hadn't failed her when she hired him. Discovering his faith in Christ had been a bonus.

Luther Pierce made her too uneasy to consider his suit. No matter how much he tried to flatter her, she couldn't forget he was doing just that — trying. Too hard, in her opinion. And Tony might be right about the man's character, even though she wasn't quite ready to believe he'd stolen the Rocking C cattle.

Tony, on the other hand, refused to stay in a tidy slot on her list of acquaintances. He attracted her more than any man she had ever met — and for more than his good looks. There was something infinitely charming about a tough man who tempered his rough edges to avoid offending his mother. Then too, the lingering grief over the loss of his father spoke of powerful emotions, deep and true.

Of course, at times she wished she had never met him. He riled her faster than any other human ever had. But those times grew fewer as she came to know him better. She had learned his pestering was only a flirtatious game to him.

That very fact concerned her.

Was Emma falling for a rogue's appeal? Was Althea's matchmaking having an influence on her?

Emma couldn't discount the possibility that the Lord might mean for them to make a match of it. If so, she didn't want superficial feelings to cloud her thoughts. No sane woman should decide her future based on a fleeting attraction.

She had still more to consider. Like Tony's lapsed faith.

When the door opened behind her, Emma jumped, startled.

"May I join you?" asked the man in her thoughts.

Glad for the darkness that hid her response to his voice, Emma nodded. "Here," she said, scooting sideways. "There's room for two."

With powerful grace, Tony dropped down at her side and studied the sky. "Nothing like the peace of a Texas night. . . ."

"Hmmm . . . I don't know. I find God's peace greater still."

"Must everything come down to God for you?"

"I gave my heart to Christ and made him Lord of my life a long time ago. He comes before anyone and anything else."

Tony shot her a quizzical look. "Even when he fails you?"

"He never has, though I fail him frequently."

"Lucky you," he muttered, bitterness in his tone.

With a prayer for guidance, Emma placed her hand on his arm. "Tell me about your father."

He grew tense under her touch. "What's there to tell? Rustlers shot him when he caught them stealing his horses. He lost too much blood. The doctor said nothing short of a miracle would save him. I prayed for that miracle, but God didn't listen to me. Or to Mother."

Tony's pain was so deep, so raw, that Emma felt wave upon wave roll off him and batter her senses. Again, she prayed for the right words, those that might ease Tony's misery, that might lead him back to God.

"I don't think God hardened himself against your prayers," she said. "Although I can't know why he didn't spare your father's life, I do know the God I serve. He would never abandon you or act capriciously."

Tony scoffed. "He took a good man's life, while every day he lets thieves, murderers, and worse get away. That seems capricious to me."

"God took your father's life, Tony? A moment ago you said he died from gunshot wounds. These things don't make sense to me, either, but God never promised everything would. As his children, we're called to seek his will and follow it, no matter what."

Tony didn't respond.

Taking a breath for courage, Emma continued. "Did you ever wonder what your father's future might have held had he lived? Obviously, his injuries were serious. Perhaps God, in his mercy, called your father

313

home to spare him years of pain and suffering. Eternity with the Father seems far better under those circumstances."

Tony's sharp intake of breath told Emma she had touched a raw nerve. *O Father, use my words to your good. Don't let them push this man farther from you.*

"How could you say that?" he asked, his words rough as a rusty horseshoe. "How could Mother say the same thing back then? How could death be better than life?"

Thank you, Lord. If a mature, godly woman like Althea voiced the same thought to her son that many years ago, then surely Emma wasn't too far off. "What kind of life would you have wanted for him, Tony? A pain-filled existence, justified only because *you* wanted him at your side?"

He rose in a rush. "What are you accusing me of?"

Emma forced herself to remain seated. "I didn't accuse you of anything but adolescence. Youth is selfish, and back then you couldn't see beyond your wants and needs to what was best for your father."

"Oh, so it was selfish to want my father alive and well?"

"Not at all. But it might have been selfish to want him barely alive and ailing, just because you refused to see God's kindness in sparing your father pain."

"I needed my father," he ground out.

Tears filled Emma's eyes. A knot tightened her throat. "No one says you didn't. We all do. But not everyone has an earthly father to fill that need. That is why in his Word God promised to be a father to the orphan, a husband to the widow. He promised his love would be sufficient for us."

"I can't trust a love that only takes, one I can't see."

"How can you not see his love? He watched over you every time you put yourself in danger. Better than any earthly father could. Even after you turned your back on him. He has loved you unconditionally all this time."

As Emma spoke, Tony paced the length of the porch. Since he didn't speak, she went on, her heart brimming with all she wanted to share. "He has always been the Father he promised to be. He's reaching out to you even now, waiting for you to love him back."

"You call me selfish?" he asked, anger heating his gaze. "As far as I'm concerned, God took away the father I loved. Yet according to you, he demanded that love from me then and does so even now."

Emma knew what she had to say next would be difficult for Tony to hear. "In the Bible, God proclaims himself a jealous God.

315

He doesn't want his children to hold anything higher than him, not even love for an earthly father. The God of Scripture wants our love, our obedience, our trust, our faith. Everything. In turn, he will meet our needs, abundantly and far exceeding imagination."

"I haven't seen any evidence of him meeting my needs."

"Why don't you try seeking him in your daily walk? in his Word? I know you'll find him. And his providence."

Shaking his head, Tony descended the stairs. "No, that's not solid enough, not real enough for me."

"That's right," Emma said. "God wants you to accept him on faith."

Taking another step toward the bunkhouse, he again shook his head. "I can't believe in what I can't see or feel."

"Then you want to touch Christ's wounds, like Thomas."

Tony kept moving. Then he paused.

Rising, Emma felt his yearning, his indecision, his confusion at what she had just said. She wished there was something else to say, to do, but the walk with Christ was one Tony would have to undertake on his own.

As she watched, he shrugged and, with heavy footsteps, walked to the building beyond the corral.

If nothing else, Emma knew she had made him think. "Dear God, I pray I haven't made matters worse."

Breakfast the next day brought only a muttered *"Buenos días"* from Tony, which left Emma fretting over the effect of their conversation the night before as she set yet another pot of beans on the back of the stove for their supper.

Shortly after Emma went to dust the parlor, Althea came downstairs and swiped her cloth. "What —"

"Go!" Althea ordered. "I can certainly try my hand at dusting. You have worked too hard since we got here. Antonio just walked past the corral with Rattlesnake. Tell him I said he should take you for a ride around your spread."

"Goodness! What's come over you?"

"Why, dear, I'm tired of watching you work yourself to the bone. It's high time you saw your inheritance. I doubt you've gone beyond the outbuildings."

"True, but —"

"No buts. Tell Antonio he's to do as I say, or he'll have some explainin' to do. I'll have a picnic ready so you needn't be in a hurry to get back."

"I warned you to stop matchmaking."

Althea pretended innocence. "Who's to say I'm matchmaking? I only said it's past time you saw your ranch. And Antonio is more than capable of showin' you around."

Emma took a step back, shaking her head. "I don't buy a word you're saying. Tony won't want —"

"What won't I want?" Tony asked as he strode inside. He headed for the kitchen. "It's dirt-dry out there. Have you made tea or lemonade today?"

"Water," Emma said, seeing an escape. "We have lots of water. Let me fetch some for you."

Althea blocked her way. "I'll make a pitcher of my lemonade, Antonio, if you'll take Emma for a ride around the ranch. We have worked the poor child so hard. Why, she hasn't had a chance to see her land."

"*My* land," he said, shaking his head. "I have work to do."

"So do I," Emma piped in.

"Nonsense," Althea countered, her jaw set. "You will both take a ride to . . . to . . . oh my, yes, to that pond nearby. For a picnic. Now go on and don't argue."

To his credit, Tony didn't.

Neither did Emma, although she liked the plan no more than he. And so, less than an hour later, she found herself lurching atop a beautiful roan mare. Tony had insisted the animal was gentle enough for a first-time rider.

Emma's rattled bones weren't quite that sure.

As she bounced on the horse, though, the stark beauty of the land stole her heart. Drawn in broad lines and occasional hills, its colors ranged from the red-yellow dust to the silvered green of occasional sagebrush. As they approached the watering hole, she made out the darker smudges of what Tony called scrub juniper.

She had expected grass, since everyone called the land a prairie, but when she asked about it, Tony said it had been overgrazed. After three dry years, not much grew around here. His cowhands had driven the cattle farther out where the animals were more likely to find food.

After riding side by side for a while, and despite sporadic conversation — where he voiced frustration at the lack of progress in his search for Jubal's missing cattle — Tony hadn't let his gaze meet hers. Emma knew he was trying his level best to avoid a repetition of last night's revealing exchange. She didn't blame him.

He had bared his soul.

And, she suspected, her words probably had struck him as harsh. If nothing else, she had sounded dogmatic. Surely he hadn't expected her to sermonize. Not if he'd come out to the porch for yet another of his regular light flirtations.

Emma sighed. No wonder she had never married. She had a most unusual way with men. Tony was the first one in a long while who had paid her any attention — and attracted her in turn — and she had just spent an evening preaching to him. Her only excuse lay in knowing how badly he ached and how surely Christ could heal those wounds.

"We're almost there," Tony called out a short while later, interrupting her thoughts.

"My sore bones are most grateful."

"So is my stomach. Any idea what Mother packed?"

"The rest of last night's beans, I'm sure, and probably some bacon, but it's anyone's guess what else she tucked into that basket."

"We'll soon find out."

Before long, Tony looped his horse's reins around the low-hanging branch of a scruffy juniper set between two massive boulders by the watering hole, then went to help Emma from her mount. She held out her hand but he ignored it, wrapping his hands around her waist and lifting her down to his side.

When she looked up, their gazes met for the first time that day. The moment grew long . . . longer.

Then his cocky smile broke out. "Maybe this wasn't such a bad idea," he said, leading her to the water's edge. "A free afternoon with a lovely lady at my side. And food — plenty of it, I hope."

Emma took his words as her cue. "I'll see to our lunch."

With shaky fingers, she returned to her horse and pulled down the basket from behind her saddle. Lifting the lid, she withdrew a bright red tablecloth. A number of bowls covered with white napkins followed. At the bottom of the hamper she found a bottle filled with a cloudy liquid.

After ensuring both horses drank their fill from the pond, Tony made himself comfortable on a corner of the scarlet cloth. "What did you find?"

"The bacon, your mother's refried beans and tortillas, dried-apple pie, and lemonade," she counted off. "And since she knows your appetite, your mother packed plenty."

"A feast, then."

No sooner did Emma hand him a full plate than Tony speared a chunk of bacon with his fork and aimed it for his mouth.

"Wait!" she cried. "Grace first."

Although he frowned, Tony didn't argue. Emma quickly offered thanks for the meal. At her amen, he dug in with gusto.

Emma took her time enjoying the food, the rugged beauty of the land, the sound of the water licking the edges of the pond, the soughing of the horses' breath. She especially savored the pleasure of Tony's company, even though they ate in silence.

Although she wanted to know if — and what — he had thought of their talk, she didn't dare broach the subject. She would have to wait patiently until he chose to discuss such matters again.

It appeared silence suited him fine right then. After eating, he leaned back against the tree trunk, dropped his hat over his face, and made it clear he wasn't open for conversation.

Emma nearly laughed out loud. If Althea could see them now! The picnic wasn't playing out quite as her friend had planned.

Respecting Tony's desire for privacy, she responded to the lure of the watering hole. She removed her shoes and stockings and dipped in her toes. It was a blazing hot day. She sighed as the water cooled her flesh. "Bliss."

Suddenly, a horse's shrill neigh shattered

the peace. Turning, Emma saw her mount rear up, crying in agony.

Tony ran to the mare and spoke in gentle tones. As she bucked, the reins tethered to the tree cut into the animal's neck, and she shook her head violently, trying to free herself.

"What happened?" Emma cried.

"I don't know! Something must have spooked her." He tried to edge closer, dodging flying hooves. "Whoa, girl. It's me. Here, I have something for you."

When Tony dug in his pocket for the promised treat, the animal bucked again, this time snapping the tethers. When she found herself suddenly loose, the mare fled in a cloud of dust.

Tony jumped on his mount and took off in pursuit, calling over his shoulder, "Wait for me!"

"What does he think I'm going to do?" Emma muttered. "Stroll home?"

She sat on one of the many smaller rocks scattered around the ten-foot high boulders at the side of the pond, slipping her toes into the water once more. The pool looked deep at this spot, and Emma wondered what swimming might be like. She had never learned, but she'd heard of ladies who traveled to the ocean and, after taking lessons, deemed it an unparalleled delight. On a day this hot she could well believe it.

As she studied her reflection in the water, the dry wind rumpled through strands of her freed hair. Deep in her thoughts, she lost track of time. What a pleasant spot —

Suddenly Emma hurtled through space. She screamed as the water at her feet rushed up to meet her face. She tried to yell again, but her mouth filled. Pain at her back told her something had hit her, pushing her in. She fought to rise, but her dress weighed her down, and a heavy weight pressed against the top of her head.

Dear God, help me. I'm drowning.

Something held her underwater.

Her lungs began to burn. Dots of light danced across her eyelids. Her arms grew weary. Was she dying?

As suddenly as she had flown off the rock, the pressure on her head vanished, and Emma bobbed to the surface. "Help —"

She went back under, then resurfaced. "Help!" she cried, flailing, reaching for something — anything — to hold on to.

Strong hands hooked under her arms, and Emma knew she had been rescued. She felt herself lifted. The water fell away.

Then everything went black.

Riding harder than he'd ever ridden, Tony

felt panic at the sound of Emma's scream. As he approached the water hole, his heart pounded furiously. Emma was struggling in the dark pond. Her gasped plea for help sliced through him.

He feared he was too late as she went under again. Diving in, he grasped her under the arms and pulled her to safety. As he carried her out of the water, Luther Pierce rode up, his face bright red.

"Whaddaya doing to Miss Emma, Mex?"

Tony ground his teeth. "Saving her from drowning. What does it look like?"

"From where I'm sitting, it sure looks the other way."

Tony fought to control his anger and focus on Emma's well-being. "Are you accusing me of hurting her?"

Pierce arched an eyebrow. "You'd own the Rocking C outright if she died. . . ."

Tony placed his precious burden on the red tablecloth. Emma's cheeks were white as paper, her closed eyelids mapped with tiny blue veins. She looked fragile, vulnerable, and her breath hardly rippled her chest. He hoped he'd gotten to her in time.

When he found her pulse, he turned to Pierce. "I'm going to do you a favor and ignore what you said. For Emma's sake. If you care about Miss Carstairs, I suggest you keep those thoughts to yourself and help me get her home. We can have this out later."

"That's a promise, Mex."

Tony reluctantly released Emma. He mounted his horse and held out his arms, letting Pierce place Emma in them. It took all his willpower not to slug the man whose hamlike hands strayed over Emma's back, her waist.

Then with Emma cradled close to Tony's heart, they rode for the Rocking C. The ride gave Tony time to wonder how Luther had arrived just when he did. What had the man been doing at the Rocking C's watering hole? Had he tried to hurt — drown — Emma?

Anger boiled in Tony just at the suspicion. But this wasn't the time. All that mattered now was Emma.

At the ranch house, Tony set up his vigil in the parlor, joined by his praying mother. Pierce paced the room in front of the sofa where Emma lay, every so often muttering empty accusations. Sparing his unwanted guest the rare glance, Tony continued to study Emma's too-pale face. He hated feeling helpless.

Tony's mother, deep in conversation with her Lord, seemed untouched by their neighbor's venom. Every time Rattlesnake tried to usher Pierce out of the house, the rancher dug in his heels, stating his need to keep an eye on Emma — for her well-being, as he put it. At least he hadn't accused Tony of attempted murder again.

As minutes ticked by, Tony remembered the horror he experienced as his father lay dying. Because this vigil felt so much like that other, he continued to hold Emma's hand. He could only bear the wait if he could feel her pulse.

Studying the waxy face before him, Tony relived the worst moments of his life. Was he about to lose Emma as he had lost his father?

Surely not.

He remembered what she had said the night before, how she believed God had spared his father a slow wasting away by permitting his death. Emma's case wasn't the same, was it? Recovery from near drowning wouldn't sentence her to a miserable future, would it?

Tick-tock. The clock on the oak sideboard marked the passing minutes. *Tick-tock.*

As he listened for a sign that might bring him hope, Tony again heard his mother's whispered prayers. Something deep inside urged him to join her, to ask for divine intervention that Emma's life be spared. But reason stepped in and held him back.

What was the use?

Tony feared he wouldn't survive placing his trust in God, only to be let down once again. At that moment, he realized how much Emma had come to mean to him. The sassy, gun-toting, prissy, preachy Eastern spinster had burrowed her way into his heart, making him care. Maybe more.

She couldn't die. Not Emma. Surely God wouldn't let him down again —

"Wha-what happened?" she suddenly whispered.

"Emma?" he asked, not daring to believe.

"Tony . . . the water . . . the horse . . . what —"

He placed a finger on her colorless lips. "Hush. You had an accident and fell in the pond."

"Weren't no accident, Miss Emma!" Luther Pierce blasted.

Tony tried to silence the man, but he would have none of it. "I went to check out the watering hole before I took my cattle there, Miss Emma, and I heard you cry out for help. When I got there, I found this here Mex drowning you. He would've done it, too, if I hadn't showed up when I did."

Tony's mother looked shocked. Rattlesnake rushed to her side.

"No, Mother," Tony said, "of course that isn't so —"

"Tony . . . ?" asked Emma, trying to sit up.

"Now, don't you go moving just yet, Miss Emma." In his rush to reach Emma, Pierce elbowed Tony aside. It was all Tony could do to keep from slugging the man.

Pierce wasn't done just yet. He plumped up two of the pillows on the sofa and stuffed them under Emma's back. "You've been through too much, ma'am. You need your rest."

Either Pierce was stupid, or he had no idea who he was dealing with. Maybe he couldn't smell danger worth spit. Tony fought the desire to shoot him dead, knowing this wasn't the time to even the score. His voice turned deadly. "She needs to rest. And that's why you're leaving, Pierce."

The rancher took Emma's hand and rubbed a thumb over her knuckles, paying Tony no mind. "Well, ma'am, I was hoping to give you more time to get used to my ways, but knowing the kinda danger you're facing all by your lonesome, why, it's best if I speak straight right now."

Emma shook her head, clearly confused. "What are you saying, Luther? Tony wouldn't hurt me —"

"Miss Emma, he's wanted your ranch all

along. What would come easier than to get it by killing you?"

Tony took a step toward Pierce. "I'm warning you, get your lying hide off my land. Right now."

"Who says I'm lying?"

"I do."

"I'm to believe the man who tried to kill my Emma?"

"You're a fool. I wouldn't hurt anyone —"

Suddenly, silence reigned supreme.

Pierce smiled.

Tony's mother moaned.

Rattlesnake prayed.

Tony realized what he'd been about to say. What he wished, for the first time in his life, he could say.

Pierce gave a chuckle. "I'll bet you've killed plenty in your time, Mex. What's one more, when there's a rich spread at stake?"

Tony clenched his fists, his jaw. "I didn't hurt her. I would *never* hurt Emma."

"It's all right, Tony," Emma whispered. "I know you wouldn't hurt me —"

"Now, Miss Emma, you can't be so sure. I saw him. And that's why we should get hitched up right away. I can protect you better once you're Mrs. Luther Pierce."

Again, silence descended.

Tony watched as his mother jumped away

from Rattlesnake's protective hold, surprising everyone. "No!" she squealed. "You can't marry Emma. Why, she and my son are to be married. The weddin' is on . . . on . . . . Saturday. Yes, this Saturday afternoon."

Pierce's gaze narrowed. "What was that?"

Tony smiled at his mother, then he took a swaggering step toward the now-agitated cowpuncher. "You heard her. Emma and I will be married come Saturday afternoon."

Ruddy cheeks puffed under angry blue eyes. "Bu-but, that *can't* be!"

Hoping Emma wouldn't let him down, Tony said, "Of course it can. Why don't you ask the lady herself? Tell the man, *querida,* won't you marry me in four days?"

Emma's sapphire eyes darted from Tony to Pierce and back to Tony again. Confusion darkened their depths. To Tony's dismay, he thought he saw fear there too.

She took a deep breath, "I . . . I . . ."

Mother bustled up to Pierce. "There. You see? Poor child can't even string a sentence together." With determination, she grasped his arm and pulled. "Get along with you. Emma needs her rest."

To Tony's amazement, the rancher let himself be dragged to the door. Ramming his hat onto his dark blond hair, he turned and, with suspicion in his eyes said, "I gotta see this wedding before I believe it. You got yourselves a guest."

"Fine," said Mother, opening the door. "We shall see you Saturday. Now go." Turning to Tony and Rattlesnake, she added, "You, too. A bride needs rest before the wedding."

With a glance at his befuddled "bride," Tony reluctantly followed Pierce. Strange how Emma hadn't objected. Had the near drowning hurt her more than it seemed? Or did she have other things on her mind? Things that made her hold her tongue?

Chapter Six

Guitar notes woke Emma Saturday morning as the rosy hue of dawn brightened the shadows in her room. "Again?"

Rising, she yawned and approached the open window. What she found this time surprised her even more than the discovery of Tony's talent.

Outside, four men in tight, dark, exotic-looking suits and huge-brimmed black hats joined their voices in song as they played various instruments. Tony stood closest to her and strummed his guitar. One of his companions plucked the strings of something that looked like a cross between a guitar and an orchestra bass. Another wrought rich bursts of sound from a trumpet, and the last sent a bow flying over violin strings. Their music was sweet, romantic, very different from the heart-rending tunes Tony had played before.

"Buenos días, querida," he called when he saw her, giving her his rogue's smile. His fingers continued their nimble dance over taut strings.

Emma rubbed her temples. Ever since they'd gone on that fateful picnic, nothing seemed sane. She remembered Luther's wild accusations, Tony's strange proposal, then the flurry of activity that turned her days into a dreamlike haze. Althea had taken over, relegating Emma to the parlor sofa, where she was expected to rest and recover from her near drowning.

When life became an unreal string of hours, she sought refuge in her Bible. No one bothered answering her questions and, in truth, Emma hadn't asked many. For suddenly she found herself betrothed to a most intriguing, handsome man. One who had come to mean a lot — perhaps too much — to her. If this was a dream, she wasn't sure she wanted to wake up, even if waking up was the most reasonable, wisest thing to do.

The men played on outside her window.

Emma had read Scripture and prayed for hours on end. Finally she decided to view these unexpected turns in her life as God's intervention.

All but her unexplained dousing in the pond. Emma remembered the pain in her back before she flew into the water. And she would never forget the pressure on her head that held her under the water's surface. Someone had tried to kill her. But who?

Although she didn't want to believe them, she had to consider Luther Pierce's accusations against Tony. She had. Ever since he'd voiced them. Over and over again.

Tony wanted the Rocking C. He had from the very start. It would be simple enough to keep the ranch after her death.

Emma glanced at the musicians. Tony's gaze was fixed on her, a smile on his lips. Had he tried to kill her? The more she thought about it, the less likely it seemed.

Realizing she was ill equipped to run a ranch single-handedly, Emma had stopped thinking of sole ownership. In fact, as Tony held the title and ran day-to-day operations, she couldn't imagine him feeling threatened by her presence any longer. And he had said he'd resigned himself to sharing the Rocking C with her.

Although occasional pangs of anxiety pierced her, she had to admit they weren't due to suspecting her future spouse of attempted murder. True, he had killed before, but only in his pursuit of justice, and she hadn't done him harm. She had even told him she would leave the ranch if the Lord led her to do so.

Tony might be stubborn, infuriating, and an unrepentant tease, but Emma didn't think he was plotting to become a widower in the immediate future.

She didn't deny someone had tried to kill her. It just hadn't been Tony. Of that, she was reasonably sure.

Of course Tony had muttered plenty of accusations of his own, featuring Luther Pierce as the thwarted murderer. And he insisted Luther had the missing Rocking C stock, even if he couldn't prove it yet.

Could Luther have tried to kill her? But why? Especially if he already had her cattle. And she had agreed to let him water his animals at the Rocking C pond.

Well, Tony *had* made her retract her agreement, but would Luther try and kill her for some water? That seemed ludicrous. Water was . . . *water*, for goodness sake! Hardly worth murdering a neighbor for, no matter what Tony said about the value of water in this arid part of Texas. Besides, Luther had come to court her, had seemed so taken with her. He had even proposed. Had he tried to kill her? As he'd accused Tony of doing?

Emma didn't know. She only knew someone had tried to kill her. *But who, Lord?*

Then she remembered something. Something that didn't seem right. Tony had said Luther had shown up at the pond only seconds after he pulled Emma out of the water.

What had Luther been doing in the vicinity of the pond?

She remembered Luther's words shortly after she came to in the parlor. He'd said, "*I went to check out the watering hole before I took my cattle there.*" But all of this had happened *after* Tony made her write the letter telling Luther he couldn't water his herd at the Rocking C's pond. Luther shouldn't have been near the pond that afternoon. Was he the one who tried to kill her?

Her heavenly Father had given her no answers to her many questions yet, and at times she wondered if the accident had addled her mind. After all, she was marrying Antonio Alvarez. And she barely knew the man!

How had it all happened so fast?

And she hadn't even objected!

Did she want to object? Would she rather remain a spinster than marry a man who attracted her mightily? One who could rattle her with a glance, a smile? One she feared she would love with every fiber of her being until the day she died?

One who wanted her ranch more than he wanted her? Who didn't share her faith in Christ?

Increasingly, Emma feared she had left her wits in the water. And since there was a chance she might be suffering from rampant lunacy, she had asked the Father to set things back to their proper order. She would place all her trust in him.

In the meantime, she would pray she wasn't making the greatest mistake of her life.

"Tony," she called during a lull in his singing, "what are you doing out there this early?"

He again flashed his wonderful smile. "I've brought a mariachi band to my bride, of course."

"Then I'm not dreaming?"

He chuckled, and his companions laughed. "No, *querida*, I'm serenading you, as a Mexican man serenades the woman he plans to marry. The word *mariachi* comes from the French *marriage*, you know."

"We *are* getting married? Really and truly?"

"Forever and ever."

"You mean it?"

"Just wait and see! I sent one of the hands to San Antone to find us a preacher, and Reverend Matthews will be here no later than three o'clock this afternoon."

"The lace veil your mother loaned me . . . it's real, too?"

"Real as can be. Spanish and Mexican *señoritas* wear mantillas on their wedding day. My grandmother wore it, and now Mother will loan it to you, just as *Abuelita* loaned it to her when she married Father."

Emma fell silent, enjoying the music and thinking of the traditional mantilla she would wear. One song ended, another began. The brilliant voice of the trumpet led off in a clear ripple of notes. The strings followed, joining the melody. Emma watched and listened, charmed in spite of herself. She couldn't imagine anything more romantic.

A borrowed mantilla to wear. A mariachi serenade. The morning of her wedding day.

Her wedding day . . . Emma Carstairs and Tony Alvarez were getting married.

Running a finger around his tight clerical collar, Reverend Matthews cleared his throat. "Dearly beloved . . ."

Emma stood frozen before the man of God, Tony's warm fingers around her cold ones, and listened to the words she never thought she would hear. She remembered little of the morning — beyond the kiss Tony tossed her at the end of his last song. That long-distance sign of affection had carried her through Althea's fussing. The older woman had played with Emma's hair, arranged her best ice-blue silk dress to exacting standards, and finally, pinned the magnificent lace mantilla on her upswept coiffure to ensure its proper drape.

Eventually, the bridegroom's mother had stood back and deemed Emma ready. *"Ever so ravishing, dear."*

Tony had arranged for the mariachi to stay for the ceremony, and they had played as Emma entered the parlor on Rattlesnake's arm just moments ago. The ranch hands, scrubbed and with slicked-back hair, stood awkwardly around the parlor, sheepish grins on their faces.

To her dismay, Luther Pierce had stared from his vantage point by the front door. His presence hadn't helped her jittery nerves. Especially now that she suspected he'd been the one who'd tried to kill her.

". . . voice your objections, or forever hold your peace," said the reverend. Emma held her breath. With a glance, she saw a glowering Rattlesnake move closer to Luther.

Emma felt a tug on her hair where Althea had anchored the borrowed veil. Turning, she saw her friend pull one end of the mantilla toward Tony, then lay it over his shoulders. "A tradition, dear," Althea murmured. "To symbolize the union."

Tony smiled warmly, tenderly, at Emma, and emotion filled her throat. *Is this truly happening, Lord?*

"Do you, Emma Carstairs," asked Reverend Matthews, "take Antonio Mallery Alvarez to be your lawful, wedded husband? . . ."

Emma's heart pounded wildly. At the proper moment, she whispered, "I do."

Turning to the groom, the minister repeated the vows. Tony's voice rang out clear and strong. "I do."

"Then in the name of our almighty Father, I pronounce you husband and wife. You may kiss your bride, Mr. Alvarez."

Tony did. Gently, his hand cupped her cheek, and his lips touched Emma's. At that moment she felt precious, cherished, special, and she dared dream it might all be real. Hope glowed in her heart.

Conversation during supper — prepared and served by the housekeeper Tony had hired when he gathered his mariachi in San Antonio — turned to ranch matters. In a roundabout way, the name *Luther Pierce* came up.

After helping himself to another serving of beans, Rattlesnake slathered a chunk of bread with butter. "Well, boy," he said, waving his knife through the air, "Pierce sure didn't like you marrying our Miss Emma today."

Tony chuckled. "No, he didn't, but there

was nothing he could do about it. Not even while he watched."

Rattlesnake nodded. "The ranch is safe now."

Emma placed her fork on her plate. "The ranch, huh?"

Both men turned her way. "He can't try and marry you for it anymore," said Tony, satisfaction in his voice. "You're a married lady. *My* wife."

Emma tapped her fingers on the table. "So *Luther* can't marry me for the ranch any longer?"

"Nope!" both sang out.

"Because *you* just did."

"Yep," said Tony, adding a chicken leg to his plate.

Emma's temper got the best of her. Rising, she pushed the chair out behind her. "How come?" Striding briskly, she headed toward the bedroom wing of the house. "What made it wrong for *Luther* to marry me for the ranch but right for *you?*"

Not waiting for Tony's response, she stormed into her room and slammed the door. A second later, it shook under his pounding. "Let me in!"

"Absolutely not! I don't *ever* want to see you again."

"Emma! You can't do this. I'm your husband now. At least open the door. We have to talk. About the ranch, the wedding . . . I don't know, we can talk about anything you want to talk about. Just don't lock me out."

Hurt and anger brought scalding tears to Emma's eyes. Tony's pleading was difficult to ignore, especially when she so wanted him to explain himself, to make things right. She took a step toward the door.

Tony's fist crashed down on the wood again, bringing her to a standstill.

"Besides," he said, "where do you expect me to sleep tonight?"

Anger edged out her hurt. "Where you always sleep. In the bunkhouse." Taking a shuddering breath, she fought back the sobs. "I only regret we don't keep pigs. You belong with them!"

"Emma . . ."

"Don't threaten me, *Mr. Alvarez*. And go away! Preferably back to New Mexico with your . . . your mari-a-chiii . . ."

Sobs ripped from her throat. Tears fell in earnest. With shaking fingers, Emma unfastened the tight bodice of her wedding gown and undressed. Wishing never to see blue silk again, she wadded it in a corner of the wardrobe and pulled on a white lawn nightdress.

Emma had never expected to spend her

wedding night alone, locked in her room, crying her heart out. But that was what happened when a woman took her eyes off the Lord for even the smallest fraction of time. A charming, serenading louse caught her attention and broke her heart in two.

After an endless, sleepless night, Tony watched the sunrise from the bunkhouse window. He couldn't remember feeling such anger before. He could just throttle his irritating, exasperating, infuriating Eastern priss of a wife. He could also kick himself for handling last night's supper conversation so poorly.

His sole excuse lay in his relief at having married Emma before she changed her mind. After her brush with death, making her his wife had become the only thing that mattered. And he hadn't planned to confess that in a room full of people.

He thought he should tell *her* first.

Now, it seemed a groom who spent his wedding night in a bunkhouse must also endure the teasing of his ranch hands.

"Hey, Boss," said Hank, "looks like your missus don't like you so well."

Billy-Bar snickered. "Nah. That's what getting hitched is all about. He best get used to the lockout."

"Boss just ain't learned to handle a woman proper-like," added Little Tex.

"Strange he can't charm a lady," said Zeb, taking mincing, dandified steps across the room, "him so purty an' all."

Tony glared at them. "Sounds like no one's getting paid this month." The men vanished without another word.

Wrapping his tattered dignity around him, Tony headed for the house, seeking food and forgiveness — not necessarily in that order. Nothing seemed as important as putting the sweet, dreamy smile back on Emma's lips. The smile she wore when he serenaded her yesterday morning. A smile that made him feel ten miles tall, mountain strong. The smile that said a splendid future spread out before them.

He wouldn't stop until that smile was in place again.

With determined strides, he made his way to Emma's room — *their* room. Raising his fist to knock, he realized the door stood slightly ajar. "Emma?"

Silence greeted him.

"Are you in here?" he asked. Opening the door, he found the room empty. The spread lay smooth over the bed, her shoes sprawled below, her Bible on the floor where it seemed to have fallen. Across the open book lay a piece of paper, a message in black ink scrawled across it.

Tony knelt to pick up the sheet. The first five words chilled him, and nausea filled his gut.

I have your wife, Mex. If you want to see her again, sign over the deed to the Rocking C.

It couldn't be. No one was so twisted as to kidnap a woman on her wedding night.

Tony scanned the note again. Despite his unwillingness to believe what it said, the sense that had served him so well for so long assured him it was true.

Pierce had Emma. He wanted the ranch that badly.

Tony went for his gun, then remembered it was no longer there. He had sworn never to use it again. But this was different, wasn't it? He had to get Emma back. And make Pierce pay for what he'd done.

Emma had been gently reared out East. Tony imagined her beautiful blue eyes filled with panic, her delicate fingers shaking with fear, her chin tilted with pride — a pride that might land her in still more trouble.

"I'm coming after you, Pierce," he muttered, crushing the paper in his hand. As he turned to leave, however, inked lines on Emma's open Bible caught Tony's attention. He picked up the book and began to read the marked verses.

> *Unto thee will I cry, O Lord my rock;*
> *Be not silent to me:*
> *lest, if thou be silent to me,*
> *I become like them that go down into*
> *the pit. . . .*

He stared at the words that seemed written for him. When God had turned deaf to him, Tony became like those who plunged into a pit. A pit of defiance, violence. Of sin.

Why had he not seen it before? Had God let him slog through the pain and the ugliness so that when faced with more of the same he would realize just how low he had fallen? Did God liken Tony's violence to that of the criminals he had hunted? The verse from his childhood memories again pierced his thoughts.

Thou shalt not kill.

Tony *had* killed, and the moment he realized what Pierce had done, he'd reached for his gun.

Revenge. Tony had sought revenge for years, calling it justice. Yet even he knew that God reserved vengeance for himself alone.

So what was he going to do now? He couldn't let Pierce kill Emma. And he sure wasn't going to hand the ranch over to the man. What should he do?

Tony's heart pounded out her name. *Emma.* Spirited Emma. She was what really mattered.

O God, the helplessness. He, Antonio Alvarez, was helpless to save his wife. Unless he again took up his gun. And he knew she wouldn't want him to. No matter how much Pierce deserved a bullet.

What should he do?

Time seemed to stop. Tony's head swirled with battling thoughts. He had to save Emma. But how?

He again turned to her Bible. *Hear the voice of my supplications, when I cry unto thee, when I lift up my hands toward thy holy oracle. . . .*

He had done that once before. He had voiced his pleas, lifted his hands to God. But his prayers had gone unanswered. Could he trust God again? Would he risk losing Emma?

Tony remembered her words. *"He doesn't want his children to hold anything higher than him. . . ."* If Emma was right, he couldn't hold pride in his abilities higher than God. Or faith in his aim, his skill with a gun. And if he carried that concept to its farthest reach, then Tony couldn't even hold his fear higher than God. He couldn't let the fear of losing Emma matter more than God.

Dare he . . . ?

The forlorn black shoes caught his eye. Pierce hadn't thought of protecting Emma's feet from the rough Texas terrain. Who knew where he had taken her? And what hardship he would subject her to. What injuries he might inflict on her.

"Emma . . ." Tears stung Tony's eyes, sharp tears, fearful tears. The tears of a man in love, of a man who had sinned, who needed forgiveness. . . .

"O God," he sobbed, the cry rending his heart in two. "Forgive me, Father. I was wrong. I was a child, a selfish, blind child. And I refused to grow up. Don't let Emma pay for my sins. Help me save her. I-I love her, you know."

He laughed through his pain. "Of course you know. You sent her to me." The extent of God's blessing suddenly hit him. "Thank you, Father, for that precious gift. Please help me save her. Show me what to do. Guide me to her. I want her to know I love her."

"Antonio?" Mother asked from the doorway. "Is something wrong?" Then she spotted his tears. "Dear God!"

"Pierce took Emma. He wants the ranch in exchange for her life."

She fell to her knees, tears pooling in her eyes. "Oh, Father, help us . . . help *her.*"

Tony reached out a hand. Althea took it. "I asked, Mother. I prayed for his help and forgiveness."

"Thank you, Father!" she exclaimed, a sob breaking from her lips. She squeezed her eyes shut. *"Thank you,* Jesus."

Tony smiled despite the ache in his heart. "I thanked him for the gift of Emma. I-I also asked for his guidance, Mother. I don't know how to get her back."

"Wait on him, Son. His work is perfect, and his ways just."

"But what if —"

"Hush, Son. Have faith. If he's brought you back to his side, why, he can certainly show you how to get our Emma away from that . . . that monster."

"I just hope he answers *soon.*"

"Let's pray, Son. God's answer is already there. We only need to discern it." In quiet tones, she began praising God for the miracle he had performed.

Hesitant at first, Tony echoed her words.

Then, still holding her hand, he joined her ... and he knew. Deep in his heart, as if a silent voice had spoken, Tony knew exactly what he had to do. "It's time," he said. Leaning toward her, he kissed his mother's cheek. "Thank you for the years of prayer —"

"I love you, Son. I always have. Now, go and get that pretty wife of yours. If the Father has spoken, step out in faith and bring our Emma home."

"Hey, Pierce!"

Nothing had ever sounded sweeter than Rattlesnake's scratchy voice as Emma lay bound and gagged in a heap on the floor of Luther's outbuilding. The filth shocked her. As did the deplorable condition of the cows sharing the structure with her.

But nothing mattered now. Help had come.

"Whaddaya want?" Luther answered in his no-longer-charming fashion.

"Get your lazy men and your sorry hide to the Rocking C pond," Rattlesnake answered. "Your stock's sucking up our water. And it sure looks like someone's messed with their brands. Makes a body wonder what the sheriff would say."

Luther had kidnapped her, and all Rattlesnake could talk about was cows and the blasted watering hole?

"Nothing wrong with the Leaning P brand," Luther countered. " 'Sides, Miss Emma gave me the nod to water my animals there."

Cows again. She expected no better from Luther, though.

"*Missus Alvarez* ain't home just now, and she sent you a letter sayin' you ain't welcome at the Rockin' C pond. The boss don't want your stock drinking his water either. Fact is, he's gone for the sheriff."

Indeed. Her new husband thought only about cows and the ranch. It looked as if Luther had done Tony a favor by taking her off his hands.

"I told you Miss Emma said I could —"

"The *boss* said if you don't get your mangy cattle off Rocking C land, he'll take back everything you've taken from him."

Well! Perhaps not *just* the cows . . .

Luther cursed. "I didn't take nothing of his!"

Emma heard hoofbeats start off. Oh no! Not Rattlesnake.

In a fading voice, Rattlesnake yelled, "Fine, Pierce. Sheriff'll be there soon enough. He can check the brands."

Men! All they cared about was cows, even as she lay trussed like a Christmas goose — with yet more dumb cows.

"Fine," Luther conceded. "Smitty, Bob, Wilson! Let's go get the stock."

Dear God, what would happen to her? Didn't *anybody* care?

Althea did. The dear lady must be frantic by now.

From outside the shed, Emma heard men calling, then hoofbeats departing. The men had left for the Rocking C.

She had been scared when Luther came in her window, his revolver aimed at her heart. But she had hoped Tony would save her. He had tracked outlaws for a living. Found them too. And although he said he'd sworn off guns, surely he had a trick or two for a time like this.

Despair hovered near, but Emma wouldn't let it take root in her heart. She had to trust her heavenly Father. After that sham of a wedding, an annulment shouldn't be too difficult to obtain. God had to have something better in store for her than death by filth, surrounded by cows.

The door of the shed opened a crack. A sliver of summer sun cut through the darkness, and Emma's heart picked up its beat. She had to be ready. A woman never knew when the opportunity to save herself might come knocking.

She heard what she had thought never to hear again. "Emma?" Tony called.

Her heart stopped.

"*Querida,* are you in there?"

Her fickle heart started up again at the sound of the reprobate's voice. He sounded worried, though. Maybe close to panic. Too bad Luther had stuffed a rag in her mouth. She couldn't answer, but she could move. Sort of. At least she could wriggle and make the matted straw beneath her rustle.

He must have heard her, for he opened the door wider and stepped inside. "Who's there?"

Emma tried to scream. It came out like a sickly bleat.

"Emma!" Tony cried, relief in his voice. How he knew it was her, she had no idea.

She heard a boot hit wood, then a yowl of pain. "I can't see you," he muttered. "Make more noise."

She did.

Moments later, she was cradled in his arms, her bindings loosed, the gag removed from her mouth. Huge sobs racked her, and Tony kissed the tears off her cheeks.

"I was so scared, *querida,*" he murmured. "I thought I'd be too late. I could never have forgiven myself if anything had happened to you."

Between whimpers, she asked, "How did you get in here? Did he take all his men to the Rocking C pond? He has so many hands. . . ."

"Shh, don't talk. Everything's going to be fine. The Rocking C hands helped me lure Pierce's cattle — *our* cattle, as I suspected — to the watering hole. They were so parched, it didn't take much to move them. Then Rattlesnake threatened Pierce with the sheriff —"

"I heard him leave with his men," she said, surprised by how content he seemed just to cuddle her — in enemy territory. "Shouldn't we leave, though? They'll be back soon."

"No, they won't. The sheriff *was* waiting for them. Those brands were changed recently. The sores hadn't healed yet. Plenty of evidence to lock him up. Don't need to prove he tried to drown you."

"I suspected Luther was the one."

"Yep."

"He tried to blame you."

Tony looked earnestly into her eyes. "Did you believe him?"

"Of course not." Emma gazed at him in wonder. "You really came for me? . . ."

Tony looked hurt. "Of course I did! What kind of man do you think I am? I wouldn't let *anything* happen to you."

"You wouldn't? Even after taking care of Pierce? Even if the ranch is safe now?"

A touch of red livened Tony's tanned cheeks. "I'm so sorry, *querida*. And ashamed. I should have told you the truth last night. I care more for you than the ranch. I-I love you."

Emma glared at him. "How can you say that? Wasn't it enough to humiliate me before everyone last ni—"

He kissed her. The warmth, the softness, the tenderness in his touch wiped her doubts away. It spoke volumes about the man she'd married. His kiss wasn't about cows.

When he ended the caress, he smiled that dizzying, rattling smile of his. "Will you listen to me now?"

She nodded, smiling back.

"I thought you should be the first to know. I wanted to tell you when we were alone in our room, as man and wife." He shrugged. "It seemed more romantic that way. Instead, you forced me to tell you in this sorry excuse for a barn."

"Don't blame me for your poor timing!"

"Has nothing to do with timing. If you hadn't shut me out of our room, Luther

356

wouldn't have taken you away. None of this would have happened. We should have been together. It was our wedding night, you know."

Emma arched an eyebrow. "And why should I have let you in that room last night? You didn't think it timely to tell your bride you cared *before* the ceremony."

"What did you think that serenade was all about? I *love* you. Why, I don't know — except God sent you to me, and you're the greatest miracle he's worked in my life."

Emma's eyes opened wider. "Tony . . . ?"

He bent down for a quick kiss. "I owe you thanks, Mrs. Alvarez. That talk of yours sure made me think a lot."

Emma closed her eyes, joy filling her. "Praise God!"

"Amen to that."

She wasn't sure she was taking it all in. "Did you make peace with your mother, too?"

Tony donned a smug look. "We cried, we prayed, then she pushed me out the door. She wanted nothing more than for me to bring you home."

Emma wriggled to a sitting position, realizing for the first time how intimately they were pressed together. And how well she liked it. Nestling against Tony, his strong arms securely around her, felt wonderful. She didn't think she'd ever get up. Stretching, she placed a kiss on his lips.

Surprised him plenty.

"So?" she asked.

"Ah . . . er . . . so . . . what?"

"Are you going to take me home?"

Tony blinked. He studied Emma as if wondering what to do with her. Then he gave her a squeeze. "On one condition."

"And what would that be?"

"That you promise you won't shut me out of our room again."

Love surely evident in her eyes, Emma shook her head. "No, my love, I'll never shut you out again. Not from our room or from my heart."

"Whew!"

Frowning at his smart response, Emma asked, "What was that about?"

"I wasn't sure you loved me."

"Of course I do."

"You never said."

"You never asked."

"Neither did you."

"Ah, but you're a man."

"What does that have to do with it? When I told you I loved you, you didn't say a thing. You're the orneriest, most stubborn —"

She kissed him again.

Author's Note

When I learned about this anthology, my imagination flew back to my teenage years. I grew up in Venezuela, where my father was an executive for an American corporation. Summer afternoons, instead of watching soaps (yes, they are *everywhere*), I would turn the television to the wonderful old Mexican movies that were my alternative. Nothing seemed more romantic to an adolescent than handsome *rancheros* serenading *señoritas* with the help of a mariachi band.

Except perhaps the power held by the said *señoritas!* The hopeful suitor knew that if she opened her window, the lady accepted his suit. If, however, the window remained closed, he knew better than to try again. While Emma wasn't familiar with this custom, by opening her window, she let Tony know she wasn't indifferent to him.

As a Christian, I am deeply moved by the symbolism in the mantilla tradition. Before the couple speak their vows, her attendant drapes the bride's veil over the groom to represent the union they are pledging.

The promises we speak at our weddings are as vulnerable as a piece of lace. If we are careless or negligent, they will snag, unravel, and become as nothing. Ah, but if we build our marriages on the foundation of faith in Christ, then our unions will be as rich and intricate and beautiful as handmade lace.

Writing "Something Borrowed" was a labor of love and a prayer of thanksgiving. I hope my words convey that to you, my readers.

Something Blue

Catherine Palmer

And I say unto you, That many shall
come from the east and west, and shall
sit down with Abraham, and Isaac, and
Jacob, in the kingdom of heaven.
MATTHEW 8:11

Chapter One

Louisiana, 1876

"You have come to the wrong place, *chére!*" The old boatman shook his head and chuckled as he paddled his flat-bottomed *bateau* upriver. "You just like a crawfish 'bout to fall into a pot of gumbo. *Mais oui*, you gonna land in some hot water now!"

As the hired guide laughed, Astrid Munsen rocked the baby in her arms and prayed the raucous sound wouldn't wake little Edvard. Dear Lord, why had her husband chosen to leave the blue fjords of Norway to settle in this forsaken place? Astrid had long known that Ole Munsen lacked wisdom, but she had never thought her husband foolish. Now she was not so sure.

Never in all her life had she seen a landscape more bleak and miserable. Heat radiated down on the fetid, swampy river, which in turn gave up a powerful smell of rotting vegetation and stagnant water. Clouds of mosquitoes swarmed. Moss-strewn trees crowded the marshy edge, and hidden birds squawked in the branches. Astrid sucked down a breath of dank air as she blotted beads of perspiration from her temples.

Ja vel, God's mysterious ways work always for the good of his children, she thought. At her father's bidding, Astrid had married Ole Munsen, and she had made the best of the unpleasant arrangement. God had rewarded her faithfulness with a beautiful son. Though loath to do it, she had dutifully agreed to follow her husband to a new world. Months after Ole's departure and the subsequent birth of her baby, she had packed up little Edvard and sailed away from her beloved homeland. And God had blessed her with health, peace, and newfound friends during the long, lonely journey.

Now she must unlock the trunks of Norwegian dishes, blankets, tools, and furnishings Ole had taken with him, and she must create a home for her family. It would be a beautiful, clean little Norway in the midst of all this swamp, she had decided. Astrid would learn all she could about the people who had given her husband employment and lodging. With God's grace, not only would she live comfortably in this place, she would find joy here.

"Please, what is gumbo?" she asked the

boatman, wondering if she had misunderstood his slow, lazy speech. "I study English very hard, but I do not know this word."

"You don't know gumbo, *chére?*" His dark eyes widened in surprise. "Where you come from again?"

"Norway." Astrid lifted her chin. Despite the fact that her wool dress was stuck to her legs and her clogs had filled with water, she wanted the boatman to think well of the newcomer. "In Norway, we do not put gumbo into a pot. We put in porridge or soup."

"Gumbo *is* soup — made outta chicken, sausage, and crawfish," he said, steering the *bateau* toward the bank. "It's a mix, *chére*, like this country. Here in Louisiana, you got Cajun, Creole, black man. You got swamp, bayou, prairie. You got the rich man, like that Creole over there."

He pointed across the river to an opening in the trees. Down a long straight path stood a large house. Painted white, it boasted a deep front porch and six soaring columns. A flight of steps rose to the porch, and on either side stood a stone urn filled with flowers.

"Flowers!" Astrid gasped, the memory of her summer garden bursting into her thoughts. "I love flowers."

"*Oui*, Emile Fontenot has enough money to waste puttin' flowers in a pot. Me, if I'm lucky, I put gumbo and jambalaya in a pot. I used to be a city man workin' for the parish, but I gave it up. Now I got nothing to my name but this *bateau* and the money you paid me to bring you here — and I'm happier than ever. Oh, Louisiana is a spicy gumbo, sure enough. Swamp and prairie. Cajun and Creole. Poor and rich. And then there's Gage Ancelet. Look there, *chére*."

He thrust his chin in the direction of a small wooden dock a short distance upstream. Astrid searched the marshy bank until she spotted a dark, hunched shape in the river. *Gage Ancelet* — the name of the man who had hired Ole! Astrid dug into her pocket for her husband's letter giving directions to their new home. Despite the heat, a chill of anticipation surged through her veins. She was here at last.

"Gage Ancelet, he's not poor like me or rich like Fontenot," the boatman said. "He's got himself some fine prairie land, a good stretch of bayou, and the best horses you ever saw, *chére*. Ancelet is rich in *joie de vivre*, you know?"

Astrid studied the unmoving figure in the water. "I do not know this *joie de vivre*."

"I reckon not. But you 'bout to find out."

He gave her a gap-toothed grin. "Quiet now. We gonna slip up close and watch Ancelet catch him a fish."

"The man is fishing?" Astrid straightened to get a better look. "Where is the net? I cannot see even a rod."

"Hush, *chére*." The boatman held a gnarled finger to his lips.

The boat drifted closer to the man who crouched in the water, his head and arms submerged. Astrid frowned. Would he never move? Did he not need to breathe? Norwegian fishermen labored from boats, using huge nets to haul in mackerel and cod. In the icy rivers, they caught trout and salmon. In Norway, working fishermen made a busy, noisy sight. Nothing like this strange, predatory silence.

"*Mais oui!*" Ancelet suddenly burst upward, spraying water in every direction. In two hands, he raised a yard-long, whiskered fish that thrashed its silver tail in combat with the human enemy. The river churned to froth. The fish flailed. Ancelet struggled to keep his grip firmly planted in the heaving gills.

"Come now, my little *barbue!*" he cried. "Stop your fussin'. You already lost this fight."

"It's a good one, Ancelet!" the boatman

called. "And look, I bring you another pretty catch."

The man turned in the water, focused on Astrid, and nearly dropped the fish. "Gabriel . . . but who is this?"

"A lady come alla way here for a *visite*," the boatman said. "Come from Norway Parish."

"Norway?"

Biceps straining and water streaming from his black, curly hair, Gage Ancelet peered at Astrid. Uncomfortable at his bold scrutiny, she clutched Ole's well-worn letter in her hand and hugged the sleeping baby even closer. Quiet, quick, and canny enough to catch a fish with his bare hands, Ancelet was as fit a man as she had ever seen. But his form held none of the Norwegian male's great slabs of flesh, barrel chest, and thighs like tree trunks. Instead, each muscle formed an individual mound, and each sinew stood out clearly visible beneath deeply tanned skin. A wet cotton shirt clung to his broad, square shoulders and chest. With piercing black eyes and a potent strength, the man inspired a sense of fear that knifed through Astrid's stomach.

She wondered if all that dark power would erupt in fury at her unexpected intrusion. Instead, Ancelet's mouth broke suddenly into a wide, dimpled smile. *"Bonjour,"* he said, lifting the now-tired fish even higher. "Welcome for the *visite!*"

"Takk . . . uh, thank you." Her thoughts in a jumble, Astrid managed to call out in English as the *bateau* passed by, "You have a nice fish, Mr. Ancelet!"

The flatboat bumped against the dock, and the old boatman tossed a rope over a wood piling. When he leapt out, the rocking jerked the baby awake. His fists knotting into tiny balls, Edvard scrunched up his face and began to whimper. If his mama didn't do something fast, that rosebud mouth soon would emit an ear-breaking cry.

"Ah, *min egen sónn,* my own son," Astrid murmured as she rearranged the blanket around the sweaty little body. She considered pausing to nurse Edvard a little, but she abandoned the idea. Once settled in Ole's snug house, she would take time to nourish and comfort her son. "Shh, baby, soon you will see your *far.* Don't cry now. We are home at last."

Gathering the plump child against one shoulder, she tried to stand up in the wobbly boat. She wanted Ole's first sight of his son to make a good impression, and a fussy, hungry Edvard would not please a man as impatient as Ole. *Ja vel,* he would have to get used to it. A baby could not be silent always. At ten months, Edvard was heavy and awkward to lift, but Astrid struggled slowly to her feet.

"Give me the little one, *chére*." Gage Ancelet was kneeling at the edge of the dock, his arms spread toward her. "I'll take him for you."

Astrid hesitated. "But the fish?"

"On the *galerie*," he said, indicating the open porch that ran the full length of a house set in the middle of a small clearing. "Come on now, lemme have that child before you drop him in the bayou and a gator eats him for supper."

Without allowing her time to respond, he set one bare foot into the *bateau* and scooped Edvard from her arms. "Hoo, you're a fine little thing, huh?" Standing on the bobbing dock, he lifted the baby with both hands, much as he had done the whiskered fish. He held the child high overhead and jiggled him back and forth. Edvard beamed. "That's a boy, now. You don' wanna cry your first day on my beautiful *vacherie*. No, sir. You cry, I'm gonna have to cry, too."

A smile tugging at her lips, Astrid clutched her wool skirt and reached for the dock. Gage tucked the baby into the crook of one arm, knelt again, and stretched out a hand. "Take hold of me, now," he said, his dark eyes meeting hers. "I'll help you, *chére.*"

"The boatman —"

"Gone to look roun' the kitchen for some gumbo, no doubt." He extended his fingers. "Gabriel brought you here, and his job is done, *oui?* Time for gumbo. You lemme help you, *chére.*"

He was smiling as Astrid stepped close enough to allow him to slip his arm around her waist. *Amazing that a man should have such dimples,* she thought. *And such strength.* With no sign of effort, he lifted her up onto the dock and set her on her feet.

"Now then, *chére,*" he said as he un-wrapped Edvard's blanket, "you gonna tell me why Gabriel brought you alla way up the bayou to my dock?"

Astrid held out the crumpled letter and repeated the two sentences she had been practicing for months. "I am Astrid, the wife of Ole Munsen. He works here."

Gage's face sobered as he looked down at the letter. "Ole Munsen," he repeated softly. "You're his wife?"

"Those are the words I said. Where is my husband?"

His big hand stroked over the baby's

wispy golden hair. "This is Ole Munsen's son?"

"*Ja,* he is Edvard." Astrid swallowed at the dismay that had begun to tighten around her throat. "Ole Munsen lives here. I know it. He wrote in this letter to me the names of your river and your house. I travel from Norway with Edvard to make a home in this place. Where is my husband, please?"

Gage shifted from one foot to the other. "I have something to tell you now. Maybe you want to walk up onto my *galerie* and sit down?"

"No." Astrid tried to breathe. "Tell me here."

"*Mais non,* I got three good chairs on my *galerie.*"

Astrid swallowed hard. "Ole Munsen has gone away from this place?"

"That is true . . . in a certain way." He brushed a drop of water from his chin and patted the baby's back. "You sure you don' wanna sit down in the shade?"

"Please tell me where is my husband."

Gage Ancelet's dark eyes went as soft as chocolate. "Ole Munsen died two months ago, *chére.*"

Astrid's blood sank to her knees. A nauseating chill swept over her. Stars danced across her vision. And then Gage Ancelet's arm locked around her a second time. "Come on to the house," he murmured. "You better cool down, put your feet up, drink somethin'."

In a mist, Astrid floated onto the deeply shaded porch and sank into a cushioned chair. Someone slid a stool under her feet. Slipped off her wet wooden clogs. Tucked a pillow behind her head. Draped a damp rag on her forehead.

Ole Munsen was dead. Dead. But it couldn't be. He had written her the letter. He had told her to come. She had sailed away from her mother and father, her village, her flower garden. All these many miles, she had brought her baby —

"Edvard!" she cried, sitting up.

"I got him, *chére.*" Gage Ancelet stepped through the doorway onto the porch, the baby still tucked in the crook of his arm. "Eddie and me, we're cookin' up some gumbo for supper tonight. Don' you worry."

Astrid slumped back into the chair. Not worry? Her thoughts tumbled through her head. To make this journey, she had spent all the money her parents had saved and the little Ole had sent. Now she was here alone, penniless, homeless. Unexpected anger surged through her. It was just like Ole Munsen to do such a thoughtless thing! He

373

had never been a responsible husband. And now look!

She squeezed her eyes shut. No, she was being unjust. Surely Ole had not intended to die and leave her in such a predicament. What had happened to cause his death? Perhaps he'd grown sick, or he'd been injured in some terrible way. Poor Ole!

"Like to taste my *andouille?*" Gage said, emerging onto the porch again. He held up a fork on which he had speared a chunk of sausage.

Astrid's stomach rolled. "No, *takk* — thank you."

"Feelin' any better?" He pulled a chair to face her and sat down. "I know it's a bad shock about your husband. When my papa took sick last year and nearly died, I thought Mama was gonna fall to pieces. She loves that man so much. A husband and a wife, blessed in marriage with children and a home — now that kind of love is sent from God, no doubt."

Astrid let the comment pass. How could she fully explain the circumstances of her marriage? Her union with Ole Munsen had been arranged by the two fathers for the purpose of joining their farms and resolving an ancient dispute over the right to fish in a certain fjord.

Astrid had not loved her husband. She had never found much reason to respect the man. But she had fulfilled her role as his wife with faithfulness and hard work. Her joy had come in the anticipation of children, and for that purpose even Ole Munsen had some use as a husband. Now Edvard would never know a father, brothers, or sisters. And she would bear no more fruit.

"How did Ole die?" she whispered.

A veil passed across Gage's face. "*Mais* . . . he . . . he passed on at a place down the bayou some. I don' know exactly what happened. We gave him a good wake. He's buried out on the prairie. I'll take you there."

Astrid shook her head. "Later. Now I must think. I must make a plan."

Confusion drew the man's coal black brows together. "Plan? You don' wanna mourn a little? Maybe weep some tears for that man you love?"

"The Bible says there is a time to weep. Now is not the time."

As her parents had taught her, Astrid buried her emotion beneath a facade of cool control. She turned her attention to her son. Edvard had sunk both his hands into Gage Ancelet's curly hair and was tugging with all his strength. The man just kept staring at

Astrid and patting the baby's bottom as though holding a wriggling little boy in his arms was the most natural thing. Perhaps it was.

"You have children?" she asked him.

"Someday. I run two farms, *chére*. No time for my own children yet. But we have plenty of babies roun' here. Families live all up and down the bayou."

"In Norway, the care of children is for women."

"*Mais oui,* but this ain' Norway."

"*Ja,* this I can see." She scowled at the fetid river. "It is nothing like Norway."

"I don' know much about that place, but I do know God gave this land to my people a hundred years ago after we lost our homeland in the north. It's a good country. We have all we need here — crawfish, catfish, okra, muskrat. We have our families, papas and mamas —"

"*Ja,* you have big hot gumbo here!" Astrid cut in, her reserve evaporating. "You have Cajun and Creole and bayou and one thousand things I don't know! You have insects as large as birds. You have stink of rotten water." She glanced over at the blank-eyed fish lying beside the door. "You catch the fish with hands. You wear no shoes on feet. Man is cooking sausages and holding babies. *Det gir ingen mening! Vi gjór ikke det hos oss* . . . we not do this in . . . *Norge* . . . Norway. Oh, I cannot make English words!"

She bent over and buried her face in her hands. Dear God, what was she to do? Where was she to go? How could she ever survive? She must find a way to get back to Norway. Somehow she must earn passage home for herself and Edvard. Or could she beg the money from this stranger who once had taken in her husband?

Oh, how could God have let her fall into such a trap? She had trusted him! She had been so sure he held her in the palm of his hands. Had he abandoned her now in this forsaken place?

"Don' cry, *chére*," a low voice said.

When a warm hand wrapped around her damp, stockinged foot, Astrid jerked upright. Gage Ancelet was looking into her face with his chocolate eyes and dimpled smile. Edvard's small golden head was tucked into the hollow of the man's shoulder. Gage stroked the ball of Astrid's foot with his thumb, and the pressure sent a shiver of relaxation through her limbs.

"Why you wear those wood shoes?" he asked.

"In Norway . . . is how we do." Uncomfortable with his indiscreet touch, she tried to move her foot.

"Wet sand feels mighty good on bare toes," he said, moving his fingers up to rub each one. "I'll tell you somethin' else. I'm gonna take you over to stay with my parents. You get outta that wet wool skirt and put on a nice cotton dress, the world's gonna look a lot better. You and my folks come on over to my house tonight. Eat some gumbo —"

"No gumbo!" Astrid pulled her foot from his hand and tucked her legs under the chair. "I have to go home. Give me Edvard."

"He's sleepin' now, *chère*. Let him rest."

"But I must give him milk."

Gage let out a deep breath. "I fed him a little *couche-couche* in the kitchen. It's a kind of cornmeal cereal we mix with syrup. Eddie ate it right up. But if you wanna feed him on top of that, it's OK by me."

He handed her the drowsy baby and got to his feet. Afraid he might see the fear and worry in her face and realize she was close to tears, Astrid gave the man the steeliest glare she could muster. "Go away now, please, Mr. Ancelet," she said. "It is not your business."

"I reckon you're right about that, *chére*." He nodded and walked to the edge of the porch.

Astrid studied the tall, lean-muscled silhouette of the man who had held her son. A dark certainty filled her heart. Gage Ancelet knew the story of Ole Munsen's last days on earth. He knew the circumstances of her husband's death. Perhaps he had even been the cause of it.

Astrid cuddled Edvard close and began to rock. This was her problem. Ancelet had no concern in the matter. He was a stranger. A confusing mixture that both beckoned and repulsed her. He spoke words of kindness, yet his speech hid the truth. He was warm in his manner, yet his appearance intimidated her. His smile radiated joy and light, but his land was a place of darkness.

Worst of all in this frightening world into which she had fallen, the one man who could determine her future was Gage Ancelet.

"I must go away from this place," Astrid Munsen said as she walked beside Gage down the narrow path to his mother's house. "I must take Edvard back to our own people."

"*Mais oui,* you would feel better to be with your parents in this time of sadness." Gage glanced at the woman's face for any indication that her mourning might begin soon. A little sob? A few tears?

Carrying her bright-eyed baby, Astrid marched stoically onward. "Norway is our home. We have our own language. Our clothing. Our traditions. Edvard must learn these things."

Gage lifted an eyebrow at her reasons for wanting to return to her homeland. A baby must grow up Norwegian? Why? The little ones who played along the bayou liked it well enough here. He winked at the rosy-cheeked baby whose broad smile revealed a set of tiny seed-pearl teeth. Gage enjoyed this child with cornsilk hair and hands like soft, plump *beignet* dough. Edvard Munsen was a plucky fellow to have sailed across the ocean with his mama. In fact, the mama herself was courageous to have undertaken such a journey with no one but a baby.

"I think Eddie could be happy catching crawfish in the bayou," Gage offered. "He'd learn the children's games. In *cache-cache la bague* they hide a ring —"

"In Norway, children ski on the snow," she cut in. "Edvard must learn to ski, and there is no snow here. I will go home."

In spite of her chilly demeanor, Astrid Munsen fascinated Gage. In an icy sort of way, she was the most beautiful woman he had ever seen. When he had turned around in the bayou and spotted her sitting in that *bateau* with old Gabriel, he could have sworn she was glowing like an angel in an altar painting.

It must have been her hair. White-gold, it framed her face in waves and draped over her shoulder in a thick braid that hung to her waist. Most Cajuns Gage knew looked a lot like he did — dark hair, dark eyes, and deeply tanned skin from hours in the sun. This golden rope of Astrid Munsen's was so rare as to seem almost miraculous. Her eyes — the blue of washed indigo — shone like jewels. Her skin was as white as a magnolia blossom. In fact, she was altogether unreal.

"In Norway," she was saying, "we have good strong houses, square and tall. Inside, we keep beautiful things. Painted bowls, we have. Big, wooden beds with feather mattresses. Trunks filled with —"

She caught her breath and stopped walking.

"You all right, *chére?*" Gage asked, pausing beside her.

"I have thought of a reason for hope." She reached out and took his hand. Her eyes shone with an intense blue light. "My things — stools, bowls, plates. Ole Munsen carried my things from Norway to put into our house in America. Do you know where is my biggest trunk? I must find it. It is very large and wooden — and blue. Oh, Mr. Ancelet, do you know where is this blue trunk with rosemaling on every side?"

Gage didn't like the trend of her questions. The more she pried into her husband's past — his possessions and the activities of his last days — the closer to the truth she would come. And the less she knew, the better.

"I reckon Munsen might have left some stuff over at Mama's house," he said.

"Why there?"

"I hired him to work her farm. He slept in her loft." Uncomfortable at keeping truth from Astrid, he glanced away a moment before adding, "He slept there most nights, anyway."

"It is a *blue* trunk standing on four short legs," she said, as though she had hardly heard him. "I must find that trunk. It is painted over with rosemaling — leaves and flowers curling all around. Can you not remember this blue trunk of Ole Munsen?"

Gage withdrew his hand. "Listen, *chére*, I'm a busy man. I work hard. I got crops, cattle, and my horse-breedin' business. Your husband came lookin' for work, and I took him on. That's all. He and I didn't exactly —" He bit off his words. "Yonder is my parents' house. Maybe Mama saw that blue trunk sometime."

They started walking again, and Gage lifted up a prayer for the right words to say to this woman. For several years now, he had given every trouble in his heart to God. He prayed about all things, big and little — from his desire to improve the bloodline of his horses to the loneliness that filled his nights.

After his wife died in childbirth so many years before, Gage had never felt such confusion. He had rowed down to New Iberia on Bayou Teche and wandered through the town looking for ways to stop the ache in his heart and find answers to his questions. When he had reached the point of desperation, he stumbled on a peddler selling used books and trinkets, and he bought himself a Bible.

He read it cover to cover. Then he read it again. Finally, on his knees, he gave the emptiness in his heart to Jesus Christ. Once he had been forgiven and made whole again, he found many of the answers he'd been looking for. He had gone back to his *vacherie* and returned to work.

Still — despite the fullness of his heart and the busy clamor of the Cajun community around him — he felt a loneliness he could hardly understand. As he did with all his problems, Gage took that need to God.

And Astrid Munsen with her golden hair had come floating down the bayou right to his dock.

"Your houses are not like houses of Norway," she said as they approached the small home his grandfather had built by hand so many years before. "My house with Ole Munsen does not stand on posts. It does not have stairs on the outside. We do not make the roof coming down in front for snow and rain to fall onto people's heads. I think the roofs of this land are not good. In Norway, we have better roofs."

Gage shook his head and reached out to draw a line across Eddie's velvety cheek. This boy's mama sure wasn't the answer to his prayer. Though she had not yet wept for her dead husband, her heart belonged to Munsen. Equally significant to Gage, she despised this rich, steaming land he called home. She had stated her intent to find a way to return to Norway immediately, and he had no doubt she would succeed. The blue-eyed angel would not grace this bayou many days. Even if she did not love her husband, and even if she learned to like the bayou, Astrid would never step willingly into Gage's arms.

He knew too many things. Events that had

happened. Words that had been spoken. Deeds that had been done. He could never permit himself to draw close to Astrid without revealing the truth. And as bearer of that truth, he would forever be rejected by her.

When he glanced at the baby again, he saw a mirror of Astrid's blue eyes in the child's face. "*Mais oui*, Eddie," he said. "I better settle you and your mama down here and head back home. I got myself some gumbo on the stove."

Chapter Two

"A *blue* trunk?" Marie Ancelet took a sip from her coffee cup and then placed it back onto the wide, flat arm of the old rocking chair in which she sat. "I don' know about a blue trunk. Maybe we can ask Pierre. My husband will be comin' in from the field directly."

Gage's mother was a small, wiry woman with sharp brown eyes and curly black hair threaded with strands of silver. Her simple cotton skirt was clean and ironed, but her apron had been patched in two places. Astrid always kept her own embroidered aprons starched as stiff as paper, and she would turn them into dishtowels before she would consider sewing on a patch.

"Do you have in this house *any* trunks from Ole Munsen?" Astrid fanned herself with her husband's letter and tried to keep an eye on Edvard, who was crawling around to explore the large front porch. She felt sure her son's knees would be full of splinters soon, and she worried that an insect might sting him or that he might put something poisonous into his mouth. Practicing the good manners her mother taught her, she had sat for nearly an hour with Marie Ancelet, sipping coffee much too strong and hot for the sultry day and discussing one thing after another of no importance. Astrid was ready to scream.

"I believe your husband may have left some of his things roun' the house someplace," Marie said, her voice as languid as the river that coursed past her front yard. "Why you say you need that blue trunk?"

"It will help me get the money to buy my passage back home to Norway."

"*Mais non,* I don' remember a blue trunk. But I think I saw Mr. Munsen sitting on a painted chair one time, and I'm sure he had a few pretty dishes of his own. You know, he never did much like the food I cooked him. Said he preferred lutefisk, whatever that is."

"It is *torsk,* the codfish, soaked in lye."

"Lye? Lemme tell you somethin' now, *chére.* Lye will kill you!" Marie rocked a little faster, the coffee in her cup splashing from side to side. "You better not eat nothin' soaked in lye. Not even a codfish."

"But in Norway, lutefisk is —"

"You not in Norway, *chére.* You here now. You with us."

Frustrated, Astrid looked into Marie's

eyes. She understood now where Gage had come by that deep chocolate color — and how swiftly it could alter to a hard, impenetrable shade that revealed nothing. The moment the man had been able to rid himself of his unexpected visitors, he had returned to his own farm. He had not even bothered to bring her luggage himself, but he had sent the boatman, Gabriel, down the bayou with it to the elder Ancelets' home. Clearly Astrid made Gage uncomfortable, and she felt certain the reason was his own guilty knowledge of the truth about her husband's death.

Marie's eyes softened again as she reached out and patted Astrid's hand. "I never saw a young lady so flustered," she said. "Ever since you got here, you been wound up like a top. Now, you just settle down and relax. I'll take good care of you and that baby. I raised a son and four daughters right out here on this *galerie* — and I never lost a one. Drink some coffee. Lay your head back. Rest a spell."

Astrid let out a breath and closed her eyes. In her mind's eye she could see the solution to her problem — the wooden trunk her father had built for her when she was but a child. Her mother had painted it a soft grayed blue. Her oldest brother, a skilled artisan, had added the intricate and elaborately intertwined acanthus leaves, roots, branches, and flowers that were the hallmark of Norwegian rosemaling. On the front stretched a blank space into which Astrid had planned to paint the name of her husband and the date of their marriage.

Ole Munsen had sailed away with the trunk before she had time to complete the inscription. But Astrid knew the large wooden chest held the answer to her prayers. A secret panel inside the lid of the blue rosemaled trunk could be slid back to reveal a small niche. On the day before Ole's departure, Astrid's father secretly placed a solid gold filigree *sólje* brooch into the compartment. It was a gift, he told her. A memory of Norway that his beloved daughter should wear when she joined her husband in America.

Now Astrid understood how God had planned all along to rescue her. *Thank you, Father!* she prayed, peace filling her soul at the knowledge of the wonderful provision of both her earthly and her heavenly fathers. *Thank you, and forgive my lack of faith.* She would find the gold brooch, and she would sell it. Then her journey home could begin. All she had to do was locate the blue rosemaled trunk.

"Mrs. Ancelet, you must show me my husband's things," she exclaimed, standing suddenly from the rocking chair. "I have rested enough."

"*Oui, oui.*" Marie rose and shook out the folds of her skirt. "I could tell right off you weren't gonna give that nap but a minute."

"Surely we have been sitting nearly one hour."

"I don' much think about time, *chére*. Fact is, roun' here most folks take a slow pace. Kinda gives us time to appreciate the world God made. The moss, the live oak, the bayou — they take their growin' and movin' along in a leisurely manner. We don' put too much stock in possessions, either. Now, there's them that would disagree. Take Emile Fontenot. You ever heard of that Creole?"

Clenching her jaw, Astrid nodded. She knew her hostess was about to launch into another lengthy discourse that would further delay any search for the blue rosemaled trunk. "I have been told of the man," she said. "He lives across the river. Are my husband's things inside your house?"

"Emile Fontenot is busy like you," Marie drawled as she arranged her patched apron over the folds of her skirt. "Goin' here, goin' there, runnin' roun' and roun'. Lemme tell you, that man's gonna fluster himself into an early grave. And he *loves* his things. He gets on the train, takes himself over to Lafayette, Baton Rouge, even New Orleans once or twice a year. He comes back with crystal chandeliers, beds with curtains hangin' all roun', tables made outta marble, and statues of folks who ain' wearin' a stitch of clothes! Not a stitch!"

"He is a rich man," Astrid said. Though she didn't like it that Marie compared her to Mr. Fontenot in his busy and materialistic manner, she was pleased to have discovered her first prospective purchaser for the gold brooch. "Does Mr. Fontenot like jewelry?"

"*Mais oui!* Rings and cuff links and chains. But I can tell you things even more terrible than this." She leaned closer. "He brings women out to his house for the *visite*. City women. Men too. They all come for *bals de maison*, grand dances with food and music. They stay two weeks. Sometimes more."

The look in Marie's brown eyes told Astrid all she needed to know. Emile Fontenot's big mansion was considered the center of every vice, and the man was looked upon as wickedness itself. Had she any interest in this community, Astrid might have cared to learn more. But her goal was to leave as quickly as possible — and Mr. Fontenot might be her avenue to freedom.

"Fontenot has his eye on Gage's horses," Marie confided. "Everybody roun' here knows my son can work miracles with a horse. He's got a gentle hand, you know?"

Astrid nodded as she scooped up her son. Gage certainly had known how to calm Edvard. The memory of his big brown hand cupping the child's golden head flooded her heart. "Your son is kind to helpless ones, Mrs. Ancelet," she said.

"*Oui, chére.* Gage is the best boy a mama could ever wish for." Marie sighed. "If only I could get him to look roun' and see there's more important things than runnin' these two farms and takin' care of his horses. Ever since his wife and baby died in birthin', all that boy does is work, work, work."

"How long is he a widower?"

Marie's face sagged into lines of sorrow. "Many years now. He was just a boy — maybe nineteen or twenty — when his wife and the baby girl passed on. Now Gage is almost thirty. Alla time he works on the *vacherie* to fill up his loneliness. He don' do useless business like Fontenot, but hard, heavy work. I want Gage to find himself another wife. Have children. Oh, Gage would be a wonderful papa. But he waits. He tells me he's lookin'. Do you know that all my daughters are married? And Gage has danced barefoot at every wedding!"

"Today I saw his feet," Astrid said softly. "I believe your son has no shoes."

"Of course Gage has shoes. Lotsa shoes." Marie stomped into the house, suddenly obliging her guest to scurry to keep up. "Last year he bought himself a fine pair of boots in New Iberia. Don' you know why he has to dance barefoot?"

"No, Mrs. Ancelet. I know nothing of your customs." Astrid scanned the large, airy room. Chairs upholstered with animal skins, a rough-hewn table, and a spinning wheel stood near a tall stone fireplace that served as a cooking hearth. Wooden shelves held crockery dishes and preserved goods of all kinds. The white walls had been plastered with every sort of illustration imaginable — pictures, newspaper clippings, labels from perfume bottles, old calendar pages. On the fire, a large black cauldron bubbled with a spicy smelling soup. Astrid's stomach turned over in hunger.

"They call my Gage a slacker these days," Marie said. "They forget he had a wife a long time ago. If a Cajun ain' married before all the younger children is hitched up, people say they's a slacker. Everybody knows my Gage ain' a slacker 'bout nothin'. But when he has to dance barefoot, it makes me so mad I could just spit."

Astrid glanced over in surprise. Such an expression! These Cajuns were the roughest, most uncivilized people she could ever imagine. Perhaps Emile Fontenot was impatient and worldly, but at least the Creole gentleman had a sense of decorum. He had planted flowers in his urns, and he understood that a bed ought to be hung with curtains. These things were important, and Astrid felt all the more determined that Edvard should grow up in a society where he could learn proper manners and polite speech.

"I do not see the blue chest here, Mrs. Ancelet," she said. "Have you other rooms?"

"*Mais oui,* I have other rooms," Marie replied. "This is no simple *cabane.* My husband's father built it with his hands, and Pierre added the loft and the *galerie* in the back. This land has belonged to the Ancelet family since the first arrival from Acadia in the north. When Gage became a man, my husband divided his land into two farms, in our Cajun tradition. But then . . . then my beloved Pierre . . . one day last year he took sick. After that Pierre ain' been able to work the land like he used to. Now Gage runs both farms. Lemme tell you, that boy is a good son. The best. But I do long for the time when Pierre was fit . . . healthy . . . and Gage, he loves his papa. . . . Oh, it's a terrible thing to watch someone you love go down. . . ."

Astrid's desire to continue searching through the house was tempered by the sympathy she felt for the woman whose pain was so raw. She jiggled Edvard to calm him as Marie struggled to compose herself. How odd it was to see emotion displayed so openly. In Norway, Astrid's family and friends had kept their feelings under guard, fearful to reveal weakness by weeping too much or laughing too loud or shouting too angrily. But these Cajuns she had met were so bold with their joys and sorrows. Marie's tears trickled down her cheeks until Astrid could hardly contain her impulse to lend comfort.

"Perhaps your husband will grow better soon, Mrs. Ancelet," she said, setting the wriggly baby on the floor. She took a step closer and reached out to lay a hand on the woman's shoulder. "God will give you comfort."

"*Oui,* you're right," Marie cried, throwing her arms around Astrid and burying her face in the younger woman's shoulder. "Gage tells me alla time to give these worries to God, but I fear the day I lose my Pierre. Oh, I have my daughters and their babies all up and down the bayou, but they won' ever make up for the love of my Pierre. My beautiful Pierre! You must know what I feel, *chére,* losin' your husband as you did. It's that love, that precious love. . . . How can we ever get along without it?"

"The love is not . . ." Astrid held the trembling woman tightly as she searched for words. "Ole Munsen and I did not have the love of you and your husband. We marry for business, *ja?* The two papas make the marriage. Is for the farm and the fishing."

"Mais non!" Marie stepped back and took Astrid by the shoulders. "Then you ain' known the wondrous joy of real love. Lemme tell you, *chére,* when God puts two people together like he did Pierre and me, there's nothin' better in all the world. It's strong, you know. That kind of love can roll right over every problem that comes along in a family. And problems do come! Oh, they do! Fussy babies, nothin' to eat, maybe a fire or a flood, somebody gets bit by a snake — a husband gets sick. But when you got God's love pourin' down into your marriage, you gonna win. Pierre and I gonna be

in heaven one day, and that's the greatest comfort of my heart."

Astrid swallowed at the lump in her throat. "It sounds very nice, Mrs. Ancelet."

"Nice? Lemme tell you what I'm gonna do for you, *chére*. I'm gonna pray you find a good husband who loves you the way Pierre loves me. A boy like my Gage." She caught her breath. "Maybe you and Gage find love together, *oui?* He's such a fine man —"

"*Nei, jeg har* . . . I have . . . *annet å gjóre* . . . I have other things to do," Astrid fumbled. Oh, why did her English always fail her at the worst times? "I must not . . . cannot marry. I will go back to Norway."

Before Marie's plans could twist her into more knots, Astrid pulled away and hurried after Edvard. Marriage had not been a pleasurable experience, and she would never consider it again. Now she had her son to love and care for. Edvard would fill her heart, and the child would have to be enough.

She knelt and lifted her son away from the edge of a basket of kindling he was exploring. The very thought of marrying a man from this place filled Astrid with dread. No, she must find the blue trunk. She must get back to Norway.

"This is the room where Pierre and I

sleep," Marie was saying as she pushed open a door on the rear wall of the main room. "In the evenin', cool air blows straight through the house, front to back. You couldn' ask for a better place to live."

Astrid glanced into the room with its wooden bed and mosquito netting draped from a hook in the ceiling. A cursory survey told her there was nothing Norwegian among the sturdy cyprus chairs, chests, and footstools. Then Marie led her back onto the front *galerie* and up the outside stairway to the loft.

"My daughters used to sleep up here when they were little," Marie said as she and Astrid stepped into the room with its sloped ceiling. "We call this the *fillière* because of all the girls, you know. When Gage hired Ole Munsen to help Pierre with the farmin', we let him stay in the *fillière*. I ain' been up in years."

Her heart hammering, Astrid walked around the small, dimly lit space and searched for the object of her hope. A row of low beds had been built for the Ancelet daughters. Ole had probably slept in one of them. Strange to think of him living in such a place. Again she wondered why he had come to this sultry land. Why had he chosen this place to forge the future of his family?

Astrid could not fathom her husband's reasoning.

"Mrs. Ancelet," she said evenly. "Do you know how my husband died?"

The woman shrugged and shook her head. "Gage told us it happened over in New Iberia. It was an accident, I think. *Non* . . . maybe something else. I'm not sure, *chére*. Ole Munsen was gone a lot. We hardly ever saw him. This may pain you to hear, but you might as well know your husband didn' pull his weight roun' the farm. His heart wasn' in it, you know. He liked the town much better."

Astrid pondered this revelation as she walked around the room. Against one wall stood two of the smaller trunks Ole had taken with him from Norway. Both had been painted with bright rosemaling, but neither contained the secret niche. Astrid lifted the lid of the brown trunk and ran her hands over blankets and sheets that she and her mother had carefully stitched through the winters of many years. Beneath them lay a feather bed, goose-down pillows, and even a small rug.

"Mrs. Ancelet, what did my husband do when he went into the town?" she asked. "Please, you must tell me the truth."

The older woman busied herself straightening her apron. "Ole Munsen first came down the Mississippi to Louisiana on one of those boats, you know. Those boats where folks . . ." She motioned with her hands as if she could explain without words. "And anybody who wanna keep on with that kind of thing can just go into town, you know. . . . *Mais,* you better ask Gage to tell you alla story. He knows everything."

"*Ja,* I believe he does." Astrid bent over the second trunk, a deep red color. Inside, she found her dishes — wooden bowls her brother had carved and painted, pottery, utensils, and iron cooking pots. Some of the clothing she had packed away was still wrapped in linen. Under the dishes lay a stack of white aprons, two wool skirts, and five embroidered blouses.

"I will take these things with me when I go," she said. "I can use them in my home in Norway."

"There's that painted chair I remembered." Marie pointed toward a corner of the room.

"*Ja,* my father made this chair. Is a good one. He will enjoy to see it again when I return to Norway."

"I reckon so." Marie made a turn around the room. "But . . . I don' see that blue trunk."

Astrid swallowed. "No. It is not here."

She fell silent as she stood in the cool upper room holding her son and staring at a patch of sunlight on the floor. Selling the two trunks and all the possessions inside them would not give her the money to get even halfway home. She and Edvard would barely make it to New Orleans, let alone across the Atlantic Ocean.

Had her hope of rescue been just an illusion? Had God deserted her after all? Was she as truly alone as she felt?

"Why don' you come on downstairs, *chére?*" Marie's soft voice broke into her thoughts. "I can hear Pierre comin' in from the field. He always whistles a little tune, you know. You gonna like my husband. You rest a while with us, and you'll start to feel better. Couple days from now, everybody roun' this part of the bayou goin' over to the *fais do-do* and dance a little, sing a little, eat some gumbo. You come with us and have some fun."

Astrid shook her head. "No gumbo."

"Ever tasted it?"

"No, but —"

"*Mais non!*" Marie's face broke into the same dimpled grin her son displayed. She swept Edvard from Astrid's arms and gave the baby a loud kiss on the cheek. "God has blessed us so much! Here in Louisiana we have the *joie de vivre,* you know? We love life! We love to be happy the way the good Lord intended."

Linking an arm through Astrid's, the older woman turned her toward the stairs. "Tonight, you gonna taste my jambalaya I got cookin' on the stove," Marie went on. "You gonna taste Cajun. You gonna taste love!"

"But, please —"

"Maybe Gage will come over. As we say here on the bayou, you and Eddie, Pierre and me, we gonna *passer un bon temps!*" Laughing, Marie urged her guest down the steps. "We gonna have us a good time!"

<hr />

After two frustrating days in which she watched life move as slowly as the bayou outside, Astrid had come no closer to finding a way home to Norway. Though she had visited Ole Munsen's grave, and she had finally accepted that her husband was truly gone, she felt greater turmoil than ever. No one around her seemed the least bit ruffled by their unexpected and clearly discontented guest. Marie meandered around the house, sweeping a little, occasionally tossing something into the pot on the stove, and sitting long hours on the *galerie* with her black coffee. Pierre came and went from the fields, always whistling as though nothing troubled him. Gage appeared now and again, played with the baby, stirred his mother's gumbo, spoke a few words to Astrid, and then vanished. These Cajuns were nothing like her bustling, energetic Norwegian family.

The night had cooled as Astrid sat in the main room of the little house and watched Edvard stacking and tumbling a collection of blocks that Pierre Ancelet had brought in from his woodshed earlier that evening. Citing exhaustion and a need to think about her future, she had declined to accompany Marie and Pierre to the dance this evening. They had been unable to convince their guest even to set foot outside, and so they had gone without her. But now Astrid regretted the loss of their company. The silent house, the creeping shadows, and the eerie noises from the trees and river outside intensified her loneliness.

But what else could she have done? It wouldn't be proper to go off to a dancing party. She couldn't leave Edvard here alone, and she certainly couldn't take him into the midst of a crowd of strangers, exposing him to foreign sounds and smells — perhaps even to dangerous diseases. Responsibility demanded that she separate herself and remain aloof from anything that could cause further problems for herself and the child.

Astrid folded her hands and tried to pray. God could see the past, present, and future. He must have known she would find herself in this predicament — surely he did not expect her to stay here. He had created her so different from these people. He had prepared her for another sort of life. She was Norwegian! She loved cold weather, snow, huge pine trees, and food that didn't burn your tongue going down. These Cajuns with their swampy river and their *joie de vivre* were too unusual to comprehend. Certainly God expected his children to love one another, but he couldn't expect them to mingle in such a close fashion. Could he?

A loud thump on the *galerie* sent Astrid's heart into her throat. She stared up at the rifle hanging over the door and realized she had no idea how to load or shoot it. "Edvard!" she whispered, kneeling beside the baby. "Come to your *mor!*"

"Miz Munsen, you in there?"

It was Gage Ancelet's voice. Crouching on the floor, Astrid gathered her son into her lap and wrapped both arms around him. "I am here," she called.

"Evenin'." The door swung open, and the man stepped into the lamplit room. Tall, dressed in a white shirt and dark trousers, Gage turned his focus on the pair huddled in the center of the room. His glossy black curls gleamed as he knelt and held out his arms. "Eddie, my little *beignet!* How are you tonight?"

With a coo of delight, the baby pushed out of his mother's lap and crawled across the floor. Gage picked him up and swung him into the air. "What you doin' here alone with your mama, boy? Don' you wanna come dance with me? See alla pretty little girls?"

"Edvard is tired," Astrid said. The baby's bright blue eyes and happy giggle belied every word. "And . . . and I need to pray."

"Pray?" Gage's smile carved deep dimples in his cheeks. "I didn' know you were a godly woman, Miz Munsen."

"Why not?" She clutched the small silver cross that hung from a chain around her neck. Wasn't her faith obvious?

"Me too," he said. "I bought a little Bible over in New Iberia. Been readin' it front to back alla time. Romans, these days. You ever read that book? Lemme tell you, that fella Paul knew some things. He's talkin' about sin and faith. Jew and Gentile." Gage laughed. "It's like Norway and Louisiana, *non?* So much between you and me is different, but I reckon since we got the same Father we're the same inside. In the heart, you know?"

Astrid nodded numbly. The very sight of her golden-haired, sapphire-eyed son so happy in the brawny brown arms of this Cajun showed how little such differences mattered. To Edvard, Gage Ancelet was warm, strong, and fun. That he ate gumbo, lived beside a swampy river, and spoke in muddled French was of no importance at all. Christ had said we must become like children. . . .

"Paul talks about some mighty strange things, too," Gage said. "Like the beautiful feet of those who come to bring good news." With a chuckle, he lifted a muddy boot. "Not too beautiful, but I got some news for you anyway, *chére*. I come alla way back here to take you and Eddie to the *fais do-do.*"

"Oh, but I cannot go." Astrid knotted her fingers. "I told your mother and father —"

"*Mais oui,* but they forget how it feels to sit around lonely. Not me. I know all about it, and I don' wanna leave you here by yourself."

"But Eddie — Edvard —"

"The boy comes too! Roun' here everybody goes dancin'. The children, the parents, even the dogs join in. Don' you know what *fais do-do* means? It's a kind of Cajun baby talk, you know? *Fais do-do* means, 'Shh, go to sleep.' We have a room roun' the back we call *le parc aux petits* with beds for the babies. Nobody gets left out, especially not a widow just arrive for a *visite*. Come on with me, Miz Munsen. You gonna have fun."

"I am very hot in your country, Mr. Ancelet. I cannot think about dancing."

"You better take off alla that wool you got on. I don' recollect that we ever had snow on the bayou, and I reckon it's not gonna start tonight. Go on up to the *fillière* and put on somethin' cool. Eddie and I, we'll wait for you on the *galerie*." As before, he stretched out his hand to her. "Lemme help you, *chére*."

Filled with confusion, Astrid placed her hand in his and gathered her skirts. As she rose from the floor, she met the man's deep brown eyes. Was Gage Ancelet as good and kind as he seemed? Or did he know secrets about her husband's death, as she had imagined? Most important, could she trust him to help her find a way home to Norway?

"I will go with you, Mr. Ancelet," she said, deciding suddenly. Perhaps in a lighter atmosphere she could convince Gage to tell her the whole truth about her husband, his fascination with towns and boats, and his untimely death.

As she left the main room and climbed the *galerie* staircase to the loft where she would sleep, the thought of dancing brought mingled excitement and trepidation to her heart. In Norway, she had loved the festive celebrations and holidays. But here . . . in the heat . . . with Gage Ancelet . . .

Astrid opened the trunk she had brought with her from home and took out a summer-weight skirt of deep forest green, a clean white shirt, and an embroidered red bodice. As she dressed, tied on her apron, and gave her wavy hair a fresh braid, she caught herself idly wondering what Gage Ancelet thought of her appearance. Did her long golden hair seem as foreign to him as his thick black curls did to her? Did her pale skin, blue eyes, and high cheekbones repel him? Or did her features fascinate him — as his did her?

Flushing at the very thought of his strong arms slipping around her on a dance floor, Astrid pressed her fingertips against her temples. She had known she was a widow but a few days, and already her focus had wandered from the loss of her husband to the intriguing presence of another man. This could not be right. God would not be pleased.

On the other hand, she had hardly lived as Ole Munsen's wife before he sailed away to the New World. He had left her pregnant and without income; he had written her but two letters in all the months apart; and then he somehow had managed to die. To mourn such a man for months on end would be dishonest. And no matter the circumstance, Astrid always lived in truth.

She started down the stairs again. What was true now in her life? Hesitating, she listened to the sound of Gage Ancelet's deep male voice humming a French lullaby to little Edvard. A man who could catch a fish with his bare hands, a man who could manage two farms at the same time, a man who could turn a baby's whimpers into giggles . . . such a man could not be all bad, no matter how strangely he spoke or what he chose to eat or what he might know about the life and death of Ole Munsen.

Gage's words echoed through Astrid's thoughts, "Lemme help you, *chére.* . . ." She recalled the way his thumb had caressed her damp foot, the way his shoulders strained the seams of his shirt, the way his dimples transformed his face, and her heart began a languid dance of its own.

Astrid whirled around on the staircase and raced back into the *fillière*. Throwing open her trunk lid, she pulled out a carved mirror and pinched her cheeks until they were pink. Then she tugged wisps of curly hair from her braid to soften her features with the tendrils. She dug around in the trunk until she found a bottle of scent. Carefully, she touched the fragrance to her neck and wrists.

Drinking down a deep breath of humid air, she squared her shoulders. *"So much between you and me is different,"* Gage Ancelet had said, *"but we're the same inside. In the heart, you know."*

Could the God who reigned in Astrid's soul live also in Gage's? Could she let go of her worries and trust the Lord to guide her through her predicament? Was it possible that God could take this confusion and create from it something wonderful?

The very idea was so different, so fascinating that Astrid shivered in spite of the heat as she set off down the stairs to meet her escort to the dance. It was time to see if she could find the *joie de vivre*.

Chapter Three

"Kick off your shoes," Gage called over his shoulder as he led Astrid into the large hall that served as a gathering place for the Cajun community up and down the bayou. The room was filled with his friends and relatives, all dressed in their bright party best. Those too old or too young to step out on the dance floor had joined the gathering to sample the good food and music. Gage bent over and started to tug off his boots, glad to be rid of the heavy footwear. When he noticed that the band was faltering and the dancers had stopped, he straightened. What had caused a hush to fall over the crowded room?

"It is I," Astrid whispered, pressing close against his side. "I am a stranger. They stare at me."

"*Mais,* they better mind their manners," he murmured back. Then he raised his voice. "Everybody, we got Miz Astrid Munsen here for a *visite.* She's the widow of Ole Munsen who worked for my parents. She comes alla way from Norway, and she don' talk English as good as we do, so be nice, *non?* And this here's Baby Eddie."

He took the little boy from Astrid's arms, lifted him over his shoulders, and danced around in a circle. If anything could win these people past their inherent distrust of strangers it was a child. Sure enough, in a moment half the women in the room swarmed over to ooh and ahh at the baby's gold hair and blue eyes. Eager to fuss over him, they smiled and nodded at Astrid and reached for the child.

"Is OK?" Gage asked Astrid. "They gonna pass Eddie roun' and play with him till he gets so tired he falls straight to sleep."

She nodded uncertainly. "But if he cries —"

"They'll feed him a little *couche-couche,* don' you worry." He slipped his arm around her shoulders as the loud music started up again. "Mama said you ain't been eatin' much since you came, *chére.* You gotta be hungry. Come on over and try some gumbo."

"No, thank you." Her blue eyes flashed. "We do not eat such a soup in Norway. The sausage, the chicken, the fish all mixed together is not good for the stomach. And when I smell, I think you have put many spices into the pot. I use only a little salt to cook our food. Maybe some butter."

"Your tongue's been sleepin', *chère*," Gage said. He steered her through the swirling, colorful throng of dancers toward huge cast iron pots that stood over the fire. Bubbling red beans and rice, jambalaya, and *court bouillon* filled the room with the aroma of heaven itself. "You taste some of this *gumbo filé*, you gonna wake up to what's really good, and you ain' never gonna go back to the old way. Here's a bowl, a spoon, and a glass of root beer to cool you down."

"I do not drink beer, Mr. Ancelet." Raising both hands as if to ward off the evils of Cajun cuisine, Astrid shook her head. "Strong drink is not good, and wine is a mocker. The Bible says this."

"Root beer is made outta sassafras, *chère*. It don' have a drop of alcohol in it." He dipped a spoonful of gumbo and held it out to the woman. She leaned toward it, sniffed, and took a half step backward.

"In Norway, we eat mostly white food," she said, her eyes on the spoon as if in fear he might slip it into her mouth. "*Lefse* is made of white potatoes. *Lutefisk* is the white codfish. Our cake is white, our porridge is white, even our meatballs are cooked in white cream. Please, Mr. Ancelet, I cannot eat this gumbo."

Gage looked down at the spoon and tried

to imagine his world through Astrid's blue eyes. Dancing with babies, going barefoot, eating cayenne peppers might seem strange to her — as strange as wearing a tightly laced bodice, wooden clogs, and wool stockings seemed to him.

"It's OK," he said with a shrug, turning the spoon toward his own mouth.

"Wait." Her hand clamped down on his wrist. "*Ja ja,* I try." In one gulp, she downed the spicy liquid, bits of okra, and chunks of crawfish. Her eyes went as wide as a pair of blue china teacups. A scarlet flush spread up her neck and onto her cheeks. Beads of perspiration popped out across her forehead.

"Give me root beer!" she gasped, grabbing the glass from his hand. In three swallows, she drained it. "Is very spicy," she panted. "Very hot."

"You OK?"

She moistened her lips. "I think . . . *ja,* is good gumbo."

She allowed Gage to fill her bowl and seat her at a table among a group of old men telling Cajun tall tales and jokes. At first her bites were small and her sips of root beer frequent. But the more she ate, and the redder her face grew, the more she relaxed.

"I will take off my shoes now," she announced, setting the empty bowl into a wash bucket. She flashed him a broad smile. *"Ja vel,* I think now I am little bit Cajun . . . *non?"*

"Mais oui," he said. *"Ja."*

Entranced, Gage waited as Astrid stepped into a corner away from the crowd to slip off her heavy wooden clogs and discreetly roll down her wool stockings. Would he have had the courage to taste codfish soaked in lye, the food his mother had informed him Norwegians ate? Would he have forced himself to survive on white foods with no flavor, the way Astrid had made up her mind to eat brightly colored dishes with too much flavor? He could not say he would fare as well as she, and he didn't know many who would. Certainly her husband had not.

"May I have this dance?" he asked, slipping his arm through hers.

"You will have to teach me, Mr. Ancelet. In Norway, we play the violin, but it does not sound this way. Also, we do not make music with accordion or triangle — and certainly not with spoons and washboard."

Gage could see she was trying her best not to giggle at the assortment of instruments the band was using. He pulled her close and led her onto the floor. As he turned her into the dance circle, he put his lips against her ear and said, "It's OK to laugh, Astrid. On the bayou, we look for the good God gave us in this life. We laugh alla time. You know what we say? *Laissez les bons temps rouler* — let the good times roll."

"*Mais oui!*" she said.

Out of breath, Astrid leaned against a rough wooden post and sipped from a glass of root beer. She had been to countless celebrations of *Syttende Mai,* Norway's Constitution Day, with its parades and fireworks. She had enjoyed Midsummer's Eve bonfires by the fjord. And she had watched her father tie a Christmas tree to his fishing boat's mast for *Jul.* During all these holidays, she and her Norwegian friends had feasted and danced. But never once had she taken off her shoes, unbraided her hair, and whirled around and around for no other reason than *joie de vivre.*

Hours ago she had laid Edvard in a cradle in the back room. A bevy of grandmas that included Marie Ancelet sipped coffee and gossiped as they rocked the children to sleep. In the main room, Astrid had danced with more men than she could imagine living on the swampy bayou. Gage had claimed her twice as often as any other, and in between the dances, he escorted her around the room introducing her to everybody. Altogether, she felt flushed and exhausted — and happier than she'd been in years.

"Miz Munsen," Gage called out, hauling a strapping younger fellow across the room by a suspender. "I want you to meet Revon Bouleur. He's the brother of my sister's husband. You remember Gloria, the second youngest? She's married to Bernard Bouleur. Now Revon, he works over on the farm of Jacques Domengeaux, who's my father's cousin by marriage."

Astrid covered her mouth with her hand to keep her lips from twitching. "Mr. Ancelet, I have come to believe that everyone in this room is somehow your relative."

He looked around as though pondering this concept. "You know, *chére*, you might be right on that one. Anyway, Revon asked me if it'd be all right to dance with you, but I told him he's too young. What do you think?"

Shaking the boy's hand, Astrid gave him a warm smile. "Roun' the bayou, everybody dances," she said, mimicking Gage's lazy accent the best she could. "The children, the parents, even the dogs join in."

"You makin' fun of me now?" he asked, his brown eyes glowing.

"Me? *Mais non!*" She linked her arm through Revon's and started for the dance floor.

They were halfway across the room when the young man suddenly tensed. "Wait, Miz Munsen. We got a visitor."

All attention turned toward the front door, and the crowd fell silent a second time that night. In an instant, Gage was at Astrid's side. He wrapped a protective arm around her and motioned Revon away.

A brown-haired gentleman with long sideburns and a thick mustache stepped into the hall. Two men joined him, one at each side, while a third waited behind in the shadows. The first lifted his beaver skin top hat and gave a practiced bow. *"Bon soir, mesdames et messieurs,"* he said in a cultured French accent. Astrid knew immediately this must be Emile Fontenot, the Creole landowner who lived across the bayou from Gage.

"Evenin' Fontenot." Gage squared his shoulders. "What brings you to the *fais do-do?*"

"Am I not welcome among my neighbors?" The man sniffed. "My friends and I were out riding this evening. We crossed the bayou upstream, heard the music, and thought we'd drop by."

"You're welcome anytime — long as you don' try to *faire le macaque*."

"It is you Cajuns who make monkey-shines." The Creole's pale green eyes focused on Astrid. "I see you have other visitors. A most enchanting addition to your gathering." He waved a gloved hand. "Carry on, please."

After a nod from Gage, the music resumed, and dancers moved back onto the floor. Revon started for Astrid, but Gage's brief signal sent him away to find another partner. Astrid sensed tension between Emile Fontenot and Gage, and curiosity kept her from heading for the back room to check on Edvard.

"Ancelet, will you step outside with me?" Fontenot asked, indicating the door. "I wish to speak with you in private."

Gage eyed the Creole's three husky companions. "You bringin' your friends along?"

"*Oui*, and you may bring yours." He gave Astrid a smile. "Madame, may I have the pleasure of your acquaintance?"

"I am Mrs. Astrid Munsen." Embarrassed at her disheveled appearance, she pushed her hair behind her shoulders as she extended her hand. "I come from Norway."

"Such a long journey!" Fontenot took her fingers, bent over, and lightly kissed the back of her hand. "Welcome to Louisiana."

Discomfited at the man's gallantry, Astrid glanced up at Gage. His brown eyes were as hard as stone, and his grip on her shoulder felt like a vise. As the group exited onto the long *galerie,* she wished she had not discarded her shawl along with her clogs. Even though the night was all but suffocating and Gage's arm stayed firm around her, she felt suddenly vulnerable. The last thing she desired was to be caught in the midst of trouble.

"I'll come directly to the heart of the matter," Fontenot said, taking a long brown cigar from the pocket of his frock coat. "Have you considered my offer regarding Petit Noir, Ancelet?"

"There's nothin' to consider. I told you that already. 'Tit Noir is not for sale."

Astrid glanced at the row of horses hitched to the long porch rail that lined the *galerie.* Petit Noir was Gage's black stallion, the horse on which he had brought her and Edvard to the dance. Gage was understandably proud of the creature, and on their trip to the *fais do-do* he had told Astrid the horse's history. Named after a tiny cup of black coffee, Petit Noir had grown into a masterpiece of muscle and speed. Gage's devotion to the stallion had been evident from the moment Astrid set foot in the stirrup.

"I repeat my counteroffer, Fontenot," Gage said. "It's a good one, a benefit to both of us. You send Papillon over to my place, and I'll put her in the breedin' barn with 'Tit Noir. The first foal is mine, the next one is yours. It's a fair deal."

"*Au contraire.* With each year, Papillon is older and the risk of failure grows. Why should I give you the first foal? What if she has no more?"

"Life is a risk, Fontenot."

So this was about horses. Astrid had seen Norwegian men in similar debates, and it intrigued her to realize that — despite customs and languages that might separate them — people were not so very different. Eating, drinking, dancing, doing business, working hard, making marriages, and rearing children kept people busy from Norway to Louisiana. Even more intriguing, Astrid realized that during the debate it had come to matter to her which of these men prevailed. Instinctively, she had taken the side of Gage Ancelet.

"You need the money," Fontenot was saying. "You have two farms to run and nobody to help you. Take my offer, Ancelet."

"Take mine, Fontenot."

"How can you be so stubborn? You have

many other horses, and I know you can train them to round up your cattle. But it's a shame to waste the talent of Petit Noir on a prairie *vacherie.* He can have a great future if you'll sell him to me. I'll see he's well treated. With the money I pay, you can buy another stallion and several mares. It's a good offer, *non?*"

Gage waved away the cloud of smoke from his opponent's cigar. "You can make no offer I will accept, Fontenot. 'Tit Noir stays with me. But if you want to send Papillon over to my *vacherie,* I'll look after her. I'll even train your foal. A better deal you won' find anywhere. Think about it."

Without waiting for the Creole to give him an answer, Gage turned Astrid toward the door. "Come on, *chére,* it's time we roun' up the old folks and Eddie."

"Mrs. Munsen," Fontenot called, "I believe I have something that belonged to your late husband. If you will do me the honor of a *visite,* I'm sure we can arrange something. I'm afraid I'll be away for a couple of weeks. At end of the month, perhaps?"

"Something of Ole's?"

"*Oui.* Nothing important, but perhaps you would find it of sentimental interest. I would be honored to show it to you. Will you come?"

Was it possible Fontenot had the blue trunk?

Astrid glanced at Gage. Despite the affinity she felt for this man, if Emile Fontenot had the trunk and brooch, she could pay her passage back to Norway. God had given her a responsibility to Edvard, to her family, even to the memory of Ole. A woman could not dance away her life, could she?

"Thank you, sir," she said. "If I am still in Louisiana, I will come to your home on the last day of this month."

"What?" Gage exploded. "You ain' goin' over there, Astrid. Fontenot is a man who —"

"Ancelet, why should she believe anything you tell her about me?" the Creole cut in. "It's obvious to everyone which of us is the better educated, the more mannerly, the wealthier. While you're some mixture of French with Indian, German, Spanish — who knows what? — I'm pure French. We were born on the same bayou, but we're worlds apart. You'll never besmirch my character with anything you say. I am — and I always will be — your superior. *Bon soir.*"

Tipping his hat, Fontenot stepped off the *galerie* and, with his three companions, vanished into the darkness. Astrid stiffened, stunned by the Creole's insults to her escort.

"I am sorry —" she began.

"Don' worry, *chére.*" He touched her under the chin. "It's not a problem."

"But I am your guest. I should not go against your wishes."

"My guest, *oui,* but not my slave." As they reentered the hall and Gage started through the crowd toward his father, he glanced over his shoulder and gave her that dimpled grin. "You do whatever you want, *chére.* I'm gonna trust God keeps your blue eyes open wide. You'll see the truth between me and Fontenot."

Truth? What was the truth? Astrid pondered the question as she gathered up her shoes and stockings, fetched the sleeping Edvard from the back room, and helped to settle the baby with Pierre and Marie Ancelet in their small carriage. As Gage lifted her onto Petit Noir's back and climbed up behind her, she felt no nearer an answer.

Everything seemed upside down. She had planned to isolate herself in her husband's new home, to create a little Norway in America. It was to have been a place where her children could grow up with the same values — even the same food, furniture, and clothing — she had known as a girl. She expected to brush against the language and culture of her American neighbors, but she would never join them in any real way.

Could it be that this plan had evaporated with a bowl of hot gumbo and the music of a washboard? Astrid leaned back, and her head came to rest against Gage Ancelet's broad chest. She jerked upright again. Was she losing her senses? Had exhaustion and desperation driven her half mad? Could the mere presence of a strong-shouldered man shatter every concept she had held to be true?

What was truth? If she clung to the illusion that all things Norwegian were superior, she was like Emile Fontenot with his claim of French purity. *Dear God, can you understand my confusion? Do you know what it means to leave one world and enter another? — a place you don't belong?* The answer was so obvious, Astrid laughed aloud.

"Somethin' funny, *chére?*" Gage said.

"I was thinking about Jesus," she said, "how he left heaven and came to earth."

"I never thought of that as a real knee-slapper myself."

"But he is just like I am in this. Do you not see it? Christ left his home and traveled to a new place, very different, sometimes difficult. He did not reject the land or the people."

"*Mais non,* he loved us."

Astrid swallowed hard as Gage's words sank in. Could she ever open her heart wide enough to love these people of the bayou as Christ loved them? Again, the answer stood out as brightly as the moon in the night sky overhead.

Already she had come to care about Marie Ancelet and feel invested in her world. Would Marie lose her beloved Pierre? Could she survive without her husband? Astrid had adored Pierre immediately with his long white mustaches, gnarled hands, and gently whistled tunes. All the cousins, aunts, uncles, and babies at the *fais do-do* had endeared themselves to the stranger in their midst. And Gage Ancelet? The moment he lifted Edvard into the air on the bayou dock, she had felt some unexplainable sense of connection with the man.

"Mr. Ancelet," she said, turning her head until she could see his face, "one thing confuses me still. Why did my husband choose to live with you? What did he find that caused him to love this bayou? And please . . . you must tell me . . . how did Ole die?"

Gage fell silent. The sound of the horse's hooves on the spongy path mingled with the song of cicadas and the hum of night insects. A fog had slipped inland, its white fingers twining through the moss that hung from the live oaks. Keenly aware of Gage's presence, Astrid realized she was almost breathless to hear the sound of his voice. The thought that he might take her hand again or touch her hair sent a shiver of anticipation through her. Why had she never felt this with any other man? Why now? Why *him?*

"Ole Munsen came down the Mississippi on a boat," Gage said.

"Your mother told me this." Astrid recalled the woman's efforts to convey a message without words. "What kind of a boat was it?"

"*Mais,* it was a . . . a pleasure boat." He paused and drew hard on the reins as a group of riders emerged from the trees onto the path. The nearest wore a top hat and tails. "Fontenot, what you want now?"

"A wager," the Creole said. "A race to the bayou. Winner takes all."

Gage gave a grunt of disgust. "I don' make wagers with anybody, Fontenot. I ain' gonna give up 'Tit Noir so you can run him at the tracks and take other folks' money, and I got Miz Munsen here, besides."

"Let's see what that stallion of yours can do, Ancelet. I think all the talk I've been hearing is just that. Talk. Give him free rein, and if he can beat my Capitaine, I'll hand you the finest horse you ever saw."

"I'm ridin' the finest horse I ever saw," Gage said. "Go on, now."

"What do you boys say?" Fontenot turned to his companions. "Don't you think we ought to have a race?"

As if that were a signal, one of the men jabbed the black stallion's flank with a sharpened stick. With a whinny, the horse reared, his legs pawing the air. Gage leaned hard against Astrid, holding tight as he struggled to control his mount. The moment the stallion's hooves hit the ground, he bolted.

Flung forward across 'Tit Noir's neck, Astrid grabbed handfuls of black mane. She could hear the other men laughing, the thunder of hooves, the screech of startled birds in the trees overhead. Beneath her, the stallion had erupted into a machine of muscle and bone, pumping hard, blowing steam, hurtling down the path like a runaway locomotive.

"Go, Ancelet!" Fontenot cried as his own stallion galloped past 'Tit Noir. "Don't let me win, *caouane!*"

"Turtle!" someone shouted from behind. *"Caouane!"*

"Don' worry, *chére*," Gage said through gritted teeth. "I ain' gonna let you fall."

Astrid had ridden her father's plodding

plow horse, but never had she felt anything like this burst of pure energy racing uncontrolled through the trees. As if by some magic, Gage gradually harnessed the horse's power, guided the creature onto sure ground, and transformed the heedless flight into a flat-out, streamlined sprint toward the bayou. In a moment, 'Tit Noir nipped at Capitaine's heels. Then they galloped side by side. Finally the black stallion surged ahead, thundering down the open road.

"Yah!" Gage shouted as he pulled the horse to a prancing halt at the edge of his dock. "Yah, 'Tit Noir, good boy! You all right, Miz Munsen?"

Astrid sat up and tried to catch her breath. "Fontenot," she said, puffing, "he will try to fight you. He will take the horse."

"Ah, look at him comin' now. Hey, Fontenot! What happened to your horse? A turtle spooked Capitaine or somethin'?"

Gage's laughter filled his chest, and Astrid could hardly keep from letting out a cheer of victory. The Creole chuckled as he guided his own stallion to the dock.

"*Oui*, Ancelet," Fontenot said. "You beat me fair and square. I never saw such a horse. Petit Noir belongs in a fine stable like mine. What do you say I up the price? Maybe double?"

"You think I'm gonna give up 'Tit Noir who can carry two riders and still outrace your best horse? Not for double or triple, Fontenot. Go on home and pour yourself a cup of strong coffee. You better wake up and see what's what."

Fontenot shook his head. "You're more stubborn than I am, Cajun. And a lot more foolish. But I tell you what now, you won the race, and I'm a man of my word." He dismounted. "Winner takes all. Here's Capitaine."

Astrid gaped as the man held out the reins to the beautiful roan stallion. Gage whistled. "Pretty horse, Fontenot," he said, "but no thanks. I got a fine stallion already, huh? Tell you what, though. You bring Papillon across the river and let me breed her with 'Tit Noir. Then we'll have us a deal."

The Creole appeared to ponder this for a moment. Then he shook his head. "No deal. Capitaine or nothing, Ancelet."

"Good night, Fontenot." Gage turned the horse in the direction of his house. "And tell your *camarades* anybody gets a stick in the back end next time, it's gonna be them."

"I'll see you at the end of the month, Mrs. Munsen!" Fontenot called out. "Come on the thirtieth at four in the afternoon. We'll

430

have tea in my gazebo."

Before Astrid could respond, Gage guided 'Tit Noir onto the narrow trail that led to his parents' home. "Papa's gonna be tryin' to figure out where we are in a minute," he said. "He'll have turned the carriage off on a side road back a ways. They won' know what to think."

"Edvard will wonder where I am. I must put him into his bed myself."

"*Oui, chére.*" He chuckled. "That baby was the star of the show tonight. Everybody loved him. Me especially. You know somethin' else, Miz Munsen? You're a fine dancer. You gotta nice way of steppin' out there on the floor."

Confused as to the proper response to this bold compliment, Astrid resorted to smoothing out her skirt. How wonderful it must be to have the freedom to say exactly what you felt. Gage loved Edvard. He thought Astrid was a wonderful dancer. What would she say if she could find the courage to speak her thoughts?

She studied the strong brown hands that gripped the horse's reins. *Those are beautiful hands,* she would say. *I love your hardworking hands, Gage Ancelet. I love your people and your food and your music. I love —*

"My words embarrass you?" Gage asked.

431

"In my family, we do not often speak our thoughts aloud."

"Why not?"

Astrid pondered the question. "Perhaps we are afraid we will say too much."

"I don' know what's too much. A person oughta say what's on his mind. It clears the air, you know. If I don' tell you I'm crazy about that baby boy, you'll never know it. If I don' tell you I like the way you dance, and I think your hair is the prettiest I ever saw on a woman, maybe you'll go back to Norway and never hear the truth." He lifted a strand of wavy golden hair. "When I first saw you, *chére,* I thought your hair was a glowing light. I thought maybe you were an angel. And now I know I was right."

Astrid caught her breath and squeezed the clumps of black mane in her fingers. "In the Bible, God sends angels with messages for his people. I am not an angel. And I think God's message comes from you to me, Mr. Ancelet."

"What can you learn from me? Not much besides how to cook a good gumbo, make some root beer, dance a few Cajun waltzes."

"Exactly," Astrid said. "You teach me to open my heart and see others with the eyes of God. You teach me to laugh. And you teach me to speak my own feelings."

"What are your feelin's, Astrid?"

Aware the conversation had slipped into an intimate tone, she struggled to bring it back to a polite distance. "I feel confused why you did not take Capitaine from Mr. Fontenot. He is a good horse."

"And the first day that stallion turns up in my barn, Fontenot's gonna haul me off to jail for a horse rustler. *Mais oui,* it's true. You don' know that Creole like I know him. He's a clever man. He wants to run 'Tit Noir on the track, make himself some money. If he can find a way to get his hands on my horse, he'll do it."

"I think you want to put your hands on his mare Papillon."

"She's a beauty. She comes from a line of fine quarter horses that are good racers and even better workers. If I could breed her with 'Tit Noir, whose ancestors have lived in Louisiana since who knows when, then I'd have my dream — beautiful horses with the hardiness to survive in our climate. They'd sell well. I could set Mama up for the rest of her life. I could hire some hands to work Papa's farm. But it ain' gonna happen. Fontenot will make sure of that."

"Maybe you are right." Astrid shook her head. "But still I must go to his house. If I am ever to get money for my journey to

Norway, I must speak with Mr. Fontenot. Perhaps he has what belongs to me. And if I can sell it, I can pay for my passage."

Gage was silent as the stallion approached the *cabane* where Marie and Pierre Ancelet stood waiting. In the moonlight, Astrid could see little Edvard — awake again — perched in the old man's arms. Her responsibility for her son all but overwhelmed her. She must not be swayed by an evening of fun and dancing. She must choose Edvard's needs above her own "feelings." The boy deserved an education, a loving family, strong traditions, and the certainty of God in his life.

This bayou *joie de vivre* allured Astrid. Gage Ancelet's deep, languid voice stirred her. But God had given her a child, and she must think of Edvard's future rather than her own.

"I reckon I'd do most anythin' I could for you, *chére*," Gage said. He stopped the horse and climbed down from his place beside Astrid. When he lifted his arms to her, she slid down into his embrace. Though his parents were watching, he held her for a moment. "I'd do most anythin' but find you a way to leave this bayou."

She glanced up into his brown eyes and read the earnest passion in them. Then he tossed his arm around her shoulders and whistled up at the trio on the *galerie.*

"Eddie, my little *beignet!*" he called, striding toward the steps. "You shoulda see your mama ridin' 'Tit Noir! She's quite a woman, *n'est-ce pas?* Quite a woman!"

Chapter Four

"You gonna let Gage take you across the bayou?" Marie Ancelet asked. Hands on her hips, she was assessing Astrid's garb, a light-weight blue wool skirt, white blouse, and green embroidered bodice. Her dark brown eyes moved from the silver *sólje* brooch at Astrid's neck to the wooden clogs on her feet. "You better let Gage stay with you alla time. You don' know that Emile Fontenot."

Astrid lifted Edvard away from the rickety porch chair he was trying to climb and snuggled him. "I go there only for tea, Mrs. Ancelet. My purpose with Mr. Fontenot is only to find my blue trunk."

"But what is his purpose with you, *chére?*" Gage stepped up onto the *galerie*. "You better think about that before you go."

Surprised Gage had appeared in the middle of the afternoon, Astrid couldn't conceal her pleasure at seeing the man. In the two weeks that had passed since the dance, she had grown accustomed to Gage's presence around his parents' home. He made small repairs — replaced a rail on the porch, tacked down a few loose shingles, and oiled the water pump outside the kitchen door. He dropped by to eat supper or have a drink of sassafras tea in the evening.

Often, Gage sat with Astrid on the moonlit *galerie* while Edvard played with his blocks. Their talk was light and filled with laughter. She found herself awaiting those moments with the same eagerness she had known as a child anticipating the approach of *Jul* with its feasting and presents. Gage was a gift, an unexpected, rare blessing she had come to treasure. And every day, when he stopped with fresh food for his parents, she made a point of admiring the fruit of his labors.

"I see you bring many big fish this afternoon," Astrid said as Gage carried a string of perch onto the *galerie*. "With your hands you caught these fish?"

"The *perche* you catch better with a line." He paused and studied Astrid. "You look beautiful, *chére*. Fontenot is gonna try to reel you in."

"But I am not a fish." Astrid touched her hair, hoping the high knot on her head would stay in place. It pleased her that Gage approved of her appearance. Of course, he always spoke his mind, and in the past days he had been more than open about his appreciation.

"You not a fish, but that man will try to eat you up anyway," Marie said. "Better take Gage with you. He's a good one, my boy. He can protect you from that Creole."

"Fontenot don' want me roun' his gazebo, Mama." Gage hung the string of fish on a nail in the porch post. "He invited Miz Munsen across the bayou for tea."

"I don' know why you wanna go over there," Marie said to Astrid.

"But you know I have asked all the neighbors and searched in every shop, and I cannot find my blue rosemaled trunk. I have hope that Mr. Fontenot has it. Then I can get the money for my ticket to Norway."

"Why you goin' back to that cold place anyhow? Alla that snow and ice and nothin' green growin'. You told me yourself the sun don' hardly shine half the year. Stay here with us, Astrid. We'll take care of you, huh, Gage?"

The man's brown eyes were soft. "I reckon you know that, Miz Munsen. You been with us awhile now. You seen our life —"

"You belong here!" Marie's lip trembled. "I don' like to think of you goin' off someplace. What we do without you? What we do without little Eddie? You been helpin' me with the washin' and cookin'. You eat our food. You even learned to sing the lullaby my beautiful Pierre taught you. You a part of us now, Astrid."

Gage laid a hand on his mother's shoulder. "Mama, people come and go. You gotta trust she's been prayin' about this. She's gonna do what she thinks is the right thing for her and Eddie."

Astrid swallowed. *Had* she prayed about this? She had prayed for strength, prayed for patience, prayed for health. She had lifted up her family and friends to her heavenly Father. She had stood beside Ole Munsen's grave and prayed to God for the wisdom to raise his son in the best way. But this decision to go or stay . . . did she really have a choice?

"I must return to Norway," she said. "To stay here alone was never my plan. God sent me to America to help my husband, but now I have no reason to remain." She handed Edvard to Mrs. Ancelet and kissed the baby's cheek before turning to Gage. "I thought I would go to the dock and look for you, but now you are here. Perhaps you will row me across the river?"

"That's why I came, don' you know?"

As they walked down the path that ran

439

along the bank toward his dock, Gage shoved his hands into the pockets of his trousers. Even though Astrid attempted a lighthearted demeanor, she sensed the heaviness in Gage's mood as he strolled beside her. Uncharacteristically silent, he didn't whistle or even look around. When he turned to her to speak, his eyes burned.

"Tell me somethin', *chére*," he said. "Back at the house, you told us God sent you here to help Ole. Is that right?"

"*Ja*. Of course."

"But before you ever set foot on that ship, God knew your husband had passed on. That means the Good Lord must have had another plan in mind when he brought you down here to my bayou."

"Another plan?" Astrid lifted her skirt and stepped over a puddle in the path. "But I came to live with Ole and make his home."

"So you're sayin' maybe God made a mistake lettin' you come? The bayou, my folks, the *fais do-do*, everythin' is kinda like a little jag in the road of your life? Once you get back to Norway, you gonna put us away like a memory of an accident. My bayou is like a root somebody trips over, or a bottle of spilled salt, or a cracked window pane. Somethin' that wasn' supposed to happen?"

Astrid stopped and studied the thick

brush on every side, the tangle of creeping vines, the lacy moss that hung from each tree limb. Heat crept through her wool skirt and petticoat. Her skin beneath her tightly laced bodice was damp. She shook her head. "I don't know why God sent me here. But how can it be right? All is so different for me. It is good for you, but for me perhaps it is a mistake."

"This *ain'* a mistake, Astrid." Gage swung on her and caught her shoulders in his powerful grip. "It ain' a mistake. Maybe you didn' plan what's happened, but not one thing since the moment you floated up my bayou has been a mistake. God knew you were comin' here to me. His hand holds both of us. When I look into your blue eyes, when I listen to your sweet voice, when I hear you laugh, I feel full inside — full in the places that been empty a long, long time. You ain' a mistake in my life. So am I a mistake in yours?"

Astrid held her breath as his dark eyes searched hers. Could she speak the truth? Could she tell him how she had come to anticipate the moment every morning when she would hear his deep voice ring out in greeting? Could she express the delight that filled her when he played his mouth harp and danced around the kitchen with Eddie, his little *beignet?* Could she honestly tell him how it blessed her to know a man who honored God with his work and his words?

"You are not a mistake," she said, praying she could find the English words to express herself. "But from the day I came here, I feel confused. First I think this is a very ugly place with bad air and too much heat. But now, I lie in the bed, and I love to listen to the sounds of the night. Now I wake and enjoy the smells of black coffee and *couche-couche* from your mother's kitchen. First I think all the people are strange with talking the mix of French and English, catching fish with hands, wearing no shoes. Now I understand that Pierre and Marie are good people, as fine as my own parents."

"And me?"

She could hear her heartbeat hammering in her ears. "You are . . . you are good, too. You work hard. Love your family. Love God."

"Love you."

"Gage —"

"You know it's true, Astrid. How it happened, I don' understand. Everything I did before now, I took my time. I searched my land three months for just the right wood to build my house. Last spring I went up and down the bayou lookin' in every store for the best seed for my crops. I never bought a horse till I watched it workin' six months, maybe a year. But you come floatin' up to my dock, and I know right away you are a miracle. By the time I take you in my arms at the *fais do-do,* I'm sure you're the best thing ever came into my life."

"How can this be? You had a wife before."

"You had a husband. Tell me you feel the same about him as you do about me."

"No," she whispered. "It is not the same."

His strong hands slid down her arms and tightened around her fingers. "Why God chose this way — so fast and confusin' — I don' know, *chére.* I only know one thing. When I think about you gettin' back on old Gabriel's *bateau* and floatin' down the bayou, I get sick inside. Heartsick."

"Please don't say such things. You know I must go back to Norway. There my parents live. My brothers. My friends. I have a home, traditions, a language and food I love. How can I keep Eddie —" She stopped and laughed without spirit. "You see? Because of you, I call my own son a name that is not Norwegian. How can I keep Edvard from my parents? From the parents of Ole Munsen? From my child's cousins, aunts, uncles? Will Edvard never know of *lefse* or celebrate *Syttende Mai?* I must go back, Gage."

443

His jaw tightened. "I don' think it's Eddie that takes you away, *chére*. I think it's fear. You know that boy would have a good life here, but you wanna run. What did Ole do that scared you so bad you won' let yourself love another man?"

"What did he do? He did nothing — exactly nothing to make me wish for marriage ever again in my life. You knew my husband. Perhaps you knew him better than I. I was his wife, *ja,* but he never even talked to me about more than milking the cows and how much money his fish will bring in the market."

"I talk to you, *chére.*"

"But you also keep secrets from me." She assessed his reaction, aware of the sudden veil that dropped over his eyes and masked his smile. "I think you know the reason Ole Munsen died. I think you were near him at that time. Why you will not tell me the truth, Gage?"

"Sometimes it's better not to know the truth."

"Shall I leave my parents and my home forever because I listened to the sweet words of a man who cannot tell me the truth?"

"I'm tellin' you the only truth that matters. We belong together. I learned from watchin' my parents that love includes sacrifice. If I care about somebody enough, I'm gonna have to give up some things. Independence, maybe. Money, time, my own way of doin' things, maybe even somethin' more important. Jesus sacrificed his whole life outta love for us. I'm willin' to follow his example. If you somehow slip away from me, *chére*, I'm gonna leave my farms, my horses, my parents, and I'm gonna come after you. You know I will."

Astrid thought of the day Ole Munsen had sailed away without a tender word of farewell for his pregnant wife. How different this man was, and how passionate his words. But could he be correct that God had brought her and Edvard here for one purpose — uniting her with Gage Ancelet? Was such a thing possible? And how could she give her life to a man who kept even one grain of truth from her?

"Emile Fontenot waits for me," she said softly. "I must go now."

"*Oui.*" The word was unusually curt as he drew away from her and started down the path again.

Astrid rubbed her arms, shivering inside despite the steamy afternoon. She had been taught to follow her head and not her heart. But look where it had taken her — to the wedding hearth of Ole Munsen. When she reflected on their short time together, she recalled no laughter, no heartfelt words of passion, no searching looks. Certainly no sacrifice. Had her husband ever touched her outside their bed? Had he ever called her a name of endearment? Despite their shared Norwegian heritage, language, traditions, and homeland, had they ever discovered one thing in common?

Gage walked ahead of Astrid down the dock and helped her into the *bateau*. In silence, he paddled the flatboat across the bayou. She knotted her fingers in her lap and tried to pray. What was she to do? How could she see the road ahead? Which direction should she go?

"Just follow the path straight up to Fontenot's house," Gage said as he looped the *bateau*'s rope over a piling. He clambered out and offered his hand. "I'll come back for you roun' sunset."

"Thank you, Gage." Astrid could hardly bring herself to look into his face. When she did, she read the unmasked pain in his brown eyes. "Please . . . please try to be patient with me. This day I feel God is far away, and my prayers go nowhere. I cannot hear his voice. I cannot see his plan for my life. Will you pray for me, Gage Ancelet?"

"I been prayin' for you since the first day I

met you, *chére.* I ain' gonna stop now."

Overwhelmed, she stood on tiptoe and kissed his cheek. "I will wait for you here at sunset."

Terrified she might betray the flood of emotion surging through her, Astrid hurried up the graveled path toward the huge white house. She passed beneath a row of ancient live oaks and glimpsed beyond them the expanse of a huge, well-mowed green lawn. Topiaries clipped into globes and cubes lined the broad drive on which stood a pair of white mares hitched to a shiny black carriage. Breathless, Astrid finally slowed her steps as she ascended the wide staircase. She paused a moment to inspect the stone urns filled with pink and purple flowers before she tugged on the bellpull.

In a twinkle of magic, she found herself ushered out of the steamy swampland and into a fairy-tale mansion with a marble-floored hall and a curving staircase. A liveried servant took her shawl and, with a crisp bow, indicated her host standing framed in a set of multipaned French windows. Emile Fontenot straightened the lapels of his gray frock coat, smiled, and held out his arms.

"My dear Mrs. Munsen, how good of you to come all this way." Stepping into the hall, he offered his arm. "My deepest apologies. I should have sent one of my carriages down to the bayou for you. I've just been outside myself visiting my fields, and it's a mighty hot afternoon."

"*Ja,* I remember you have many horses beside Capitaine," Astrid commented. "Mr. Ancelet spoke of your beautiful mare, Papillon."

As her host showed Astrid through a series of rooms, she did her best to put the conversation with Gage out of mind and to concentrate on her goal. While Fontenot boasted about his horses, she took in the opulent furnishings. Tall, mullioned doors opened to spacious chambers in which huge chandeliers hung from plaster ceiling medallions. Curvaceous settees upholstered in brocade lined jewel-colored Oriental rugs. Brass urns and hanging planters burst with ferns and other exotic flora Astrid could not name. The walls had been hung with flocked papers or stenciled to reflect scenes from Egypt's palm-rimmed Nile. And everywhere pictures in heavy gilt frames displayed still-life scenes, raging battles, or unclothed women sprawled across velvet couches.

"You have a gazebo?" Astrid asked, flushing to the roots of her hair over one particularly revealing portrait. It was all she could do to keep from dropping the man's elbow and dashing outside. "You mentioned we might drink tea there."

"*Oui*, Mrs. Munsen. Mighty refreshing with a spoonful of honey and a sprig of fresh mint from the garden."

He led her out a final set of doors onto a brick patio. A large white-framed gazebo formed the centerpiece of a formal garden fragrant with herbs and roses. Within the glass-and-iron structure stood a table draped in white linen and set with a silver tea service. Astrid settled into a chair as a servant poured a cup of amber tea.

"Very good," she said after her first sip. "You are a kind man to invite a stranger into your house."

"Such a beautiful woman as you deserves the finest in luxuries. I can hardly believe Ancelet has stowed you away in that hovel his parents call home. Surely you're accustomed to better quarters, Mrs. Munsen."

"I am the daughter of a Norwegian fisherman, sir. Our home was always clean and tidy, but it is hardly as fine as your house."

He took a long sip of tea. In the afternoon sun, his brown hair reflected a burnished tint, and his green eyes glittered. Astrid knew most women would find such a man handsome, charming, and well spoken. But in his face she recognized a softness that one day would melt into the sagging flesh of an indulgent man. His hands were pale and pillowed from idleness, and the rosy tint of his nose betrayed a fondness for strong drink.

Though the scent of roses drifted through the gazebo and a gentle breeze rustled the fern fronds just outside, Astrid felt increasingly uncomfortable. What did this man know about Ole? Did he have her blue trunk? Dare she ask him for it? If she did, what would he expect in return? Palms clammy and stomach in a knot, she sipped at her tea while he explained the history of his family in Louisiana.

"The house was built in 1756," he said finally, "and one Fontenot or another has lived in it ever since. My ancestors came from France many years ago, and we've preserved our traditions and language in a way the Cajuns never did. I think you certainly can see we've bettered ourselves in this land, and we Creoles intend to continue our noble heritage."

"It is good to keep the customs of your homeland," Astrid said. "But perhaps also it is good to accept new ways in a new land. Better to have friendship with the others who live here than to remain apart thinking you are better than they. Do you agree?"

"Absolutely not, and if you stayed here at Fontenot even one night, I assure you, you'd change your mind." He smiled. "Luxury is better than poverty any day, Mrs. Munsen. A succulent veal *cordon bleu* is better than gumbo. A chandelier hung with Austrian crystals and fitted with beeswax candles is better than a glass oil lamp with a smoking wick. And a garden planted with roses is better than a front yard full of swamp water and mosquitoes. Can you disagree?"

Astrid traced a line around the rim of her teacup. "I think most important is what lies inside the heart of a man — and not the place where he lives."

Fontenot laughed. "A grand answer! You are a delightful young lady, and I must say I regret the unfortunate circumstance that brought you to us. Your husband was a good man."

"How well did you know Ole?" Astrid sat up straight. "Did he come here?"

"*Oui,* of course. He stayed with me many nights."

"Ole stayed *here?*"

"You sound surprised."

"I understood he was working on the cattle farm of Pierre Ancelet."

"I'm sure you know hard labor on a

451

prairie *vacherie* was not your husband's primary objective in life. His interest lay in other arenas, and I suspect he might have gone quite far had he not encountered that unfortunate streak of bad luck."

"Bad luck?" Astrid wadded her linen napkin into a ball. "Please, Mr. Fontenot, you must give me news of my husband. What were these other interests? How did the bad luck come to Ole?"

"Didn't Ancelet tell you?" He shrugged. "But surely you knew the passions of the man you married? He loved racing, of course. Pleasure boats. Gaming tables. It was the horses that drew him here to Fontenot. Would you like to see our stables? Your husband used to spend a good bit of time there."

Her thoughts whirling, Astrid permitted the Creole to escort her from the tea table out of the gazebo and down a long brick path toward his stables. Horse races, pleasure boats, gaming tables? Gage Ancelet had told Astrid that Ole came to Louisiana on a pleasure boat. Were these boats used for gambling and placing bets? As Fontenot led Astrid down the long row of stalls that housed his beautiful horses, she tried to force her mind to accept what she had heard.

Ole Munsen had not fulfilled his promise to her. He had not come to America and searched for a little farm where they could begin a new life with their son. He had not sought out the settlements of Norwegian families already living in the northern prairies. He had not even worked his way to Louisiana in order to find a job on the Ancelet cattle ranches.

Instead, he had drifted onto a pleasure boat that plied the Mississippi. No doubt winning money had kept him aboard, and fear of losing it had prevented him from leaving. When he came to the end of the river — and probably the end of his cash — he must have wandered around looking for work.

Had he owed Gage Ancelet a gambling debt? Doubtful. Gage had plainly stated his disgust with betting and games of chance. Perhaps the two men first met when Gage was looking for an employee, and Ole had come to this bayou with the intent of establishing a home at last. He had written Astrid and instructed her to follow. And then he had met Emile Fontenot.

"This is Papillon, my beautiful butterfly," the man said, indicating a well-built chestnut mare. "She's a quarter horse, and you should see her run! *Mais oui,* she's won a good many races for me. She's out of a wonderful line of champions. I paid quite a sum for her, but she was bred up north, and I don't trust her endurance in this climate. It's her offspring I'm counting on. With the right stallion, this mare could produce a racer no horse could outrun."

"You wish for a stallion like Gage Ancelet's Petit Noir," Astrid said.

"Finest horse I've seen around, and he's fast in his own right. Well, you saw that for yourself."

"*Ja,* when your friends provoked that dangerous race."

He assessed her, his thin lips curved into the hint of a grin. "I do believe you're miffed about that, Mrs. Munsen. Let's walk back to the house, and I'll tell you what I'm gonna do to make up for our monkey business. I'm gonna tell the maid to fix you up in the Peacock Room right here at Fontenot. It gets a cool breeze from the west, and it's the prettiest room in the house. You spend a few nights here, and you'll feel a lot better."

"Oh, Mr. Fontenot," Astrid fumbled, praying for the right words as they walked back into the rose garden. "I-I cannot accept such kindness. I have a baby, and he often cries in the night. I fear he would disturb you."

"Why not leave the child with Marie Ancelet? Have yourself a little rest."

"But I nurse him still." Flushing, she gripped the tea napkin as she climbed the stairs into the house. Could Fontenot not understand that she would not think of leaving her baby? Edvard was the only real joy she had known until she met the Cajuns Fontenot so disliked. "I must keep my son near me. I am his mother."

"Then send word to bring your baby to Fontenot. We'll put him in a room with the maids, and they'll tend him. I assure you, it will not be a problem. You'll relax, eat well, pamper yourself. In fact, a group of my friends is coming from New Iberia tomorrow evening. You'll enjoy their company."

"But, Mr. Fontenot —"

"Please, Mrs. Munsen. It's the least I can do to make up for your unforgivable treatment at the hands of my companions the other night."

"You wish to ease my situation?"

"Of course I do." He took her hand and kissed her fingertips. "I'll do whatever it takes to please you."

Aware this was her moment of opportunity, Astrid sucked down her trepidation and squared her shoulders. "Mr. Fontenot, there is something you can do that would help me greatly."

"Say the word, my lovely golden-haired princess." His voice took on an intimate tone as he opened a set of French doors and motioned her into a large, cool parlor. "I'm at your command."

Astrid sat down on the edge of a settee and wedged her fingertips between her knees. *Please, dear God, give me courage. Don't let me fall into a trap with this man!*

Fontenot knelt on one knee beside her and bent his head to lay a string of kisses up her bare arm. Shuddering with unexpected revulsion, Astrid scooted back on the settee. He lifted his head, a smile across his mouth. "Your request, my timid beauty?"

"You say you have what belonged to my husband," she said, jumping up from the settee and crossing her arms over her waist. "I cannot return to Norway without it. I shall write you a note of indebtedness, sir, and I promise the sum will be repaid in full. My father is a good man. A man of honor. You can trust me in this."

Fontenot stared at her, his nostrils slightly flared. Running fingers back through his brown hair, he stood slowly to face her. "Credit?" he asked softly. "I took your husband's things in payment for a debt, and

now you want me to give them back to you on credit?"

"I shall pay every penny. Please, sir, you must understand my situation. I have a small baby and no place to live. My family are all in Norway. My home is there. I have nothing here, nobody —" She caught her breath. That wasn't true, was it? She *did* have someone. Only hours before, a man had declared his love for her. A good man — a man who brought her laughter, who shared her love of children, who adored her son, and who stirred her heart — this man had laid himself bare for her.

"You have *me*, Mrs. Munsen," Fontenot said. "I've offered you my friendship, my home, my company. Surely my ears deceived me when I heard you ask for something in addition to all that. You must know I am not a bank. I'm merely a generous gentleman who offers you the bounty of his household."

"But I need to go home to Norway," Astrid said, and for the first time the words rang hollow in her ears. "I must bring up my son in . . . in the traditions of my people."

"Let me make a proposal. Spend a few days with me here at Fontenot, and we'll talk over this matter. I'm a man of business, you understand. I'm generous, but not

foolish. I won't give away something for nothing."

"But I do not ask you to *give* me anything. I shall pay it back with interest."

"*Oui,* but I think we might be able to work out another plan."

"No." Astrid turned her head and focused on the far end of the parlor. "Mr. Fontenot, I am an unmarried woman. A widow. It would not be proper for me to stay at your house. I came here to ask you for Ole Munsen's things, because I must return to —"

In the early evening gloom, her eyes made out a large square shape beneath a window. It was a wooden box. Painted in a soft shade of grayed blue. And covered with swirls of Norwegian rosemaling.

Chapter Five

Stepping around Emile Fontenot, Astrid ran to the window and knelt before the blue rosemaled chest. "This is from Norway!"

"You recognize it?" Fontenot asked, joining her.

"But of course. This design was painted by my brother. These leaves, the flowers. This is —" She swung around. "This is my wedding chest, Mr. Fontenot."

His dark eyebrows lifted. "*Your* chest? Munsen assured me it belonged to him."

"Ole gave you my wedding chest?"

"As I told you, my dear, he owed me a great deal of money. I took the trunk in trade."

"Is it still filled with our things?"

"Munsen pawned off most of what he owned. Gambling debts, you know."

"How could he do this? The furnishings for our home were in the trunk — curtains I had sewn, blankets I wove, pots and pans made by my grandfather. My mother had painted the chest blue. My brother . . . he made this very special design. It was to be . . . to be . . ."

She unwadded the linen tea napkin and dabbed at her eyes. It was not enough that Ole had betrayed her trust in him to build a home for them in America. Not enough that he had gambled away any hope of a future for their son. Not enough that he had led her here to this foreign land and left her no provision at his death. But now she must accept that Ole Munsen had robbed her of her family heritage!

"I'll tell you what," Fontenot said. "There may be a few things inside — a tablecloth and a blanket or two. Have a look, why don't you? I'll just step into the hall and instruct the servants to prepare the Peacock Room."

Astrid stifled the cry of denial that choked her as he strode out of the room. What did Fontenot expect her to do? Stay here and become his paramour in exchange for her heritage? The man was disgusting. Heart hammering, she opened the latch and lifted the trunk's heavy lid. Ole had traded the trunk for his debts — but the *sólje* brooch belonged to her. Could it be he had never discovered it? Was the answer to her prayers still inside?

Praying she could look before Fontenot returned, Astrid leaned the lid against the parlor window and found the opening to the secret niche. *Quickly, now. Quickly.* Holding

460

her breath, she slid back the panel — and there it was! Sparkling in the waning sunlight, the golden pin danced like firelight as she slipped it into her palm. Dangling leaves hung from the intricately spun vines that formed the base of the brooch. It was beautiful, unique, and valuable.

"Find anything?" Fontenot asked behind her.

Astrid closed her hand over the brooch and sucked in a breath. She lifted from the chest a set of bed linens and tablecloths she had woven years before. Mouth dry, she stood and turned to face the man. Had he seen her actions? Should she confess her discovery? Dare she offer the brooch now in exchange for money? She needed time to think, to plan . . . and yes, to pray.

"I found the tablecloth and blankets," she said. Swallowing hard, she added, "Also I found a trinket my father gave me."

"Keep them, sweetheart. My interests lie in French and Italian arts and crafts. I forgave a sizable debt for the trunk, but you can keep your other little Norwegian mementos."

"Thank you, sir."

"Now why don't we step into the hall, and I'll show you to your new quarters?"

"But I must return to the dock, Mr.

Fontenot," she replied, hugging the linens as if they could protect her from the man.

"You won't stay here?"

"I cannot. Gage Ancelet waits for me in his *bateau*."

"You'd go back to that Cajun after all I've offered you?" Fontenot's face was an angry sneer. "Maybe you're not as smart as I thought."

"Perhaps not. But I know what is in my heart, sir. I honor God, family, truth. I thank you for the tea and the gift of the things from my trunk, but I can never stay with you."

"Because I refuse to play banker?"

"I'm sorry. I must go." She hardly heard his response as she hurried toward the doors leading into the front hall. Slipping the brooch into her skirt pocket, she ran out the door and down the steps. Oh, Gage! What would he say if he knew she had found the brooch? What would he do if he knew she could afford to secure passage to Norway? And suddenly none of it mattered but seeing him.

"Astrid!" Gage's voice carried across the open space between them as she raced toward the dock. "Astrid, are you all right?"

"*Om forlatelse* . . . forgive me . . . *Hva skull jeg gjóre?* What shall . . . should I do? *Uff,* my

English goes away. . . ." She tossed the linens into the boat and threw her arms around his chest. "Oh, Gage, Fontenot owns my blue trunk! Ole sells . . . sold it to him. Traded it. Why you did not tell me about the races? the gambling?"

"Shh, now, *chére*." Gage stroked his hand down her back. "Let's get into the *bateau*, and we'll float a little. Do some talkin'."

Distraught, Astrid stepped into the flat-bottomed vessel and waited while Gage untied the rope and poled the boat toward the middle of the bayou. When they were floating freely, he sat down beside her and slipped his arm around her shoulders. For a long time they drifted, neither speaking. Finally, he took a deep breath.

"I don' wanna hurt you ever, Astrid," Gage said. "I knew if you heard the truth about your husband, you would ache inside. Maybe I was wrong, but I wanted to spare you that."

"Better to tell the truth always. You teach me this, Gage. Now, you must tell me everything."

"*Oui*, because you ask. Ole Munsen came down the Mississippi on a pleasure boat. He roamed roun' lookin' for work, ran outta money in New Iberia and found me at a seed store. I offered him a job, and he came over to the bayou to work my papa's farm. Said he had a wife in Norway he was gonna send for, and I thought that was mighty honorable. I knew what he'd been up to, but I reckoned he was lookin' to make a change now he had a job and a place to live. But not long after that, he starts roamin' roun' again, hears about Fontenot, and spends a lotta time over there. Next thing I know, he's pawnin' off all his Norwegian stuff — your trunk, too, I reckon. He stops showin' up for work. He borrows a *bateau* and goes up and down the bayou huntin' for saloons to play cards, or racetracks where he can place bets. Tells me he's gonna strike it rich one of these days. Gonna make it big like Fontenot. One time I'm goin' over to New Iberia to buy some supplies, boots and tools, you know. Munsen asks if he can go along, and I say *oui*. Why not? Next thing I know, the law is poundin' on my hotel room door sayin' there's been a problem."

"What happened?" Astrid whispered. "You must tell me."

Gage nodded. "A fight broke out down at one of the saloons. Coupla men shot at each other over a card game. Both of 'em dead."

"One was Ole Munsen."

"I'm sorry, *chére*," he said. "I didn' wanna tell you. You're good and kind, and I don'

464

like to see you hurt."

"It is all right." Astrid stared at the inky water, imagining her husband's violent death. "I know Ole took many wrong steps. He did not choose well, even in Norway."

"He chose you."

"The papas chose."

"What you gonna choose now, *chére?* Will Fontenot give back the trunk so you can return to Norway?"

"No. He wishes me to stay in his house. He thinks I will trade myself to him in the same way Ole traded away the blue rosemaled trunk."

"Did you ask him for the trunk? It was never Munsen's to sell."

Astrid shook her head. "No, I will never again have the trunk of my family. My mother's painting of blue, my brother's design of the rosemaling, the hopes I put into that chest, they are lost to me now."

Gage rubbed his palms over his knees. "Maybe this ain' the right time, but you said it's better to tell the truth always, *chére.*" He took a deep breath. "So I'm gonna lay somethin' out here, and I don' wanna hear about it till you've had time to think. But here's the truth if I ever knew it: I love you, Astrid Munsen, and I wanna make you my wife."

"Wife?" she gasped.

"Like we get married, you and me. *Mais oui,* I know you ain' hardly been here long enough to unpack. I know we ain' spent a lotta time together. But I never knew anything to be so right in my life. You fill up my heart, Astrid. I give my word of honor I'll take care of you all your days. I'll see Eddie grows up right. Listen, I wouldn' say this, but I been prayin' about it night and day ever since you got here. God knows I love you, and I wanna spend the rest of my life with you."

Trembling, Astrid laid her hand on his arm. "Gage —"

"*Non,* don' speak." He placed a finger over her lips. "You go up to the *filliére* and think over my words. Tomorrow, we talk again."

"*Ja,*" she said. "It is past the time for me to pray."

He guided the *bateau* to Pierre Ancelet's dock and helped Astrid ashore. She hesitated a moment, hoping he would take her into his arms again. Instead, he shoved his hands into his pockets and stared up at the moon.

"In Norway we say *god kveld,*" she whispered. "It means good evening."

He looked at her, his brown eyes liquid in

the lamplight from the *galerie.* "Good night to you, *chére.*"

"I thank God for you."

The corner of his mouth tipped up and formed the beloved dimple. "You ain' supposed to talk. You gotta be quiet, *chére,* or no tellin' what I might do."

She chuckled. "You gotta kiss me, *cher,* or no tellin' what I might do."

With a laugh, he caught her up in his arms and pressed his lips to hers. Warm and firm, his mouth moved across from her lips to her cheek. Shivering, she kissed his neck and drank in the scent of musky balm on his skin.

"Au revoir, mon amour," he murmured against her ear.

"Du fär leve sä vel," she whispered in return. "Take care of yourself."

"You two gonna smooch all night?" Pierre Ancelet called out from the *galerie.* "We gotta hungry baby in here decided he don' wanna eat no more *couche-couche.* Wants his mama."

Astrid brushed her lips across Gage's cheek and ran toward the house.

Gage Ancelet sat in a rocking chair on his *galerie* and listened to the night sounds. All his life he had heard those sounds and thought nothing of them. Now he could imagine Astrid lying alone in the *filliére* and marveling over the chirps, buzzes, and croaks. She was a marvel. She had brought such a freshness to his life, such excitement, such hope.

He had told her love meant sacrifice, but all his thoughts had been centered around himself and his own desires, Gage realized. He could think only of how much he loved the sound of Astrid's voice. How much he longed to catch a glimpse of her golden hair. How deeply her laughter stirred him. He was crazy about her baby, certain he would protect the child with his life. He wanted to bring them both into his home and build a family around their love.

But what did Astrid want? Any man could see she enjoyed Gage's company. She tenderly cared for his parents. She appreciated his friends. Despite her protests, Astrid had grown comfortable in her short time in Louisiana. Gage had to believe she could live here and find happiness. But did she want to? Could she give up her homeland? Could she make a new life with him? Most important, did she love him?

Gage stopped rocking and studied the silhouetted trees that lined the bayou. No, the most important thing was God's will. *What do you want, Father? What shall I do with this unexpected love in my heart?*

He thought about Astrid's dismay as she ran from Fontenot's house. The truth of her husband's betrayal played a part in her emotional distress. But of equal concern was the loss of the blue rosemaled trunk. She loved that trunk. It was her Norwegian heritage.

A chill ran down Gage's spine. If he truly loved Astrid, he must put aside his own desires. What did she want? What did she need? She had told him the blue trunk was her only hope of a ticket back to Norway. Now that hope was lost to her forever.

Lost . . . unless Gage was willing to make the ultimate sacrifice for the woman he loved.

Astrid lay in the iron bed where Gage's sisters once had slept. She listened to the melody that rose from the bayou, and she thought about the man she had grown to love so deeply . . . so quickly. How could this have happened? How could she seriously consider abandoning her Norwegian home and family for a man she had known such a short time?

She fingered the *sólje* brooch that lay on the small table beside the bed. Responsibility demanded that she try to sell the brooch to Emile Fontenot as soon as possible. Reason dictated she book passage on the first steamship back to Norway. Sanity insisted she leave behind a whirlwind passion for the stability of tradition.

But what did God want? Astrid set the brooch back on the table and stared up at the ceiling. *What will you have of me, Father God?* she prayed. *Shall I be wise and stable, taking Edvard back to Norway where we both belong? Or shall I follow my heart and dance along the bayou with the man I love?*

Or is my heart in Norway, with her long blue fjords, tall mountains, and crisp snow? Shall I never again watch my breath form a cloud in the chilly air? Will Edvard never learn to ski? Will lutefisk taste foreign on his tongue one day as gumbo did on mine?

Oh, Father, what shall I do? Astrid closed her eyes, and instantly the face of Gage Ancelet formed in her mind. True love meant sacrifice, he had said. But what must she surrender to prove her love?

⚭

Gage stepped up onto the *galerie* of his parents' home and knocked on the door. He had been busy most of the day setting his plan in motion, but he had taken time to bathe and dress in a clean shirt and trousers.

Though his heart was heavy, he couldn't deny the anticipation he felt at seeing Astrid's blue eyes again.

"Gage?" Marie opened the door and gave her son a frown. "What you mean by knockin'? You never knocked before in your life. Come on in and taste some of this jambalaya I got cookin'."

"Mama, I've come to talk to Astrid."

She pursed her lips. "*Mais,* she ain' here. Gone back over the bayou to have a *visite* with Fontenot. Took our *bateau* all by herself. I tried to stop her, but no. She's gonna do it, even though I can tell she's been up half the night stewin' and fussin' and upsettin' that poor baby —"

"Mama, why did Astrid go over to Fontenot's?"

"I don' know, but I suspect it ain' nothin' good. You shoulda seen her this mornin', cryin' half the time and laughin' the other. She told me she knows all about what her husband did, sellin' her things and gamblin' away everythin' — includin' his own life. Said she's gotta make some hard choices, but she's gonna do it. Said she prayed all night, and God told her what to do."

"What?" Gage demanded, knotting his fists. "What's she gonna do?"

"I already told you I don' know! Stop

shoutin' at your mama, or you're gonna wake that baby from his nap. What you come over here for anyway? Why you all dressed up and smellin' good?"

"Everybody's comin' round to my house for a get-together. A party. I want Astrid to be there. I need her. I have somethin' —"

"I will come." Astrid stepped from the *galerie* into the room, her blue eyes aglow. "Hello, Gage."

Unable to hold himself back, he took her in his arms and kissed her forehead. "You all right, *chére?* Mama said you went over to Fontenot's place. Please don' worry about things. I told you, I'm gonna take care of you. You don' need that man's help."

"Mais oui," she said, a smile curving her pink lips. "But why have you made a party? I hoped perhaps we could talk together tonight. Important things must be spoken between us."

"You just come over to my house. We'll talk. We'll dance." He fought the pain welling up in his chest. "Everything's gonna be all right."

"Stop moonin', Gage, and put your arms around this jambalaya," Marie cut in. "If we gotta feed a party of neighbors, we better get goin'. Papa be in from the prairie any minute now, and . . . here he comes. Is that the baby I hear? Astrid, go feed your little one. And try not to get him all worked up again. I do believe that child echoes your every laugh and every cry. Pierre! My love, come in and lemme take off your boots."

Astrid glanced at Gage before hurrying upstairs to the *filliére*. His father tramped into the house and gave Marie a big smooch on the cheek. Gage took a cloth and wrapped it around the handle of the big stewpot. Jambalaya, friends, and dancing. With God's grace, he was going to make it through this night.

Aunts and uncles, sisters and cousins, toddlers and babies, friends from all up and down the bayou gathered in and around Gage's house. Pots of gumbo and jambalaya materialized in the kitchen. A band formed on the *galerie*. Rocking chairs appeared in the living room, and baby cots materialized in the back bedroom. Astrid had no idea how everyone could eat so much, talk so loudly, and dance with such vigor in the heat. Amid laughter and singing, she wandered through the crowd passing Edvard around and sipping root beer.

Gage kept himself with the men, but whenever Astrid caught his eye, his face registered none of the joy she had seen in the past. *Why did he organize this party?* she wondered. Why set up a time of happiness when everything about him registered the gravity of their discussion the previous day? Astrid lifted her chin. *Ja vel,* it was time to make her decision known. She handed Edvard to Marie, who had been pestering her all night for a chance to hold the baby, and she started across the room.

At that moment the music stopped, and Gage stepped into the middle of the dance floor. "Alla you folks havin' a good time?" he called out.

"*Oui!*" several answered.

"Good jambalaya, Gage!" someone shouted.

He laughed. "*Mais,* I had a reason for askin' you all over tonight. Somethin' more than checkin' over the pretty girls, Revon." Everyone chuckled at the expense of the poor fellow who had been caught standing in the midst of a group of young women.

"You know we've had a very special guest with us a while now," Gage continued. "Come over here, Miz Munsen."

Astrid touched her throat. What was this all about? She smoothed down her apron as she made her way to his side. "Gage, I must talk to you in private," she whispered.

"We'll talk, but first I have a surprise for you." He took her hand. "Revon, you other fellas, go fetch it and bring it out now."

Astrid stared in amazement as the young men reentered the room carrying her blue rosemaled wedding trunk. A gasp of delight rose from the onlookers. Huge, the chest dominated the dance floor as the men set it in front of her and then stood back to assess her response. Astrid leaned over and ran her fingertips across the smooth wood painted by her mother. Slowly, she traced the delicate intertwining of leaves and flowers added by her brother. Then she straightened and looked inquiringly at Gage.

"A gift for you," he said. His eyes were liquid as he went on. "You said this trunk can help you buy your ticket back to Norway, and I reckon it'll fetch a pretty price when you sell it. You know how much I care about you, Astrid, and I want to make your happiness complete. This is the hardest gift I ever gave, but I told you I'd take care of you, and I meant it. I love you, *chére*."

Her eyes brimming, Astrid squeezed his hand and struggled to make herself talk. Somehow on this day, Gage had gone to Fontenot's house and persuaded the man to part with the trunk. All for Astrid. All so she could return to Norway and bring up her son as she had wished aloud so often. He had given her this gift — and at what price?

"How did you obtain this?" she whispered. "Gage, you have given me my heritage."

"I meant it as a way home."

"*Ja,* but . . ." Gulping down the lump in her throat, Astrid pulled an envelope from her pocket. "I also have a gift for you, Gage."

Confusion furrowing his brow, he took the envelope and tore it open. He unfolded the paper tucked inside, and as he read a strange light crept into his eyes. Finally, he lowered the letter and stared at Astrid.

"This is a bill of sale," he murmured. "It says I own a horse."

"Papillon!" she said, unable to hold back a laugh. "*Ja vel,* I buy you this mare from Fontenot today! She is yours to breed with Petit Noir."

"But where did you get the money?"

"From the wedding trunk. When I went there yesterday, Fontenot tells me I can have everything inside. I remember my father put a golden brooch in a special hiding place inside, so I take it. The *brooch* — and not the trunk — is my ticket to Norway. Last night, I think a long time about what you tell me on the bayou, about love and sacrifice. I think about my future and the life of my child. I decide . . . no, I hear God speaking to my heart words of truth. And then the decision is easy. Maybe I will see Norway again one day. But that dream I can surrender. More important is to follow the plan God made for me, to give my son the family he deserves . . . and to marry the man I love."

A roar of delight filled the room and echoed out onto the *galerie*. Gage swept Astrid up into his arms and kissed her again and again. Someone threw a quilt over the trunk, and at the urging of the crowd, Gage climbed onto it to give Astrid another kiss so everyone could see.

Flushing, she listened to the sudden cries that they marry at once. "Now!" rose the shout. "But there's no preacher! Find a broom they can jump! Where's the judge?"

Astrid clung to Gage. "How did you get me this trunk?" she asked amid the frenzy. "Fontenot said he forgave a very large debt in exchange for it."

Gage laughed. "I traded 'Tit Noir for the trunk."

"No! But I bought Papillon for your stallion, for your new breed of horses." She shook her head as the reality of his sacrifice overwhelmed her. "Oh, my love, even though you had asked me for marriage, you gave up Petit Noir to make true my dream of going back to Norway."

"That's the best stallion, but I got others I can put with Papillon. And besides, once Fontenot tries to handle 'Tit Noir a few times, he'll probably wanna renege on the trade. I know 'Tit Noir and Papillon are gonna make some babies. It's just a matter of who gets the first one." He tightened his arms around her. "The important thing is, you gave up Norway to make true my dream of a better horse breed. I reckon we must love each other a lot, *chére*."

"I reckon so."

"Wanna get married?"

"Mais oui."

Before Astrid could catch her breath, old Gabriel the boatman had climbed onto the blue trunk with them. "I ain' done this for a long time," he said, "but I still got my judge papers from the days I was a city man workin' for the parish. You two really wanna do this?"

"Oui," Astrid said.

"Ja," Gage added.

Amid cheers and laughter, old Gabriel took their hands and united Gage Ancelet and Astrid Munsen in matrimony under the laws of the state of Louisiana. Just for good measure, Pierre Ancelet shoved a broomstick up onto the trunk, and the couple jumped it in the Cajun tradition.

When the crowd had calmed a little, Gage held Astrid close and beckoned his mother to lift the baby to him. Tucking the child under his arm, he kissed the pink forehead.

"I make a promise now, before God and everybody," he said. "I'm gonna love this boy as my own, gonna teach him to hunt for crawfish and catch a catfish with his bare hands. His mama will teach him to talk Norwegian, and she'll feed us both some of that lye codfish — and we're gonna eat it!"

"Even if it kills you!" someone shouted.

Gage chuckled. "I want you all to know God made this marriage. He brought this woman to me, and I'm never gonna stop lovin' her."

"You better quit talkin', *cher*," Astrid said, affecting his drawl. "The band is itchin' to play, and your mama wants to watch you dance — with your boots on!"

At that the band struck up, and Gage leapt onto the dance floor with Astrid and Edvard in his arms. As they whirled around and around, people reached out to pin money to the bride's dress in the Cajun promise of a happy future.

"Today we both gave away the best we

had," she whispered when Gage danced her out onto the *galerie*. "You have sold your horse, and I have given up my homeland. But I am happier than ever I imagined."

"It's because God gave us somethin' we never could have bought for ourselves. He gave us our love."

Astrid smiled and laid her cheek on his shoulder. Her baby snuggled close between his parents and began to drift to sleep. Gage led his wife away from the crowd down toward the bayou. As they floated through the misty air, she listened to the night sounds and wondered at the marvels God had brought into her heart.

A Note from the Cook

Mais oui, I wanna give my sincere thanks to a coupla folks who spent a long time helpin' me come up with the recipe you just tasted: Audrey Hanson McIntosh and David Horton. Audrey also loaned her entire collection of Norwegian books for me to read through, and, for inspiration, she let me snuggle up with baby Keir, her own little blond *beignet.* I gotta tell you I owe my gratitude to O. Henry, whose *Gift of the Magi* helped me add a dash of zest to the dish, as you will know if you ever read that great story. I wanna thank my two fine sons for puttin' up with me while I stewed over this gumbo. And I offer my heartfelt passion to my husband who helped me get it to taste right, and whose love inspires everythin' I do.

To Christ be the glory —
Catherine Palmer

Author's Note

One of the many interesting Cajun wedding traditions involves gifts of money. As a way of contributing to the financial well-being of the new household, guests pin money to the bride's veil during the reception. The bride may be asked for a kiss or a dance in exchange for the money, and by the end of the celebration her veil is often covered with bills. In recent times, the groom has come to be included as well, with guests pinning money to his jacket.

The employees of Thorndike Press hope you have enjoyed this Large Print book. All our Large Print titles are designed for easy reading, and all our books are made to last. Other Thorndike Press Large Print books are available at your library, through selected bookstores, or directly from us.

For information about titles, please call:

(800) 257-5157

To share your comments, please write:

Publisher
Thorndike Press
P.O. Box 159
Thorndike, Maine 04986